D0495677

ENTREPRENEURSHIP

last date stamped below.

David Deakins FRSA

Professor of Enterprise Development
University of Paisley

with contributions from Mark Freel
Centre for Entrepreneurship
University of Aberdeen

McGraw-Hill Publishing Company
London • Burr Ridge, IL • New York • St Louis • San Francisco • Auckland
Bogota • Caracas • Lisbon • Madrid • Mexico
Milan • Montreal • New Delhi • Panama • Paris • San Juan
Sao Paulo • Singapore • Sydney • Tokyo • Toronto

Published by
McGraw-Hill Publishing Company
Shoppenhangers Road, Maidenhead, Berkshire, SL6 2QL, England
Telephone 01628 502500
Facsimile 01628 770224

British Library Cataloguing in Publication Data
A catalogue record for this book is available from the British Library

Further information on this title is to be found at
http://www.mcgraw-hill.co.uk/textbooks/deakins

Publisher: Dominic Recaldin
Desk Editor: Alastair Lindsay
Created for McGraw-Hill by the independent production company
Steven Gardiner Ltd. TEL +44 (0) 1223 364868 FAX +44 (0) 1223 364875

ISBN 0 07 709452 2ᴸ

McGraw-Hill

A Division of The McGraw-Hill Companies

2 3 4 5 CUP 3 2 1 0

Printed and bound in Great Britain at the University Press, Cambridge

Dedication

This book is dedicated to the memory of Joe Wilson, a true entrepreneur and visionary—an entrepreneur who through his inspiration was responsible for being involved in some of the research in this book. Joe died, after a courageous battle against leukaemia, as the first edition of this book was nearing completion in 1995. Much of his visionary and innovative work remains for others to build on. Without his contribution this book, and the research on which it is based, would not have been possible.

Contents

Acknowledgements

As stated throughout this book, the author is indebted to colleagues that he worked with at UCE and Paisley. He is also indebted to entrepreneurs who became involved with the research programme at UCE, especially Joe Wilson, to whose memory this book is dedicated. He would also like to acknowledge the contributions of students and participants in seminars who have helped to shape the research programme.

Special thanks goes to the reviewers who for this edition were:

Jon Beckett, Marketing Consultant
Jim Paterson, School of Management, University of Abertay Dundee, UK
Dr Martyn Pitt, School of Management, University of Bath, UK
Richard Scase, Canterbury Business School, University of Kent, UK
Colin M. Souster, Department of Marketing, University of Luton, UK

Introduction to First Edition

This book has arisen for a number of reasons. Firstly, a gap has been perceived in the literature concerning entrepreneurship and small firms, between the more practical start-up guides for small firms and would be entrepreneurs and the more academic literature associated with research with entrepreneurs and small firm owners which has burgeoned with the increased attention paid to the small firms sector in the 1980s and the 1990s. This book seeks to fill a need which was recognized through the provision of an Enterprise Studies course at Birmingham Polytechnic (now University of Central England—UCE), and later at the University of Paisley, placing the academic and research contributions in the context of the reality that small firm owners/managers and entrepreneurs face in their everyday decisions. Thus this book includes suggested practical assignments and case studies that, if used with students, will develop problem-solving skills and competencies in analysis. These assignments are designed to develop 'enterprise skills' in students and to build towards the completion of a feasibility study and business plan for a client organization which should preferably be for an existing small firm or entrepreneur. They can also be adapted to provide students with help for their own start-up business including a feasibility study and business plan.

Secondly, this book has been written for the purely selfish reason of disseminating research findings carried out at Birmingham and at Paisley. At UCE, a group of staff formed a small business research group in 1990. Later this became the Enterprise Research Centre at UCE, before the author left to form the equivalent Paisley Enterprise Research Centre at Paisley. Most of the research reported in this book was carried out by the author with colleagues while at Birmingham. The author is indebted to the small group of staff, mentioned in the Acknowledgements, who made this research possible. Occasionally, when people of like minds get together, a programme of innovative ideas develops as was experienced at UCE—a very productive time in terms of research undertaken and results produced. Often this research was applied and underpinned contemporary developments in courses at UCE that were being established in entrepreneurship and small firms.

Thirdly, there has been considerable course development in universities on relatively new 'Enterprise' degree courses that build upon the work of courses in HNC/HND. At the time of writing, there is also considerable development of the curriculum involving courses in entrepreneurship and enterprise in Scotland following concern about a low business birth rate in Scotland and a perceived need to encourage greater awareness of enterprise and entrepreneurship. Despite these considerable curricular developments there has been no associated growth in appropriate textbooks and lecturers often have to resort to their own specialized course materials. It is hoped that this book may be adopted as a suitable text for many of the students on these courses.

In addition, there have also been other curricular developments in Business Studies degree courses and in Business School MBAs which place greater emphasis on small firm business development and business planning. First-level courses in MBAs now offer Certificates and Diplomas in Business Development and many MBAs now (rather belatedly) contain small business and entrepreneurship modules or options. Again, although there are specialized academic texts, there has not been the development of texts that combine practical examples of case studies with theory and research. It is hoped that this text will go some way to fill these gaps and the needs of students on these new courses and modules.

Fourthly, as recognized above, it was felt that there was a need to combine theory and research with practical examples through case studies of entrepreneurs and small firms.

One of the aims of the Enterprise Research Centre at the time was to involve entrepreneurs, not only in course and curricular development, but also in seminars and the discussion of research findings. Some of the material in the book reflects contributions from entrepreneurs and small firm owners who participated in these seminars. This book also reflects other contributions from representatives of the enterprise community that attended and participated in the seminars. Too many seminars are held by academics for academics even on areas of concern in small firms and entrepreneurship. We have tried to avoid this and it is hoped that the book reflects the views of entrepreneurs and the spirit of some of the seminars that were held at Birmingham.

Although the entrepreneurship and small firm literature has begun to burgeon following the growth in importance of small firms and concern with 'enterprise' and the 'enterprise culture' in a number of advanced economies in the 1980s and 1990s, this literature is still an emergent one. In some areas, such as the finance of small firms, theory is still being developed. Unusually for an emergent academic discipline, evidence has tended to run ahead of theoretical developments. Research has tended to be carried out in an *ad hoc* way without theoretical underpinnings developed. In addition there has been a tendency to apply theory from large firms that is not always appropriate for the relationships entered into by entrepreneurs and small firm owners. Furthermore, because of the way that much of small firms' research has developed, there are also gaps in our knowledge of entrepreneurs and small firm behaviour. For example, as discussed in Chapter 1, we know little about how entrepreneurs learn and develop entrepreneurial expertise and we understand little about the process of entrepreneurship.

There are some views of entrepreneurial and small firm behaviour that are commonly held but have yet to be either underpinned by theoretical developments or are based upon, in some cases, quite limited research. For example, one convention that has recently been challenged is that successful small firm development depends upon the extent to which such small firm owners and entrepreneurs can engage in local economic networks. However, Curran and Blackburn (1) have recently shown that, for the majority of small firm owners local economic networks are unimportant. They have also commented that because of trends such as globalization, entrepreneurs are more likely to be in, and rely upon, relatively dispersed networks. A further example of a convention that has yet to be adequately challenged is that, to be successful, entrepreneurs display certain personality characteristics such as high ambition and a desire to be in control of their environment. These 'entrepreneurial personality characteristics' are discussed in detail in Chapter 1 where we question much of the convention that surrounds them.

While the small firm and entrepreneurial literature continues to emerge we can expect that there may be a number of these current conventions that will be challenged and eventually disproved or changed. As a result, at the present time we have an imperfect body of knowledge about entrepreneurial and small firm behaviour. The reader will find that the author expresses his own views about current conventions in a number of different areas in this book. Therefore, while acknowledgement is made to the contribution of colleagues at UCE, of entrepreneurs, of other participants in events at UCE and Paisley and not least of students, this book also is a reflection of the author's interpretation.

Although the research with entrepreneurs and small firms has grown with the associated literature, much of this research has been quantitative. The result is that, although we know much about the importance of small firms for the economy, we still know comparatively little about the processes of entrepreneurship and enterprise development. Much of the research has adopted a 'black box' approach to the study of the small firm owner/manager or entrepreneur. It has been concerned with measurable outputs such as the contribution of small firms to changes in employment. Although there are notable exceptions, there has not been the same output of qualitative research which is likely to increase our understanding of processes in entrepreneurship and relationships between institutions with the entrepreneurs and different firms. The emphasis (not exclusively) for research carried out at UCE has been on qualitative research—only by interviewing entrepreneurs can we begin to understand some of the processes involved in entrepreneurship and enterprise development.

The book begins by examining concepts in entrepreneurship. The first chapter questions some of the blinkered pursuit of the entrepreneurial personality. We can draw an analogy between this approach, which attempts to define the characteristics of the personality of the entrepreneur, and the current concern to identify the characteristics of the growth or 'entrepreneurial' firm. The search for the growth firm is examined later in Chapter 9. In the same way that it is impossible to identify an identikit profile of the successful entrepreneur, so it is proving impossible to identify an identikit picture of the fast-growing or fast-track small firm, despite considerable research effort to do so. We can also say that this focus is undesirable since the potential of many small firms and entrepreneurs is likely to be overlooked and may lead to the rejection of potentially successful entrepreneurs and growth firms.

Chapter 2 examines the importance of small firms for the UK economy, an importance which is now undisputed and well established. This importance is likely to increase in the future due to the increasing pace of change and the greater need for firms to be flexible, to respond to change quickly, and to be specialized. This 'flexible specialization' need and ability of small firms has been well established and will continue to account for their increased importance and contribution to the economy in the future.

Participation in entrepreneurship across different groups of society is far from even. This is the case, for example, when we examine the participation of different ethnic minority groups in entrepreneurship and enterprise. Some of our research and some of the special issues in ethnic minority entrepreneurship are examined in Chapter 4.

Sources of finance for entrepreneurs and small firms remains an area and field of study which is of major importance to successful outcomes in the entrepreneurship process and enterprise development. We examine some of the emerging theory and research in this important area in Chapters 5 and 6. This is accompanied by the complementary case study of Peters and Co., a business plan written by the entrepreneurs involved.

There are special issues that affect the process of entrepreneurship when combined with the process of innovation. For example, an entrepreneur concerned with the process of innovation requires seed capital to fund research and development (R&D). Some of these special requirements are examined in Chapter 7 and this chapter is accompanied by the Aquamotive case study, to give a real-world example of the different problems faced by entrepreneurs in the process of innovation.

Some commentators have claimed that there has been such a trans-formation in society, in the UK, in the 1980s and 1990s that we now have an 'enterprise culture' to support entrepreneurs and small firm owners. We examine the support infrastructure in Chapter 8. It is noticeable that we do have a unique infrastructure of support in the UK compared to other countries. We compare the UK system of support to that of some European countries which do not have the network of support agencies such as the Training and Enterprise Councils (TECs) or the Local Enterprise Companies (LECs) in Scotland and the Business Links and enterprise agencies.

As stated at the beginning of this introduction, this book has been compiled primarily from a course in Entrepreneurship and Enterprise at UCE and later at Paisley. Those courses built towards assignments undertaken on a consultancy basis by students on, firstly, an investigative feasibility study and, secondly, a strategic business plan. For students to undertake such work, it was necessary to be aware of different sources of information and different research methods. These are dealt with in Chapter 11. Finally, we have included a chapter on the design and implementation of the business plan. It is important to take both of these chapters together since the business plan is meant to build upon the work undertaken for the feasibility study and should be the logical outcome of research undertaken for that study.

This book has been written with students in mind. Therefore, 'learning outcomes' have been included at the end of each chapter, as well as suggested assignments and recommended reading. For students who undertake the suggested assignments, it is hoped that they can produce a worthwhile document at the end which has practical value and application—the business plan. It has not been possible to list the most valuable learning outcomes that students obtained while working on such assignments. These came from working with small firm owners and entrepreneurs. Like the students, the author remains indebted to all the entrepreneurs that have freely given up their time to help students and to make this book possible.

REFERENCE

1. CURRAN, J. and BLACKBURN, R. (1994) *Small Firms and Local Economic Networks: The Death of the Local Economy?*, Paul Chapman, London.

Introduction to Second Edition

The production of the Second Edition has provided an opportunity to introduce some important changes. Apart from the need to update the First Edition, it was decided that the treatment and introduction of new cases used in the text warranted a tutor's manual. This contains additional case material and suggested student assignments. The author has attempted to build upon the experience and feedback of the first edition and some changes have been made to improve the content and sequencing of chapters. New material has been introduced with contributions from Mark Freel. However, considerable rewriting has also been undertaken of the first edition. The major changes are given below.

The tutor's manual discusses each chapter from the second edition with the new case material. It aims to place the case material in context and it also provides supplementary material on the cases; that is, what happened. Only one case from the first edition has been retained for the second edition—Peters and Co. The other case material in the first edition has been transferred to the tutor's manual. The tutor's manual also contains new case material, which could not be incorporated into the second edition. The tutor's manual has made it possible to include additional suggested assignments, exercises and worked examples.

The reader will find the following new chapters in the second edition: Chapter 3 on business start-up, Chapter 6 on equity and venture capital and Chapter 10 on international entrepreneurship. These have been introduced partly as a result of feedback and comments on the first edition, but also to reflect the changes that have been occurring in the environment for entrepreneurs and small firms. For example, the growth in venture capital and the new equity markets has necessitated the splitting of the chapter on finance. Chapter 5 is now solely devoted to bank and debt finance.

While the remaining chapters described in the introduction to the first edition have been retained, as previously mentioned much of the material for these chapters has been rewritten. For example, Chapter 9 on growth has been completely rewritten by Mark Freel and other chapters, apart from being updated, contain new material. Chapter 3 replaces the previous chapter on business start-up from the first edition and also contains a contribution on rural environments from Alastair Anderson and Sarah Jack. Additional contributions are acknowledged from Geoff Whittam on networks.

The second edition, however, still retains the main aim from the first edition: to meet the need for a text that combines academic research with practical case material and understanding of entrepreneurs and small firms. It retains that aim, while incorporating major revisions, additional material, updating and improvements.

Learning outcomes

At the end of this introduction you should be able to:

1. Describe the orientation and emphasis of previous research into small firms and entrepreneurship.
2. Identify two areas of misconceptions in the small firm and entrepreneurship literature.
3. Appreciate the need for continuing research into small firms and entrepreneurship.

1. The Entrepreneur: Concepts and Evidence

INTRODUCTION

What makes an entrepreneur or small business owner? Is an entrepreneur different from other individuals or can anyone be an entrepreneur given sufficient resources? Can anyone set up in business or do you need to have special skills and characteristics? These are questions which have occupied researchers and theorists for some time; indeed theories on what makes an entrepreneur date from the early Industrial Revolution. We will attempt to answer some of these questions later when we examine factors that can encourage successful new business creation and entrepreneurial success. However, it is useful to review the contribution of the major theorists on entrepreneurship first. It is only when these have been examined, that we can understand the characteristics, traits and factors that researchers have sought to find in the modern entrepreneur. Later we question much of this research effort into the characteristics of the entrepreneur which can be seen as misplaced. It may, for example, be better to concentrate on the management skills which are required of business owners. Developing this theme, we consider some recent research which examines the concept of risk management and the use of insurance by entrepreneurs.

Literature concerning entrepreneurship can sometimes be seen as stemming from three sources: firstly, from the contributions of economic writers and thinkers on the role of the entrepreneur in economic development and the application of economic theory; secondly, from the psychological trait approach on personality characteristics of the entrepreneur, which is examined critically later; thirdly, a social behavioural approach which stresses the influence of the social environment as well as personality traits. Each approach is considered in this chapter, and it can be claimed that all three approaches have something to contribute to our understanding of the entrepreneurship process. However, it will be seen that the value of psychological and social approaches are more controversial. Indeed there is some dispute over whether 'entrepreneurial' characteristics can be identified at all.

There are many writers who have contributed to theories about the entrepreneur, but there is insufficient space to consider more than the major contributors. For a detailed analysis of other theorists and contributors, and the development of the theory of the entrepreneur, the student is advised to consult the recommended reading at the end of this chapter.

THE ENTREPRENEUR

If we examine conventional economic theory, the term 'entrepreneur' is noticeable only by its absence. In mainstream or neo-classical economic theory, the entrepreneur can be viewed as someone who co-ordinates different factors of production, but the important distinction is that this role is viewed as a non-important one. The entrepreneur becomes merged with the capitalist employer, the owner-manager, who has the wealth to enable production to take place, but otherwise does not contain any special attributes. The entrepreneur, if recognized at all, is a pure risk taker, the reward being the ability to appropriate profits. It is a remarkable fact that the main body of conventional economic theory has developed without a place for the entrepreneur, yet there is no shortage of writers who have contributed to the development of views on the role and concept of the entrepreneur.

The idea that the entrepreneur has a significant role in economic development has been developed by writers outside the mainstream economic thinking. Their contributions now have an important place, but it is only relatively recently that the importance of these contributions has been recognized. As attention has become more focused on the importance of the Small- and Medium-Sized Enterprise (SME) sector for economic development and job creation, so greater attention has also been directed at theories of entrepreneurship. We examine the most important of these theories which are accepted today.

The term 'entrepreneur' is French in origin, a literal meaning might translate as 'one who takes between'. There are some important French writers who contributed views on the role of the entrepreneur, the most important being Cantillon and Say. Cantillon was the first to recognize the crucial role of the entrepreneur in economic development, which was founded on individual property rights. Of the three classes in society recognized by Cantillon, entrepreneurs were the important class and were the central economic actors. The other two classes were landowners and workers or hirelings. Say also made the entrepreneur the pivot of the economy and a catalyst for economic change and development. The entrepreneur provided a commercial stage in three stages of production. In this way the entrepreneur could be seen as close to the traditional mainstream view of the entrepreneur as someone willing to take the risk of bringing different factors of production together.

Both Cantillon and Say belonged to a French school of thought known as the 'physiocrats', so called because the physical nature of the agrarian economy dominated their thinking. It could be because of this view that developments in the concept of the entrepreneur were not seen as being relevant to the nineteenth century industrial economy. It was much later before more modern concepts of the entrepreneur were developed. Some of these views have been developed within the 'Austrian School' of thought, however, this is such a wide-ranging term that there is no one particular view associated with this school for the entrepreneur. What is different, however, is that the entrepreneur is seen as being crucial to economic development and a catalyst for dynamic change. We turn now to these Austrian School writers who underpin much of the current day theories of the entrepreneur and hence much of modern day research into the characteristics of the entrepreneur.

KIRZNER

For Kirzner, the entrepreneur is someone who is *alert* to profitable opportunities for exchange. Recognizing the possibilities for exchange enables the entrepreneur to benefit by acting as a 'middleman' who facilitates the exchange. The Kirznerian entrepreneur is alert to opportunities for trade. He or she is able to identify suppliers and customers and act as the intermediary. Note that there is no necessity to own resources and profit arises out of the intermediary function.

These possibilities for profitable exchange exist because of imperfect knowledge. The entrepreneur has some additional knowledge which is not possessed by others and this permits the entrepreneur to take advantage of profitable opportunities. The information is costless, it arises when someone notices an opportunity which may have been available all the time. It can often seem obvious after the service or product has been provided, but it still takes someone with additional knowledge to recognize and exploit the opportunity.

The role of information in the market place is important for the Kirznerian entrepreneur. Market exchange itself is an entrepreneurial process, but people can profit from exchange because of information gaps in the market. In this view, the entrepreneur may be seen as little more than a market trader, taking advantage of opportunities to trade; yet for Kirzner the entrepreneur is someone who is still creative. The possession of additional knowledge provides opportunities for creative discoveries. However, in contrast to the Schumpeterian view below, anyone could potentially possess the additional knowledge and be alert to opportunities for exchange and trade.

SCHUMPETER

By contrast, Schumpeter's entrepreneur is a special person. Although Schumpeter is a writer classified in the 'Austrian School', his views on the entrepreneurial functional are quite different from those of Kirzner.

The Schumpeterian entrepreneur is an *innovator*. The entrepreneur brings about change through the introduction of new technological processes or products. For Kirzner, anyone has the potential to be an entrepreneur and they operate within set production constraints. For Schumpeter, only certain extraordinary people have the ability to be entrepreneurs and they bring about extraordinary events. The Schumpeterian entrepreneur changes technological possibilities and changes convention through innovative activity, and moves production constraints. He or she develops new technology, whereas for Kirzner the entrepreneur operates on opportunities that arise out of new technology.

Although the entrepreneur is again an important catalyst for economic change, the entrepreneur is essentially temporary for Schumpeter. Schumpeter predicted the demise of the function of the entrepreneur. Technological advance and change would be carried out by teams of workers and scientists operating in large organizations. This is because, for Schumpeter, large monopolistic firms have distinct advantages over small firms in the technological process.

The idea that large firms are more successful than small firms in new technology-based industries is more correctly attributable to Galbraith. However, this idea has come to be associated with Schumpeter, even though he was more concerned with the advantages of monopolistic market structure than with firm size. The basic concept is that the small firm entrepreneur faces considerable disadvantages in research and development (R&D); e.g., R&D is expensive; it has long development times; and teams of researchers are able to benefit by feeding off one another's ideas. If the entrepreneur is an innovator, then this argument suggests that he or she will find it difficult to establish new small firms. Technological change is carried out by large firms. The entrepreneur may still exist in large firms—the so-called 'intrapreneur'—an individual who is capable of initiating change in large firms.

The concept that the entrepreneur is someone who is different, someone who is an innovator, is important. Some writers have carried this forward to distinguish entrepreneurs (business owners who wish to develop and expand their businesses) from other small business owners who have no ambition to expand their business or wish to remain merely self-employed. The essential distinguishing feature for such writers is that the entrepreneur is a Schumpeterian innovator, although here the term 'innovator' would be more loosely defined to include a person who wishes to manage change or initiate change in some way. For example, Curran and Stanworth (1) state that:

> Entrepreneurship, rigorously defined, refers to the creation of a new economic entity centred on a novel product or service or, at the very least, one which differs significantly from products or services offered elsewhere in the market. (p. 12)

KNIGHT

The commonly held view of the entrepreneur as a calculated risk taker comes close to the view of Knight. For Knight the entrepreneur is an individual who is prepared to undertake risk and the reward—profit—is the return for bearing uncertainty and is an uninsurable risk.

The opportunity for profit arises out of uncertainty surrounding change. If change is perfectly predictable then no opportunity for profit exists. The entrepreneur is someone who is prepared to undertake risk in an uncertain world.

Knight made an important distinction between risk and uncertainty. Risk exists when we have uncertain outcomes but those outcomes can be predicted with a certain degree of probability. For example, the outcome that your car will be stolen or not stolen is uncertain, but the risk that your car will be stolen can be calculated with some degree of probability and this risk can be insured against.

True uncertainty arises when the probability of outcomes cannot be calculated. Thus, anyone can set up in business, but that person cannot insure against business failure because that particular outcome cannot be predicted with any degree of probability. The entrepreneur is someone who is willing to accept the remaining risk that cannot be transferred through insurance. We have an important distinction established by Knight which has not so far been explored in small firms' research. We include some recent research on risk management and insurance in a later section in this chapter. Issues such as the extent to which the entrepreneur assesses, accepts and transfers risk have yet to be properly explored.

This distinction helps to distinguish a small firm manager from the entrepreneur/owner. One of the characteristics of entrepreneurs (following Knight) could be considered to be the responsibility for one's own actions. If a manager assumes this, then he or she is performing some entrepreneurial functions. We can also use this distinction as a criticism of some research into entrepreneurship which concentrates solely on personality traits and ignores management skills.

These distinctions are unfortunately rarely discussed in the small firms' literature. However, an exception is provided by Shailer (2), who considers that:

> (The) entrepreneur is now a widely used term, with considerable contemporary diversity in meaning associated with the intended interests of its users. . . . Owner-managers do not necessarily fit any of the current popular definitions of 'entrepreneur'. (p. 34)

Shailer prefers to adopt the view of entrepreneurship as a process and refers to a stage of the firm when it is in owner-management. Again we have the important concept of management of the firm, the willingness to accept risks and responsibilities. If the firm grows, it is possible to transfer this entrepreneurial function, but still retain part ownership through the issue of shares. The manager, as opposed to the owner, now takes on the function of the entrepreneur. The fact that behaviour of the previous owner-entrepreneur is likely to alter has been established (theoretically) by writers such as Jensen and Meckling (3) by applying agency theory. The concept of the importance of small business management skills is also discussed by Ray (4). He considers that the search for the prototype has been ill-conceived and that: 'There is no empirical evidence or conceptual base to say much, if anything, about entrepreneurs and risk taking'. (p. 347)

Ray considers that we should concentrate on the development of skills and how managers acquire them. These concepts are too frequently ignored and this entrepreneurial and learning process has not been adequately researched.

We could say, then, that the Knightian entrepreneur is anyone who is prepared to undertake the risk of setting up their own business. However, equally it could be any risk taker (and this is a source of criticism). The entrepreneur is someone who has the confidence and is venturesome enough to make judgements about the uncertain future and reward for this is profit.

SHACKLE

Shackle's entrepreneur is someone who is creative and imaginative. Whereas Kirzner's entrepreneur perceives opportunities, Shackle's imagines opportunities. Everyone potentially has this creative ability, which is exercised in making choices.

The role of uncertainty and imperfect information is crucial for the view of the role of the entrepreneur by Shackle. Uncertainty gives rise to opportunities for certain individuals to imagine opportunities for profit. Shackle's entrepreneur is creative and original. The act of imagination is important for identifying the potential of opportunities. This potential is compared to resources available which can lead to the decision to produce, hence the act of entrepreneurship. Shackle's creative entrepreneur indicates that *creativity* is an important element in the entrepreneurship process. However, how this creative process occurs, and the factors which might influence it, remain areas that are only just beginning to be explored. A host of factors will influence an individual's ability to be creative, including personal background, education and attitudes; but it is likely that such influences will combine to affect the extent to which that individual is *prepared* to recognize and exploit opportunities. It is only recently that *pre-entrepreneurial* experiences (including education, employment and learning) are beginning to be recognized as important influences on nascent (pre-start) entrepreneurs— Reynolds and White (5). In fact the neglect of the study of important influencing factors pre-start, or the process of nascent entrepreneurship, is surprising, given its potential importance for modern economies (6).

CASSON

Casson attempts to synthesize some of these entrepreneurial attributes and concepts that have been discussed with the major writers above. Casson recognizes that the entrepreneur will have different skills from others. These skills enable the entrepreneur to make judgements, to co-ordinate scarce resources. The entrepreneur makes judgemental decisions which involve the reallocation or organization of resources.

Casson emphasizes that entrepreneurs require command over resources if they are to back their judgements and that this is likely to imply that they will have personal wealth. Lack of capital would thus be a barrier to successful entrepreneurship.

Casson's view is closer to that of Knight than other writers. The entrepreneur operates within a set of technological conditions; by making difficult judgemental decisions they are able to enjoy the reward of profit (for bearing uninsurable risk). This enables the entrepreneur to co-ordinate demand and supply under uncertainty.

In Fig. 1.1 the demand curve represents the return to each entrepreneur as their numbers increase and is part of a map of such curves. The supply curve of entrepreneurs depends on access to resources and thus on the local economy and

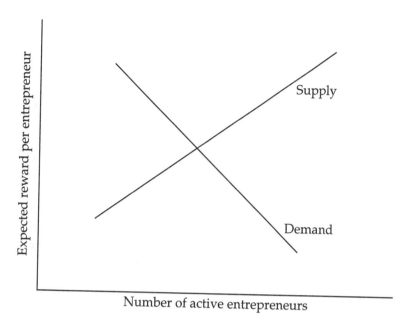

Figure 1.1   Casson's demand and supply of entrepreneurs

environment. Casson's analysis attempts to explain why in some economies entrepreneurs can flourish, yet in others there are low participation rates for people who own their own businesses. For example, in the UK, the South-East has higher participation rates of people in small business ownership than the Midlands, which in turn has higher participation rates than Scotland. The low participation rates in Scotland have been partly attributed, for example, to low home ownership which limits the amount of equity that a nascent entrepreneur might have to invest in a start-up firm (7). Thus Casson's point about the access to resources would appear to be an important one. The clear implication, when we examine such participation rates, is that the environment can be a more powerful influence than any predilection amongst the local population for entrepreneurship.

Casson's insight is to view change as an accompaniment to entrepreneurship. The pace of change provides opportunities and the entrepreneur chooses which one to back. Entrepreneurs can vie with each other as their numbers increase, the supply of entrepreneurs depending on their access to resources. The supply curve shown in Fig. 1.1 will thus depend on the propensity of any given set of circumstances and the extent to which potential entrepreneurs have access to resources. This will depend on factors such as social mobility, and institutional factors such as the ability to access capital. An equilibrium position will result as shown in Fig. 1.1 from the interaction of these factors.

A number of other economic writers and theorists have considered the development of the role of the entrepreneur; for example, Thunen who could be seen as a forerunner of Knight. Thunen recognized the function of the entrepreneur as a risk taker, risk which cannot be transferred through insurance, a theme which we will return to later in this chapter. For Thunen, however, the entrepreneur was also concerned with innovation, and problem solving.

It would be untrue to say that the neo-classical school of economists added little to the concept of the entrepreneur. For example, Marshall recognized a distinction between the capitalist and the entrepreneur through his 'undertaker' who was alert to opportunities, but also innovative in devising new methods of production.

SUMMARY

A consensus has emerged that, in conditions of uncertainty and change, the entrepreneur is a key actor in the economy. Two major lines of thinking have developed: the Knightian approach which highlights the risk-bearing and uncertainty-reducing role of entrepreneurs; and the Schumpeterian approach in which the entrepreneur is an innovator, a forger of new systems and production possibilities. Other perspectives highlight the knowledge and insight of the entrepreneur to possibilities and the role of Kirzner's middleman. This co-ordinating role has been developed and emphasized by Casson, but in addition it is clear that there are other factors that influence participation in entrepreneurship, such as access to resources and facilities in the local environment. The entrepreneurial act of business creation is part of a process that will be affected by many historical factors as well as the opportunities arising from economic change. As the pace of economic change increases, so opportunities increase; yet our understanding of the complete entrepreneurship process, and why participation rates (of different groups in society) are far from equitable, remains quite limited.

We turn now to consider some of the empirical evidence on the factors that influence entrepreneurship. As we have suggested much research effort has gone into discovering personality traits of the entrepreneur; some of this literature is controversial, since it assumes that an entrepreneur must have some special ability that distinguishes him or her from other people. Unfortunately this does not explain why there are low participation rates in entrepreneurship by women and by Afro-Caribbeans in the UK. As Ram (8) has pointed out, the Asian community has high rates of participation in small business ownership/entrepreneurship, yet this has more to do with negative factors of barriers to employment elsewhere than any predisposition for entrepreneurship.

MORE RECENT DEVELOPMENTS

The ideas and concepts surrounding the entrepreneur which have been outlined above are used as a basis by researchers for detecting traits in successful small business people and entrepreneurs. As in any scientific method, the theory can be used for developing hypotheses about the behaviour of successful entrepreneurs.

These hypotheses are then tested against the observed characteristics of entrepreneurs and small business owners in the real world. However, there are a number of problems with this approach that have been discussed above and in particular:

1. Some regions are more favoured than others at establishing successful small businesses and entrepreneurs and hence their economic development is more successful. The question of whether this is due to characteristics in the population, or due to certain aspects of the environment and infrastructure which enable potential entrepreneurs to exploit their skills and opportunities more easily, remains, at this stage, an open one.

   Research undertaken for Scottish Enterprise (9), after concern with low participation rates in entrepreneurship, showed that a complex series of factors contributed to low participation rates in Scotland. For example, the historical dependence of the population on a limited number of large employers coupled with inward investment (North Sea oil) had produced a 'dependency culture', that is, people were used to depending on large firms for employment. Thus the thought of going into business on their own account did not come easily to them. Other factors were found to be important as well, such as difficulties in accessing finance. This example shows why participation rates might be different in particular geographical areas for varying complex reasons.

2. Concern has been expressed at the existence of latent entrepreneurial talent. For example, why are there so few successful female entrepreneurs? In Scotland, a compilation and promotion of over 400 recent high growth entrepreneurs by Scottish Enterprise as 'Local Heroes' (10), to provide more role models that might influence possible or potential nascent entrepreneurs, contained only 16 per cent who were female. Why is the participation rate of Afro-Caribbeans in entrepreneurship low? Again these remain open questions which appear to have no simple solution but rather are caused by a complex combination of social and economic reasons.

   Little research has been conducted, specifically on these groups, in the UK, although a study carried out by the author and Ram (11) with Afro-Caribbean entrepreneurs suggests that motivations among this minority group in the UK consist of a combination of positive (pull) and negative (push) factors. Positive factors are associated with the attractions of entrepreneurship and negative factors are associated with limited opportunities in the inner-city and deprived urban environments.

3. Attention has focused on the role of networks in successful entrepreneurial development. For example, some research suggests that inter-firm networks contribute to successful entrepreneurship as discussed below.

We know that a high proportion of new firms fail within three years of start-up. For example, in the UK, 30 per cent of new firms cease trading by the third year and 50 per cent by the fifth year (12). In addition, there are only a small proportion that grow to employ 50 or more workers. One of the factors that might affect such limited numbers of high growth firms is the potential loss of control faced by the entrepreneur as the firm grows. New small firms and entrepreneurs that are successful are predominantly located in the South-East in the UK, which suggests that the environment and infrastructure are at least as important as the characteristics of the entrepreneur. It is also likely that the development of inter-firm networks is more advanced in the South-East than in other regions of the UK.

The inter-organizational networks that link firms after they are established have been found to be important to the ongoing success of firms (13). Efficient networks that foster good communications between firms contribute to entrepreneurial behaviour and success.

THE ENTREPRENEURIAL PERSONALITY

The second approach to entrepreneurship is to identify certain personality characteristics or 'traits' in individuals that appear to be possessed by successful entrepreneurs. The characteristics literature has been concerned with testing and applying some perceived characteristics in individuals. From this approach it is possible to argue that the supply of potential entrepreneurs is limited to a finite number of people with innate abilities, that they have a set of characteristics that mark them out as special, and have particular insights not possessed by others. This has led to some controversy and, in terms of policy, has significant implications. Obviously, if entrepreneurial characteristics are inherent, then there is little to be gained from direct interventions to encourage new entrepreneurs to start new businesses, although interventions to improve the infrastructure or environment may still have an effect. Whether an 'entrepreneurial personality' exists, however, is the subject of controversy and, despite attempts to provide prototypical 'lists' of characteristics of the entrepreneurial personality, this author remains sceptical of such approaches.

Some of these personality 'traits' are examined below, although as will become apparent the author does not accept the hypothesis that there is a limited supply of potential entrepreneurs. For example, many of the characteristics which are often said to be special to successful entrepreneurs are the same abilities and skills that could be applied to most successful managers and it is therefore difficult to identify specific characteristics of entrepreneurs.

Some of this research stems from the original work carried out by McClelland (14), who identified the historical role model influence of heroes on subsequent generations which induced a high need for achievement on the population of the subsequent generations. McClelland, however, is also associated with identifying the following key competencies of successful entrepreneurs:

- Proactivity: initiative and assertativeness
- Achievement orientation: ability to see and act on opportunities
- Commitment to others.

Much has been made of the need for achievement trait, as though this was the one characteristic that set potential budding entrepreneurs apart from others, and was, therefore, associated with successful economic development in advanced industrial countries. An implicit assumption of this approach is that the individual bears responsibility for his or her lack of entrepreneurial activity and this proposition could be used by policy makers, as discussed above, to divert interventions away from regions that have low rates of participation in small firm ownership.

Considering the work of writers on the entrepreneurship personality and those who might subscribe to the approach, we can identify certain key characteristics which have been identified in the literature as being important abilities of any entrepreneur:

- McClelland's need for achievement
- Calculated risk taker
- High internal locus of control
- Innovative
- Ambiguity tolerance
- Vision.

Some writers subscribe to the view of McClelland that the key characteristic is achievement motivation, or a high need for achievement, which can be described as a desire to excel, to achieve a goal in relation to a set of standards. High achievers are those who accept responsibility for decisions and for achieving solutions to problems, but who set standards carefully so that they can be achieved. Satisfaction is gained from finding the solution to a problem rather than with monetary reward. Yet, partly because such a characteristic is difficult to measure, the evidence has proved to be contradictory. A high need for achievement can also be important for people in many occupations, not just entrepreneurs.

Another characteristic that has been advocated is the locus of control. Individuals with a high locus of control like to be in charge of their environment and of their own destiny. Again, as with the need for achievement trait, it has not been possible to reconcile conflicting evidence of entrepreneurs with this approach to one or two important personality traits. For a critique of the characteristics literature see Chell *et al.* (15).

As we have said above, researchers have been concerned with whether successful entrepreneurs display psychological traits which separate them as individuals from others. This approach can be criticized in a number of ways:

1. It is inappropriate to search for a significant single trait.
2. It ignores environmental factors which may be more important than personality.
3. It comprises an essentially static analysis approach to the dynamic process of entrepreneurship.
4. It ignores the role of learning, preparation and serendipity in the process of entrepreneurship (these factors are discussed later in this chapter).

A further example is provided by Meredith *et al.* (16) who gave five core traits:

- Self-confidence
- Risk-taking activity

- Flexibility
- Need for achievement
- Strong desire to be independent.

Again the trait of need for achievement is represented.

In general the following traits have been suggested as important:

- Need for achievement
- Internal locus of control
- High propensity for risk taking
- Need for independence
- Deviants (see below)
- Innovative behaviour.

The deviant personality is associated with the third approach to the entrepreneur, that of the social behavioural school, associated with Kets de Vries. A deviant character is associated with individuals who do not easily fit in with their existing employment, e.g., someone who is out of place in a large firm. However, this would seem to rule out the possibility of the dynamic employee wishing to create change in the large firm, the intrapreneur.

Writers such as Timmons (17) have attempted to summarize the personality characteristics of successful entrepreneurs and to categorize traits that can be acquired and those that are more innate. While Timmons does admit that many of these characteristics can be acquired, that is through learning or from experience, Timmons also considers that there are some attributes which cannot be acquired, that are innate, that perhaps mark out 'born entrepreneurs' from 'made entrepreneurs'.

Timmons considers that both need for achievement and locus of control can be acquired along with other leadership abilities and competencies such as the ability to take responsibility for actions/decisions. Many of these characteristics are management skills. Entrepreneurs obviously need to be ambitious but need to be satisfied that they have achieved personal goals and ambitions.

We can assume that profit or monetary reward is not the only driving force behind entrepreneurs. There is also the need to build and achieve personally set goals, hence implying that entrepreneurs have a high need for achievement in order to establish a growing business or 'entrepreneurial' firm (this is discussed in more detail in Chapter 9). Similarly, the internal locus of control characteristic has been identified as an important characteristic of potential entrepreneurs. A high internal locus of control means that the person needs to be in control of their own environment, to be their own boss. It is perhaps interesting that Timmons considers that these characteristics can be acquired. This approach is one to be welcomed—many of these abilities can be taught or, at the very least, scenarios can be provided which stimulate the acquisition of these skills and abilities.

It is also interesting that Timmons considers that dealing with failure can be an important attribute of entrepreneurs. However, the ability to tolerate failure depends on the culture. In the USA failure is viewed as a learning experience and people can benefit from failure, can learn from their experience and can go on to form successful companies as a result. In Britain the culture is less tolerant of failure and too often highly talented individuals have not been able to recover from failure. The culture and environment is crucial to tolerance of failure. There is little doubt that Britain has lost many potentially successful entrepreneurs because, having failed once, they have not been allowed to recover from that failure, perhaps from an inability to raise capital having been through bankruptcy. Failure is a very valuable learning experience, as many entrepreneurs have admitted. It is a pity in Britain that new entrepreneurs are often not allowed a further opportunity so that they can benefit from their experience, apply lessons learned, and build a successful business.

In practice, many of the entrepreneurial characteristics are those associated with any successful manager or indeed with any successful individual. It is thus difficult to justify a separate set of characteristics for a successful career in entrepreneurship.

Timmons also lists attributes which are more innate:

- High energy coupled with emotional stability
- Creative and innovative ability
- Conceptual ability
- Vision combined with a capacity to inspire.

Although it may be claimed that this set of characteristics is more innate in terms of identifying people who are potential entrepreneurs, it is difficult to justify that they mark people out for entrepreneurship. Also it does not mean that they cannot be acquired. By the use of planning scenarios and problem solving it is still possible to demonstrate how opportunities can be exploited, how resources can be acquired and how creative solutions can be developed.

Some institutions and writers have attempted to develop tests of potential entrepreneurial ability or enterprise. Caird, for example, has developed a measure of enterprising traits (or entrepreneurial abilities) called the General Enterprise Tendency (GET) (18), used by the Durham Business School. It consists of a scale of different questions within the following categories:

12 which measure need for achievement
12 which assess internal locus of control
12 to determine creative tendency
12 to gauge calculated risk taking
6 to measure need for autonomy.

Entrepreneurial or enterprise tendency tests, however, suffer from the same limitations as the characteristics approach. Not surprisingly, these tests have been found to be inconsistent in their application or selection. However, subsequent work at Durham, carried out by Johnson and Suet Fan Ma (19), with an expanded scaled test with nine dimensions, appears to claim more promising results as an enterprise tendency test.

Problems arise whenever attempts are made to measure these characteristics. For example:

1. Characteristics are not stable and change over time.
2. In many cases they are subjective judgements that do not lend themselves to objective measurement. For example, how do we define being innovative? It can simply be the ability to deal with change and the ability to cope with new processes and solutions. How do we measure the calculated risk-taker? In many respects there are unsatisfactory definitions of these concepts which makes their measurement difficult to justify.
3. Concentrating on personality characteristics means that we are in danger of ignoring environmental and cultural influences which can be just as, if not more, important than any set of personality traits.
4. Placing too much importance on an inherent set of personality characteristics reduces the role of education and training. Learning can be a very valuable process that allows potential entrepreneurs to acquire skills to develop methods of business planning. While we would agree that many people are not suited to entrepreneurship, there is still much that can be learned and acquired by potential entrepreneurs and this process is far from understood.

There is a danger that these approaches can influence and dominate approaches to small firm ownership and entrepreneurship so that important influences on entrepreneurship, such as quality of the infrastructure provided in the environment, are ignored. There are a number of problems with these approaches which have been mentioned above. They include ignoring issues such as gender, age, social class and education, all of which can have a bearing on the propensity of an individual to enter entrepreneurship. Later in this chapter we turn to one of these issues for special consideration, that of gender, and we examine some of the limited research into female entrepreneurship.

THE ABILITY TO LEARN

Much effort has gone into identifying entrepreneurial characteristics and it has diverted research away from important areas concerning the entrepreneur's ability to learn from problem solving and to gain from their business experience. We do not understand how entrepreneurs learn, yet it is accepted that there is a learning experience from merely establishing a new enterprise. The learning process that is involved in business and enterprise development is poorly understood, yet programmes have been designed and interventions are made in business development. The problem with these interventions (at least in the past) is that they are often task-oriented. They are often built around particular tasks and skills in terms of business planning; for example, they may concentrate on bookkeeping or financial skills, on liquidity or controlling for debt. As such they concentrate on specific tasks of running a business. A failing of such interventions is that they do little to alter the approach of the entrepreneur to solving business problems and learning from dealing with those problems. It is not surprising that Storey and Westhead (20), from a survey of the literature, found little evidence of a link between formal training and improved performance of small firms, indicating that formal personal management development and training of the entrepreneur appears, paradoxically, to have no impact on improved performance. Gibb (21), however, proposes that development of the entrepreneur is affected by the extent of interaction with 'stakeholders' in the small firm environment, for example, customers, bankers, creditors and supply chain relationships, thus implying that intervening to improve learning from interaction and experience should improve entrepreneurial ability and performance.

> Learning better from experience implies bringing knowledge, skills, values and attitudes together to interact upon the learning process; it therefore fundamentally demands an action-learning approach. (p. 16)

Entrepreneurs who become task-oriented are those who are more likely to fail. Entrepreneurship involves a learning process, an ability to cope with problems and to learn from those problems. An ability to recognize why problems occur and to be able to deal with them, and more important understand why they occur, will ensure that the entrepreneur will be able not only to deal with those problems, but to learn from the experience and ensure that processes are put in place within the firm to ensure that either the problem does not occur again or that the firm can deal with the problem. This ability to learn from experiences involves the concept of double-loop learning (22)—a process which involves examining why the problem occurred and to learn from that process. It is a process of learning 'how to learn'.

Our limited knowledge and understanding of the interaction of learning and the entrepreneurship process remains one of the neglected areas of entrepreneurial research and, thus, understanding. This is perhaps surprising given the attention that has been paid to areas such as 'the learning organization'. Case studies of the features of learning organizations have been developed in some detail (23), yet little equivalent research has been undertaken within small firms; partly because of the lack of appropriate ethnographic and case study approaches that are capable of revealing the complex and often subtle mix of factors that will affect entrepreneurial learning. At the same time we need developments of theories and concepts that are appropriate to entrepreneurship. Learning organization concepts are derived from large organizations; more promising are developments in evolutionary approaches to learning and the entrepreneur. In part, these stem from a Schumpeterian dynamics analysis of the forces of change and attempt to explain how the entrepreneur can adapt, change and thus learn from dealing with uncertainty (24). The interaction between learning and the entrepreneurship process has been highlighted by Levinthal (25), who stresses the adaptive role of entrepreneurs as they adjust to their environment, to their learning experience and, as a result, change behaviour. The nature of learning may follow a trial and error and discovery activity, entrepreneurial behaviour becomes adapted in an evolutionary way to the discovery of information from trial and error. It is suggested that such evolutionary theories may be able to model the nature of entrepreneurial behaviour and development, although, there is a need for further work in this area.

The ability of the entrepreneur, or entrepreneurial team, to learn is crucial to their behaviour and ability to succeed. To be successful, entrepreneurs must be able to learn from decisions, from mistakes, from experience and from their networks. It is a process that is characterized by significant and critical *learning events*. To be able to maximize knowledge as a result of experiencing these learning events will determine how successful their firm eventually becomes. There seems little doubt that there are methods of enhancing the learning activity, such as the careful choice of an entrepreneurial team with complementary skills. We have suggested, however, that at present there is a need for further theoretical development, which will help to guide policy makers and, thus, interventions. Entrepreneurial behaviour is a dynamic response to a constantly changing environment. Large firm organizational theory does not capture the dynamics of learning in such an environment. Approaches that attempt to model the nature of such dynamic interaction stem from a Schumpeterian dynamic modelling of entrepreneurial response to their experience. Further work and evidence is required to develop this area.

RISK MANAGEMENT

In this section we return to Knight's concepts of risk and uncertainty and of the entrepreneur as risk taker and manager. It has often been expressed that an entrepreneur is a risk taker but 'not a gambler'. That is, they will take calculated risks, not gambles (which are seen as uncalculated risks). The author, however, does not find this helpful, since a gambler can just as easily be described as someone who does take calculated risks—a gambler knows the odds against winning, has calculated the chances of beating those odds and hence takes a calculated risk with a financial stake. It is possible to argue that there is little difference between this approach and that of the entrepreneur who has made a calculated risk by putting up a financial stake and has worked out the odds against success. We can describe first attempts to enter business, by definition, as a form of calculated gamble. The entrepreneur can minimize those risks but there is always an element of luck, of right timing. There are always things that can go wrong, after all the entrepreneur is dealing with uncertainty. This is the key insight of Knight, that the entrepreneur is dealing with uncertainty and takes risks that can be calculated just as the gambler takes his or her calculated risks.

It is more helpful to see the entrepreneur as a risk manager as this identifies one of the key concepts to understanding the process of entrepreneurship. In dealing with uncertainty, the entrepreneur has to identify, assess, evaluate, manage and transfer risk. Knight saw risk as a subset of uncertainty. Events which are truly uncertain cannot be predicted with any degree of probability. However, most events are risky; their occurrence can be predicted with a degree of probability. Some events have a greater degree of probability of occurrence than others. For example, insurance premiums in the inner city are high because the probability of damage to premises is greater than in other locations. A successful entrepreneur is someone who is able to identify, assess and evaluate the importance of the risk, say, of trading in the inner city. They are able to manage this risk either through preventive measures or through the transfer of risk with insurance, and hence make decisions about trading and market opportunities weighed against the risk of operating in a particular location. Chapter 4 examines ethnic minority entrepreneurs. In the UK there have been successful entrepreneurs in marginal economic environments. They have successfully managed the risk of operating in that environment by being resourceful, by developing coping strategies, by learning to manage within a limited ethnic market, and by developing policies that enable them to break out into mainstream markets. Understanding the process of entrepreneurship in the context of the environment and the degree of risk imposed by that environment, gives us a greater degree of understanding of what contributes to success.

A successful entrepreneur is someone who can minimize risks either through the limitation of his or her financial stake or by reducing the degree of uncertainty, so that they can be calculated accurately and decisions can be made with more reliability. He or she will want to know what their potential market is, who their competitors are, and what strategy would be best in the market place. By assessing different risks in the process of production, which includes buying materials, supplies, and assessing risks in the market, the entrepreneur engages in uncertainty reducing behaviour that will maximize his or her probability of success.

RISK MANAGEMENT AND THE USE OF INSURANCE

Although Knight identified the importance of risk taking, the entrepreneur needs to be able to assess which risks to accept and which to transfer. In this process, the entrepreneur may decide to accept some risk, reduce risk through risk management, or transfer risk through insurance. As indicated before, however, we know little of the extent to which an entrepreneur attempts to perform this function.

The availability of insurance is important because it enables the entrepreneur to transfer risk instead of accepting the full risk liability. For example, if you start in business, you will be faced with a number of risks that can prevent the business operating successfully. These include theft of stocks, fire, damage to vehicles through motor accidents, injury to a member of the public through the actions of your employees or from your products, and injury to visitors on your premises. All of these risks can easily be transferred through insurance policies and in some cases such insurance may be compulsory, e.g., employee liability. Some risks, of course, are not transferable. The risk of making losses cannot be transferred through any insurance policy, although it is possible to transfer subsequential losses from some other risk, e.g., fire. In addition, the management of risk can reduce the extent of insurance needed, and risk can also be reduced by taking measures that prevent the possibility of accidents. For example, special training for employees in health and safety may reduce the risk of employee accidents and hence reduce the amount of premium required by the insurance company.

Some firms are faced with more risks than others. For example, high technology manufacturing small firms face greater risks than service sector firms. They may have product liability risks and, if their product is protected by a patent, they also face the risk that another firm could copy their product, thus incurring expensive legal action to defend their patent.

The extent to which entrepreneurs undertake both risk management and the transfer of risks through insurance is largely unknown, yet the ability to manage risk (of which insurance is part) is an important subset of management skills for small firm survival. Two surveys of high technology small firms in two different regions, West Midlands and Scotland, utilized similar sample sizes to provide comparisons in the use of insurance by such firms (26). The results are summarized in Table 1.1. It shows that there are significant differences in the extent of the use of insurance between the top four risks and other risks that we might expect entrepreneurs to transfer through insurance and specialized risk cover.

Although the similarities in the use of insurance cover are striking, Table 1.1 indicates that gaps exist in high technology small firms. For example, we would expect the take-up rate of key man insurance to be higher. The use of more specialized insurance is also low with only 8 per cent and 9 per cent (in both areas) of firms taking out cover for the protection of patents and copyright. The low take up of patent protection may reflect a low application rate of high technology-based and innovative entrepreneurs to take out patents, which are time-consuming, relatively

Table 1.1   The use of insurance by two samples of high-technology small firms in the West Midlands and Scotland

Risk category	Percentage of firms using risk cover	
	West Midlands	Scotland
Motor and vehicles	97	91
Property and premises	96	97
Public liability	92	85
Employer's liability	90	93
Business interruption/loss of profits	72	64
Products' liability	57	57
IT and risk of computer breakdown	32	24
Goods in transit	12	5
Health and life insurance	9	n/a
Professional indemnity	8	7
Protection of patents and copyright	8	9
Key man	5	n/a
Personal accident	5	n/a
Errors and omissions cover	4	5
Engineering	4	n/a
Travel	4	n/a
Sample no. of firms	76	74

complicated and expensive. Follow-up research in Scotland indicated that 38 per cent of firms were concerned with acquiring patents which would suggest that the low take-up rates of cover are due to difficulties in the insurance environment. The existence of such insurance gaps is a matter of concern and could indicate limited risk management skills and knowledge of insurance by the high technology-based entrepreneur. Little research has been conducted with entrepreneurs in this area. However, a follow-up study by Bentley and Sparrow (27), with technology-based entrepreneurs on their perception of risks revealed that the low take up of some forms of insurance was due to 'cost reasons' in relation to overall risks, with high premiums for specialized insurance accounting for low take-up rates.

These studies have helped to raise the profile of the need for such research and highlight the importance of the relationship of the small firm with the insurance broker. In both the West Midlands and Scotland, over 90 per cent of high technology small firms turned to brokers for insurance provision and over 85 per cent turned to brokers for advice on insurance, yet interviews with brokers indicated that risk management advice, although available on a fee basis, was rarely used. The follow-up study by Bentley and Sparrow recommended that more attention should be given to education of entrepreneurs with risk management, a potential area of intervention for support agencies. The relationship with the broker was seen as important by the high technology-based entrepreneur and apart from the Bentley and Sparrow study there has been little in-depth investigation of this relationship.

Further discussions with the insurance industry and small firm representatives such as the Federation of Small Businesses (FSB) indicated that risk management and the use of insurance was an important topic that suffered from a low profile in research. A paper by the FSB (28) indicated that insurance was seen as a particular problem by their members (small firm entrepreneurs) especially in the inner city, where the difficulties in obtaining adequate cover were seen as a significant constraint in small firm entrepreneurship start-up and development. For example, insurance premiums in these areas are expensive, yet risk management measures were difficult to impose due to local authority restrictions on the extent of security provisions.

We have discussed the use of insurance in this section because it is part of a subset of management skills of the entrepreneur concerned with risk management. It fits nicely into the Knightian (or Thunen) theory of the entrepreneur as someone who has the ability to assess, evaluate and accept risk. Despite recent developments, in general we know little about the managerial skills of entrepreneurs and the process of how these skills are acquired. Entrepreneurship as a learning process, during which skills are acquired or developed, is now becoming a welcome focus for new research.

FEMALE ENTREPRENEURSHIP

Although data is hard to come by, it is generally accepted that the activity rates of women in business are much lower than those of men. For example, UK data suggests that 7 per cent of women in employment are either self-employed or run their own business. This compares to 17 per cent for men (29); furthermore these figures have remained remarkably consistent throughout the 1990s (29). However, during the 1980s, in line with other activity rates for women, the participation of women increased at a faster rate than that of men. The national picture is that women are catching up with the activity rates of men as some of the traditional barriers (for entering entrepreneurship) come down, but still lag a long way behind those of men.

Women have higher participation rates in areas such as personal services, but there are some industrial sectors which are largely male preserves and in which women still face barriers. Goffee and Scase (30) have suggested that female entrepreneurship is influenced by two sets of factors:

- Attachment to 'entrepreneurial ideals'
- The extent to which they accept conventional gender roles.

Goffee and Scase define entrepreneurial ideals as high motivation for self-advancement, self reliance and strong attachment to the 'work ethic'. Conventional gender roles were associated with a subservient role for women to the career aspirations of their partner, primarily a domestic role in supporting their male partner. Based on this distinction they give the taxonomy of female entrepreneurs shown in Table 1.2 and outlined as follows:

1. *Conventional* Using Goffee and Scase's terminology a conventional female entrepreneur is someone who is highly committed to entrepreneurial ideals and conventional gender roles. The motivation is the need to acquire earnings, but the traditional domestic role is retained. Help received from the partner is very limited.
2. *Domestic* The domestic female entrepreneur is strongly attached to the traditional gender role, but only moderately committed to entrepreneurial ideals. The motivation for start-up is self-fulfilment. Goffee and Scase argue that in this case the attachment to the traditional female role limits the development of the business because of the priority attached to the partner and family.
3. *Innovative* The innovative female entrepreneur has rejected the conventional gender role and is highly committed to entrepreneurial success. She is likely to start in areas where she may have encountered obstacles to her career.
4. *Radical* The radical female entrepreneur regards the business primarily as part of the feminist movement for equality. Thus she has a low attachment to

Table 1.2   Types of female entrepreneur

Entrepreneurial Ideals	*Conventional Gender Roles*	
	High	Low
High	Conventional	Innovative
Low	Domestic	Radical

both entrepreneurship and conventional gender roles. In these circumstances the business may be co-owned and operate as a co-operative.

Although the Goffee and Scase approach was useful it is now rather outdated as a method of classifying 'types' of female entrepreneur. In addition, the concept of 'entrepreneurial ideals' is rather ill-defined. Considerable progress has been made by women in business, but research has yet to catch up with the development of female entrepreneurship. UK research into female entrepreneurship is still limited; Watkins and Watkins (31), with a limited sample of 58 women and 43 male business owners, showed that some differences did exist, in particular that women had little prior experience that facilitated their entry into non-traditional areas. A study by Rosa *et al.* (32) showed that factors affecting female entrepreneurship were complex and depended on environmental as well as social considerations and that the influence of different factors varied across different industrial sectors. Women were less likely to be involved in co-ownership although, nevertheless, there were significant numbers of women in multiple business ownership. The researchers considered that women were fast catching up with male-dominated participation rates in entrepreneurship:

> If we speculate that women in business have started from a much lower tradition of achievement, then these figures are remarkable, and may indicate that they are catching up fast. (p. 30)

In Northern Ireland a study by Borooah *et al.* (33) found that women in the province (compared to men) tended to be younger, married and better educated; but, as the authors point out, there was considerable heterogeneity within the sample of self-employed women. This point is made also in a recent editorial by Holmquist (34):

> Another conclusion suggests that women entrepreneurs should not be treated as a homogeneous group. There are differences within the group that make all generalisations dangerous. (p. 181)

Thus it is suggested that it is dangerous to make hard and fast conclusions about the existence (or lack) of a distinctive nature for female entrepreneurship. We have also indicated that patterns are probably changing rapidly as women increase their activity rates, both in the economy generally and in entrepreneurship. However, as Holmquist also points out, traditionally entrepreneurship is 'gendered', that is, seen as masculine. Women are becoming increasingly important in entrepreneurship. There is evidence that increased female participation rates are associated with increased diversity; although in Scotland there are indications that comparatively few female entrepreneurs are associated with recent high growth firms (35). It may take more time before women increase their participation as entrepreneurs in high growth performing firms.

CONCLUSIONS

We can see that attempts to develop tests on entrepreneurial characteristics owe something to the development of theories of entrepreneurship. Shackle's creator and Schumpeter's innovator are included in the measures of creative tendency. There is Knight's calculated risk taker. The role of co-ordinator of Casson and

Kirzner is included by the need to have an internal locus of control and autonomy. These theories have been the guidelines for tests of entrepreneurial ability. Concern with the entrepreneurial personality has diverted attention away from the learning and development process in entrepreneurship and enterprise development, away from the recognition that the individual entrepreneur *acquires* skills and abilities, which are learned from the very process of entrepreneurship, as much as innate abilities. Much of this learning process is not understood. There is a need to re-focus research away from the investigation of the entrepreneurial personality, which is effectively a *cul de sac*, towards identifying the important factors, of which the environment might only be one, that affect the process of learning and development in entrepreneurship. Support for entrepreneurship can then be better informed to enable individuals to acquire management skills that enable them to learn from their experience, from their solution of problems.

There is little doubt, however, that the environment can be just as important as personal management skills for successful entrepreneurship. This has important implications for policy and the support of SMEs. Some of these issues will re-occur when we examine small business support later in this book. If the environment is not conducive then entrepreneurial talent will lay dormant. The importance of identifying entrepreneurial characteristics lies in encouraging potential entrepreneurs to start their own businesses. Schemes that give blanket coverage run the risk of persuading people to enter who are not suited to the task of controlling and running their own business (however good the business idea may be) and eventually fail. Indeed the evidence suggests that the majority of small business start-ups will fail. Policy developments in the UK have been aimed away from blanket coverage to help start-ups and more at helping existing small firms and reducing the high failure rate of start-ups.

Learning outcomes

You should be able to:

1. Understand the main theories and concepts of the entrepreneur.
2. Discuss the application of these theories and concepts to attempts to research the personality of the entrepreneur.
3. Appreciate some of the problems and limitations of research into the personality of the entrepreneur.
4. Appreciate some of the factors that influence the extent of entrepreneurship.
5. Distinguish between personality of owners and the management skills of small firm owner-managers and the importance of the distinction between ownership and management of a small firm.
6. Understand the importance of risk management and insurance to small firm development and survival.
7. Understand that entrepreneurship is a process of development, not a static state.
8. Understand the need for research into the process of entrepreneurship.

Suggested assignments

1. Undertake a small research study by interviewing small firm owner-managers about their concepts of management and entrepreneurship. For example, do they consider themselves as entrepreneurs? Small groups of students can each interview one small firm owner and discuss results in class.

2. Debate the skills of entrepreneurs. Students are each given one of two briefs indicating which case they have to argue from:

   - Entrepreneurs are special and have to be born
   - Entrepreneurship skills can be acquired and the environment that fosters entrepreneurship is important.

3. Discussion around a theme such as 'Can entrepreneurship be created?' or 'What difficulties might inner-city entrepreneurs face?'

REFERENCES

1. CURRAN, J. AND STANWORTH, J. (1989) 'Education and Training for Enterprise: Some Problems of Classification, Evaluation, Policy and Research', *International Small Business Journal*, vol. 7, no. 2, pp. 11–22.

2. SHAILER, G. (1994) 'Capitalists and Entrepreneurs in Owner-managed Firms', *International Small Business Journal*, vol. 12, no. 3, pp. 33–41.

3. JENSEN, M.C. AND MECKLING, W.H. (1976) 'Theory of the Firm: Managerial Behaviour, Agency Costs and Ownership Structure', *Journal of Financial Economics*, vol. 3, no. 2, pp. 305–60.

4. RAY, D. (1993) 'Understanding the Entrepreneur: Entrepreneurial Attributes, Experience and Skills', *Entrepreneurship and Regional Development*, vol. 5, no. 4, pp. 345–57.

5. REYNOLDS, P.D. AND WHITE, S.B. (1997) *The Entrepreneurial Process*: *Economic Growth, Men, Women and Minorities*, Quorum, Westport, USA.

6. *Ibid*.

7. SCOTTISH ENTERPRISE (1993) *Scotland's Business Birth Rate: A National Enquiry*, Scottish Enterprise, Glasgow.

8. RAM, M. (1993) *Managing to Survive: Working Lives in Small Firms*, Blackwell, Oxford.

9. SCOTTISH ENTERPRISE (1993) *Scotland's Business Birth Rate: A National Enquiry*, Scottish Enterprise, Glasgow.

10. SCOTTISH ENTERPRISE (1997) *Local Heroes*, Scottish Enterprise, Glasgow.

11. RAM, M. AND DEAKINS, D. (1995) *African-Caribbean Entrepreneurship in Britain*, Small Business Research Centre, University of Central England.

12. DTI (1997) *Small Firms in Britain Report 1996*, DTI, London.

13. BUTLER, J.E. AND HANSEN, G.S. (1991) 'Network Evolution, Entrepreneurial Success and Regional Development', *Entrepreneurship and Regional Development*, vol. 3, no. 1, pp. 1–16.
14. McCLELLAND, D.C. (1961) *The Achieving Society*, Van Nostrand, New Jersey.
15. CHELL, E., HAWORTH, J. AND BREARLEY, S. (1991) *The Entrepreneurial Personality, Concepts, Cases, and Categories*, Routledge, London.
16. MEREDITH, G.G., NELSON, R.E. AND NECK, P.A. (1982) *The Practice of Entrepreneurship*, International Labour Office, Geneva.
17. TIMMONS, J.A. (1994) *New Venture Creation: Entrepreneurship for the 21st Century*, 4th edn, Irwin, Illinois.
18. CROMIE, S. AND O'DONOGHUE, J. (1992) 'Assessing Entrepreneurial Inclinations', *International Small Business Journal*, vol. 10, no. 2, pp. 66–71.
19. JOHNSON, D. AND SUET FAN MA, R. (1995) 'Research Note: A Method for Selecting and Training Entrants on New Business Start-up Programmes', *International Small Business Journal*, vol. 13, no. 3, pp. 80–4.
20. STOREY, D.J. AND WESTHEAD, P. (1996) 'Management Training and Small Firm Performance: Why is the Link so Weak?', *International Small Business Journal*, vol. 14, no. 4, pp. 13–24.
21. GIBB, A. (1997) 'Small Firms Training and Competitiveness. Building Upon the Small Business as a Learning Organisation', *International Small Business Journal*, vol. 15, no. 3, pp. 13–29.
22. PEDLER, M., BURGOYNE, J. AND BOYDELL, T. (1991) *The Learning Company: A Strategy for Sustainable Development*, McGraw-Hill, New York.
23. KLINE, P. AND SAUNDERS, B. (1993) *Ten Steps to a Learning Organisation*, Great Ocean, Virginia.
24. NELSON, R. AND WINTER, S. (1982) *An Evolutionary Theory of Economic Change*, Harvard University Press, Massachusetts.
25. LEVINTHAL, D. (1996) 'Learning and Schumpeterian Dynamics', in Dosi, G. and Malerba, F. (eds), *Organisation and Strategy in the Evolution of Enterprise*, Macmillan, London.
26. DEAKINS, D., PADDISON, A. AND BENTLEY, P. (1997) 'Risk Management, Insurance and the High Technology Small Firm', *Small Business and Enterprise Development*, vol. 4, no. 1, pp. 21–30.
27. BENTLEY, P. AND SPARROW, J. (1997) *Risk Perception and Management Responses in Small and Medium-Sized Enterprises*, Small Business Research Centre, University of Central England, Birmingham.
28. GOODMAN, F. (1994) 'Insurance and Small Firms: A Small Firm Perspective', paper presented to Insurance and Small Firms Seminar, University of Central England, Birmingham, April.
29. MORALEE, A. (1998) 'Self Employment in the 1990s', *Labour Market Trends*, March 1998, pp. 121–30.
30. GOFFEE, R. AND SCASE, R. (1987) 'Patterns of Business Proprietorship among Women in Britain', in Goffee, R. and Scase, R. (eds) *Entrepreneurship in Europe*, Croom Helm, London, pp. 60–82.
31. WATKINS, D. AND WATKINS, J. (1984) 'The Female Entrepreneur: Her Background and Determinants of Business Choice, Some British Data', *International Small*

Business Journal, vol. 2, no. 4, pp. 21–31.

32. ROSA, P., HAMILTON, D., CARTER, S. AND BURNS, H. (1994) 'The Impact of Gender on Small Business Management: Preliminary Findings of a British Study', *International Small Business Journal*, vol. 12, no. 3, pp. 25–32.

33. BOROOAH, V.K., COLLINS, G., HART, M. AND MacNABB, A. (1997) 'Women and Self-Employment: An Analysis of Constraints and Opportunities in Northern Ireland' in Deakins, D., Jennings, P. and Mason, C. (eds) *Small Firms: Entrepreneurship in the Nineties*, Paul Chapman Publishing, London.

34. HOLMQUIST, C. (1997) 'Guest Editorial: The Other Side of the Coin – Women's Entrepreneurship as a Complement or an Alternative?', *Entrepreneurship and Regional Development Special Issue Women's Entrepreneurship*, vol. 9, no. 3, pp. 179–82.

35. SCOTTISH ENTERPRISE (1997) *Local Heroes*, Scottish Enterprise, Glasgow.

RECOMMENDED READING

BARKHAM, R. (1992) 'Regional Variations in Entrepreneurship: some evidence from the UK', *Entrepreneurship and Regional Development*, vol. 4, no. 3, pp. 225–44.

BROWN, B. AND BUTLER, J.E. (1993) 'Networks and Entrepreneurial Development in the Shadow of Borders', *Entrepreneurship and Regional Development*, vol. 5, no. 2, pp. 101–16.

BUTLER, J.E. AND HANSEN, G.S. (1991) 'Network Evolution, Entrepreneurial Success and Regional Development', *Entrepreneurship and Regional Development*, vol. 3, no. 1, pp. 1–16.

CASSON, M. (1982) *The Entrepreneur: An Economic Theory*, Robertson, Oxford.

CASSON, M. (1990) *Entrepreneurship*, Edward Elgar, Aldershot.

CHELL, E., HAWORTH, J. and BREARLEY, S. (1991) *The Entrepreneurial Personality, Concepts, Cases, and Categories*, Routledge, London.

CROMIE, S. AND O'DONOGHUE, J. (1992) 'Assessing Entrepreneurial Inclinations', *International Small Business Journal*, vol. 10, no. 2, pp. 66–71.

DAVIES, S.P. (1991) 'The Entrepreneurial Capabilities of Rural Furniture Manufacturers in Central Java, Indonesia: a framework and case study', *Entrepreneurship and Regional Development*, vol. 3, no. 3, pp. 253–67.

HÉBERT, R.F. AND LINK, A.N. (1988) *The Entrepreneur: Mainstream Views and Radical Techniques*, 2nd edn, Praeger, New York.

JOHANNISSON, B. AND NILSSON, A. (1989) 'Community Entrepreneurs: networking for local development', *Entrepreneurship and Regional Development*, vol. 1, no. 1, pp. 3–20.

REYNOLDS, P.D. and WHITE, S.B. (1997) *The Entrepreneurial Process: Economic growth, men, women and minorities*, Quorum, Westport, USA.

RICKETTS, M. (1987) *The Economics of Business Enterprise*, Wheatsheaf, London.

SHAW, B. (1991) 'Developing Technological Innovations with Networks', *Entrepreneurship and Regional Development*, vol. 3, no. 2, pp. 111–28.

SZARKA, J. (1990) 'Networking and Small Firms', *International Small Business Journal*, vol. 8, no. 2, pp. 10–21.

2. The Small Firm and the UK Economy

INTRODUCTION

The role and importance of the Small and Medium-sized Enterprise (SME) in the UK economy has been the subject of increased attention, particularly in the 1980s and 1990s. One reason for this has been the belief that a healthy and vigorous small business sector is important to the performance of the UK economy. Comparisons are often made between the UK performance and that of Germany and Japan. Germany has an important medium-sized firm sector, the Mittelstand, but both Germany and Japan have a more important and vigorous SME business sector and both, until recently, have out-performed the UK economy. A report comparing SMEs across Europe (1) commented that, in the UK, the industrial structure of the economy is still dominated by the large firm sector.

However, the role and importance of the small firm in the health of the economy is not without some controversy (for example, the importance of small firms in job creation). We will be examining some of the arguments later. The small firm sector has recovered importance since the 1971 Bolton Report pointed out a relative decline of the sector in the 1960s. Indeed the UK, at this time, had the smallest small firm sector of any advanced industrial country. First, though, it is necessary to define what we mean by the small business sector. This chapter begins with some definitions of the small business sector, examines the importance of this sector in the economy, and considers some of the issues in the debate concerning the importance of small firms for job creation.

DEFINITIONS

In the previous chapter, we saw that it can be difficult to define both the term entrepreneur and the process of entrepreneurship. Precise definitions of small firms and the small business sector are similarly elusive. Entrepreneurship does not necessarily coincide with small firm ownership, although throughout this book we will use the term entrepreneur in connection with small firms. However, the entrepreneurship concept and entrepreneurial skills can be applied to large companies. Unlike entrepreneurship, which is essentially a subjective concept, small firms lend themselves to objective definitions. For example, criteria such as turnover or numbers employed can be applied to distinguish the SME sector. The number of firms which are below certain turnovers or employee size may constitute the SME sector of the economy, although there are difficulties with comparable definitions. We might say that small firms are all those that employ less than 50 employees. However, there will be big differences in the size of firms with such a definition across different industrial sectors. For example, a clothing sector firm employing less than 50 will be much smaller than, say, an information technology firm employing less than 50 and there may well be little comparison between their respective turnovers.

The Bolton Report in 1971 (2) considered that one definition of small firms was inappropriate. Instead they recommended the following alternatives:

1. *The employee definition*   Small firms can be classified by some maximum number of employees, depending on the nature of capital intensity which varies from one industrial sector to another. Thus, less than 200 employees was considered appropriate for manufacturing, whereas less than 25 was considered appropriate for construction.
2. *The turnover definition*   Bolton gave £50,000 as a turnover definition for small firms in the retail trade—which might be nearer £1m. today. This illustrates one of the problems of a turnover definition—inflation can make nonsense of it over time. However, for temporary purposes there are advantages of using turnover definitions, since they are roughly comparable across different sectors.
3. *The characteristics definition*   Bolton gave three essential characteristics of a small firm:

    ● It has a small share of the market
    ● It is managed by its owners or part-owners in a personalized way
    ● It is operated independently.

This third definition is sometimes referred to as an economic definition. The three definitions combined were meant to be used in different circumstances. Turnover might be used in some sectors where there was some consistency in the turnover levels of firms. However, the third definition can be incompatible with some small firms which may have a formal management structure and do not necessarily have a small share of the market.

The multiplicity of criteria of Bolton has been replaced in most circumstances by a European Union (EU) definition of the small and medium-sized enterprise as an enterprise employing less than 250 employees, as revised by the EU Commission in 1996 (3). As we will see later in this chapter, this definition covers 99 per cent of all the enterprises in the UK. It is now generally accepted that there is a need to identify different sizes of firms within the SME sector. In particular, it has been recognized that very small firms are important to the economy; these are sometimes referred to as micro-enterprises to distinguish them from other small firms.

There are revised EU definitions that are generally adopted. These use the criterion of number of employees as the distinguishing factor of size according to the following definitions:

Number of employees	Size of enterprise
0–<10	Micro
10–<50	Small
50–<250	Medium

Thus the important Mittelstand sector of Germany would consist of medium-sized enterprises employing between 50 to less than 250 employees. A consensus has emerged that this is an appropriate definition. The result is that this definition is often used misleadingly in studies in the small firm sector. We can claim that the definition is misleading because it covers 99 per cent of all firms, as shown in Table 2.1. In fact, even if we reduce the definition to include only those firms that employ 20 or less, we would still capture 98 per cent of all the firms in the UK. If we are to use a small firm definition based on number of employees, the evidence in terms of firm size distribution, as shown in Table 2.1, would suggest that we restrict our analysis to firms employing less than 20 employees. Table 2.1 illustrates the importance and growth of the micro-sized firm in the UK. Comparing the UK's SME sector to other European countries seems to show that the UK still has less micro-sized firms than the EU average, as shown in Table 2.2.

One problem, at least in the UK, as a result of the importance of the micro-enterprise for small firm surveys which include SMEs (less than 250 employees) is that, statistically, inclusion of the relatively rare medium-sized firm can distort the results of the survey in terms of parameters.

Table 2.1   Firm size and share of employment UK, 1979–96

Firm size	1979 No. (000)	1979 Share of employment (%)	1989 No. (000)	1989 Share of employment (%)	1997 No. (000)	1997 Share of employment (%)
1–9	1597	19.2	2802	28.6	3519	30.2
10–19	109	7.6	92	6.0	107	7.2
20–49	46	6.9	57	7.6	50	7.3
50–99	16	5.3	18	5.8	15	5.1
100–199	15	10.2	9	7.2	8	5.3
200–499	5	8.1	6	10.6	5	7.0
500+	4	42.8	3	34.2	3	37.9
Totals	1791*	100*	2988*	100*	3708*	100*

* Totals affected by rounding.

Source: Employment Gazette, 'Labour Market Trends' (modified) February 1992 and 1997; DTI 1998 'Small and Medium-sized Enterprise Statistics for the UK 1997'.

Table 2.2   EU *v.* UK by size of enterprise and share of employment (1996)

Number of employees	EU by share of employment (%)	UK by share of employment (%)
1–9	25.5	15.4
10–49	20.7	18.6
50–249	16.4	16.4
250+	37.3	49.7
Totals	100*	100*

*Totals affected by rounding.

Source: DTI Small Firms in Britain and Eurostat data.

It is not surprising that some researchers have turned to alternative definitions in their studies of small firms. For example, a 1992 Kingston Small Business Research Centre study (4) of service sector firms used a 'grounded' definition of size adapted for the different services covered. The researchers considered what the small firm owner and representatives of the sector regarded as small in relation to the economic activities in which they were involved.

It may not be possible to define statistically the small firm or the small firm sector. As we see from the evidence given in the tables, there is no doubt that the small firm has become more important throughout the 1980s and 1990s. One of the reasons for this increased importance is its ability to respond quickly to change. As the pace of technological change has increased in society, so the ability of the small firm to respond quickly to change has given it an advantage over the large firm. This characteristic has been called 'flexible specialization' and reflects the ability of the small firm to be both specialized and respond to change. As the demands of society change, it may be that the growth in the importance of the small firm merely reflects those changed demands. In the same way that the UK labour market has changed dramatically, with employment no longer based on long-term careers with large firms in one occupation and in favour of a more 'flexible' labour force, so the structure of the economy has changed in favour of the small, flexible and specialized firm.

In such circumstances, and in the face of the increasing pace of change, it may be folly to attempt to define the small firm, because what is small, and which small firms are important, are changing anyway. We turn now to examine the evidence concerning the importance of small firms in the economy.

THE IMPORTANCE OF THE SMALL FIRM SECTOR IN THE UK

Table 2.1 shows the trends in the numbers and importance of small firms for share of total employment in the 1980s and 1990s. One striking trend is the increased numbers and growth in importance of the very small or micro firm, that employs less than 10 employees. The numbers of such firms have nearly doubled in the 1980s, and continued to increase strongly in the 1990s, as has their share of employment. It is also noticeable that the numbers of firms that employ more than 10 employees has remained virtually static during the same period. Thus most of the growth in the importance of small firms has come from the micro businesses.

Why there should have been this concentration of growth in micro firms is less clear. There are reasons associated with the restructuring of the economy. Large numbers of workers were made redundant in the early 1980s; workers who often had substantial redundancy payments and little prospect of retraining. Faced with lack of opportunity it is not surprising that many people were tempted into starting their own (micro) businesses. However, this factor alone cannot account for the growth in the importance of such businesses in share of employment. Also, because these figures are based on VAT registrations, some self employed workers may not register for VAT (because their incomes are below VAT threshold registration levels) and may not enter the statistics. The explanation of the growth of these micro-firms is more complex than simple push factors from high unemployment rates and is probably tied to underlying structural changes in the economy, as discussed above—structural changes that had been in place for some time.

Across the EU as well, there has been a significant growth in small firms that employ less than 100. According to a European study (1), between 1988 and 1993 these firms were responsible for creating three million jobs, whereas other firms were net losers of jobs, suggesting that there are significant structural changes in all European countries in favour of small firms and entrepreneurs that employ less than 100 people.

These statistics contrast with the decline in the small firm sector that had been reported by Bolton in 1971. The growth in the small firm sector began soon after Bolton reported and its revival is a longer process than that reported in Table 2.1. Factors that are put forward include the following:

1. Structural changes in the UK economy, particularly the decline in manufacturing and the growth of the service sector where a smaller size of firm is more 'optimal'.
2. An associated change in the extent of economies of scale, partly associated with technical changes which suit smaller-scale production.
3. The ability of the smaller firm to be more flexible and respond to 'market opportunities', the ability to be both specialized and flexible as discussed above.
4. Changes in government policy and the fostering of the so-called 'enterprise culture'. As discussed in a later chapter, the importance of the impact of policy is debatable.
5. Changes in macro-economic policy in favour of small firms, e.g., changes in corporation tax to ensure a fairer treatment of small firms.
6. Private sector initiatives, e.g., enterprise agencies were often established with sponsorship from the private sector.

7. A more important role for the small firm in local authority policy, e.g., some economic development units have launched initiatives to help smaller firms. Contracting out of public sector services has also encouraged the growth of the small firm entrepreneur.
8. High unemployment rates in the 1980s which forced some workers to start their own enterprise using existing skills and redundancy payments rather than retraining.

The data shown in Table 2.1 are reinforced when we examine turnover levels for small firms. Table 2.3 gives the size distribution of firms based on turnover for 1989 and shows that 97 per cent of all firms had turnover levels of less than £1 million. This gives further weight to the importance of the micro firm. Remarkably, the table also shows that 35 per cent had turnovers of less than £15 000. This makes one wonder at the nature of operation of many small firms. It will become clear that, far from being prosperous, many of these micro firms spend much of their time trying to survive from day to day (one reason why there is little forward planning in small firms). As we will see below, being in business for many small firm owners can only be a part-time occupation, generating very small turnover levels.

Table 2.3   Size distribution of firms based on turnover 1989

Turnover (£000)	Number of firms (000)	Percentage share	Cumulative percentage share
0–14	1046	35.0	35
15–49	939	31.4	66.4
50–99	345	11.6	78
100–249	339	11.3	89.3
250–499	139	4.6	93.9
500–999	82	2.7	96.6
1000–2499	56	1.9	98.5
2500–4999	20	0.7	99.2
5000–9999	11	0.4	99.6
10 000+	12	0.4	100
Totals	2989	100	

Source: Employment Gazette, February 1992 (modified).

SMALL FIRM VOLATILITY

It should be clear by now that not only do most small firms struggle to survive on very low turnover levels, many will also cease to exist. Table 2.1 may show a net growth in small firm formation, but the table also hides high volatility due to both high birth rates and high death rates of small firms in the 1980s and 1990s. These are illustrated in Table 2.4 for the period 1987–89, and shows that small and micro

Table 2.4 Small firm turbulence 1987–9

| No. of employees | Service sector | | Production and manufacturing | |
	Births (000)	Deaths (000)	Births (000)	Deaths (000)
1–4	240	166	82	62
5–9	139	133	78	84
10–19	76	101	65	95
20–49	28	45	28	55
50–99	15	28	14	34
100–499	18	42	14	50
500–999	0	2	2	12
1000–4999	3	9	2	21
5000–9999	0	6	0	10
10 000+	0	0	0	0
Totals	518	532	284	423

Source: Employment Gazette, August 1992.

NB: In 1997 births were 182,600; deaths were 164,500.
Source: Business Start-ups and Closures, DTI 1998.

firm death rates were almost as high as birth rates and this was in a boom period. It is only in the service sector in the micro firms that new firm formation exceeded small firm deaths by any significant figure. During a recession period as in the 1990s death rates will have been higher. 1997 total registrations and deregistrations still show high turbulence.

Not surprisingly, official figures show low survival rates for new firm formation. Table 2.5 shows that less than 55 per cent of new VAT registrations survive for longer that 3 years, and less than 40 per cent survive for longer than 5 years. However, it should be realized that VAT registration survival rates may not be indicative of true survival rates, since a deregistration may not indicate business closures as such, just a decision to leave the VAT register but continue trading. Registrations are difficult to compare over time due to larger increases in the VAT threshold. However, these figures are consistent with those produced independently by Cressy and Storey (5). Using a database of businesses opening an account with the NatWest bank, over the period 1988–94, Cressy and Storey claim that less than 30 per cent survived longer than six years.

These birth and death rates illustrate a side of small firm creation that is too often ignored by the Government and policy makers. The social costs associated with a drive to improve start-up rates are often high. For example, high bankruptcy rates among small firm owners and entrepreneurs, who have often pledged much of their wealth and personal assets into the business, leave many people who have lost more than they put into the business. Due to the bankruptcy

Table 2.5   Survival rates of businesses registered for VAT

Period since registration in months	Percentage surviving	Number of deregistrations as percentage of number registered at start
6	93	7.3
12	84	9.3
18	75	10.6
24	68	10.1
30	61	10.0
36	55	9.1
42	51	8.6
48	47	7.6
54	43	7.6
60	40	6.9
66	37	6.8
72	35	5.9

Source: DTI, Small Firms in Britain 1996.

laws which require secured creditors to be paid first, small firm creditors are often the last to be paid. During a recession, this situation can lead to a domino effect as one business failure forces other small firms to fail.

The problem of (low) small firm survival rates has been illustrated by Westhead and Birley (6). They show that VAT deregistrations have been highest in the older industrial areas and conurbations leading to high net losses of firms even during the boom period of 1987–90. They comment that:

> This aggregate macro-level analysis reinforces the micro-level evidence that the majority of new firms are doomed to death in their formative years. Deregistration rates were found to be markedly lower in rural environments and significantly higher in urban areas. (pp. 56–7)

High business birth rates may look impressive, but they hide the fact that many of the new starts will not survive beyond the first year of operation and most will not survive the first three years. It is a sad fact that policy makers have been too preoccupied with quantifiable numbers of new firm starts and insufficiently concerned with the quality of business start-ups that were created during the 1980s. It is only recently that there has been some belated attention given to the quality of new firm start-ups. As we comment below, greater focus on the potential of surviving and growing new firms has led to changes in policy away from blanket coverage and incentives for all new starts, incentives that in the past have encouraged new firm starts that were doomed to fail.

GROWTH FIRMS AND JOB CREATION

The gradual realization that we should be more concerned about the quality of new small firm start-ups has led to greater focus on small firm start-ups that have the potential to grow—the so-called 'fast track' new firms with the potential for job creation. There has been some controversy surrounding the job creation of small firms. Numbers of small firms' starts do not give an indication of job creation, nor do we have a picture of whether new firm starts can replace the job losses of larger firms that have continued to rationalize and cut jobs in the 1980s and 1990s. Some writers have questioned whether small firms can replace the job-creating ability of large firms. After all it takes a lot of small firms to create the same number of jobs (ignoring issues of quality and security of jobs created) as one major car plant such as the investment by Toyota in Derbyshire.

The controversy surrounding the role of small firms in creating employment stems from a paper by Birch (7) which claimed that, in the USA between 1969 and 1976, 66 per cent of net new jobs were created by firms employing less than 20 employees. However, the assumptions and conclusions of Birch have been criticized by subsequent writers. In the UK, Fothergill and Gudgin (8) claimed that firms employing fewer than 25 people only accounted for 0.8 per cent of the growth in total manufacturing output in the period 1968 to 1975. A more recent study by Daly *et al.* (9) claims that small firms employing less than 20 people were equally important (to large firms) in the UK in job creation between 1987 and 1989.

Daly *et al.* calculated a net fertility index (NFI) by dividing the firm size share of overall employment into the firm size share of net job gain. This fertility index is shown in Table 2.6 and shows that on this measure, for the period 1987–9,

---

Table 2.6   Job creation 1987–9

$$\text{Net fertility index (NFI)} = \frac{\text{Share of net job gain}}{\text{Share of overall employment}}$$

NFI by size of firm

Firm size (no. of employees)	Service sector	Production
1–4	2.7	6.3
5–9	1.0	2.1
10–19	0.4	1.0
20–49	0.8	0.8
50–99	0.9	1.1
100–499	0.9	0.8
500–999	1.1	1.6
1000–4999	0.8	0.2
5000–9999	0.3	0.3
10 000+	0.7	0.4

Source: Employment Gazette, August 1992.

the major net providers of new jobs were the micro firms that employed less than 10 employees.

These studies must be treated with caution because of a number of factors:

1. They are usually based on VAT registrations which exclude some of the very small firms (due to the VAT turnover threshold) and do not give a complete picture. (Although adjustments are usually made, it is difficult to allow for non-registrations and de-registrations that are not deaths.) As stated above, the VAT threshold has sharply increased over time.
2. Some small firm creation can lead to job replacement rather than job creation. For example, if an individual starts in business under a public sector-provided grant scheme, they may force another individual out of business (because they are subsidized).
3. Equally some of the job creation may be temporary due to state subsidies or special financing schemes.
4. We have hinted that job creation may be of low quality in small firms. Employees are often non-unionized. The evidence on industrial relations is mixed and Ram and Holiday (10), for example, show that in small family-run firms relations are not as harmonious as might appear and consist of a form of 'negotiated paternalism'.
5. Small firm owners/entrepreneurs work long hours.

It has been suggested that net job generation is accounted for by a very small proportion of new small firms. For example, only a small minority of firms will grow to employ 50 people. Storey (11) claims that out of every 100 new firm starts only a handful, perhaps 3 or 4, will turn out to be major job creators and high growth potential firms. For example, Storey comments: '. . . out of every 100 small firms, the fastest growing four firms will create half the jobs in the group over a decade'. (p.113)

Using data from manufacturing firms in the north of England for the period 1965–78, Storey shows that out of 774 firms surviving to 1978, only 5 per cent had more than 50 employees and only 1 per cent had more than 100 employees. It is not surprising that only a minority of firms will grow to any size, given that national data such as that shown in Table 2.1 indicate that 98 per cent of all firms employ less than 20 people. More important, however, is the contention that a very small number of firms will create the major proportion of new jobs. For example, Storey calculates '. . . over a decade, 4% of those businesses which start would be expected to create 50% of employment generated'. (p.115)

A study by Gallagher and Miller (12) supports the contention that a majority of jobs will be created by a small minority of firms. From a study of 2000 new firms in Scotland and 20000 in the South-East, they found that in Scotland, 11 per cent of firms created 68 per cent of the jobs and in the South-East 18 per cent of firms created 92% of jobs. However, Daly et al. (9) with national data shown in Table 2.6 for the period 1987–9, claim that the growth of employment is more dispersed and slower than the evidence given above might suggest. They claim that over 50 per cent of net job generation is accounted for by firms moving from less than 5 employees to less than 10 employees. That is, the existence of fast-track new firms or 'high flyers' is less important than has been claimed for job generation. However, the contention that only a few fast-track firms will create the majority of jobs has influenced policy. As will be seen later in Chapter 7, emphasis in policy has shifted from blanket coverage to the concept of identifying winners and helping fast-track or growth firms to achieve their potential. While this concept is sound in theory and is supported by the balance of evidence (since the Daly *et al.* data may be seen as an exception that only covers a two-year period) there has yet to emerge any consistent criteria or policy for identifying these fast-track growth firms.

REGIONAL VARIATIONS

Using VAT data, Keeble and Walker (13) show that there are very significant regional variations in the growth of new and small businesses. The data reveals a north–south divide in new firm formation during the 1980s. Table 2.7 shows that the South-East, South-West and East Anglia have much higher enterprise formation rates than the North, Scotland and Northern Ireland. These regional differences in new firm formation rates add weight to our argument in Chapter 1 that the environment is a powerful factor in entrepreneurship. Keeble and Walker model a series of factors that affect firm formation, growth and death. Significant factors for both formation and growth were local population growth, capital availability, and professional and managerial expertise. They also found that support from enterprise agencies does help to reduce the death rates. The self-employment rates for 1997 are also shown in Table 2.7 and reveal some regional variations. Although not equivalent to business ownership, these figures reinforce the view that participation rates are lower in the North and Scotland than other regions of the UK.

Recent work by Barkham *et al.* (14) on differences in regional performance and growth rates of small firms found that high growth performing firms in Northern Ireland outperformed equivalent firms from comparative regions in England. In a four region comparative study, rather surprisingly their results show that the best performing region was Northern Ireland and the poorest performing region was Hertfordshire. They compare permutations of 'pairs' of regions but the most striking comparison is between Hertfordshire and Northern Ireland. In a discussion of the possible reasons for the disparities between these two regions, the authors suggest that contributing factors include differences in operating cost, such as wages and rent. This finding that a peripheral region can outperform a southern region leads to a guarded conclusion:

> The widening of the regional cost gap in the 1980s led to a temporary
> reversal of the general tendency for southern regions to perform
> more favourably than northern regions. (p. 123)

The authors do not pursue the intriguing possibility that the performance of firms in Northern Ireland may have been influenced by the enterprise development agency, Local Enterprise Development Unit (LEDU). The regional differences are

Table 2.7   Regional variation in new firm formation rates, 1980–90 and self-employment rate 1997

Region	Number of new firms (000)	Formation rate[1]	Proportion of employment accounted for by micro firms	Self-employment rate
South-East	850	100.3	33.2	14.7
South-West	190	99.7	40.4	15.7
East Anglia	79	95.8	31.5	n/a
East Midlands	140	79.3	25.3	10.8
Wales	93	77.5	40.4	12.6
West Midlands	180	72.1	27.1	11.5
Yorks and Humberside	158	70.3	29.8	11.4
North-West	207	68.7	31.2	11.9
Northern Ireland	39	61.1	39.5	13.0
Scotland	134	55.4	30.5	10.1
North	77	55.3	29.7	8.9
UK	2147	81.4	30.2	12.5

[1] Per 1000 civilian labour force, 1981.

Source: Keeble and Walker, 1994, *Labour Market Trends*, March 1998.

assigned to 'one of the swings of fortune' (p. 137) and the authors do not ascribe to the possibility that public sector intervention can overcome the constraints imposed by limited markets in a peripheral region.

Scottish Enterprise as mentioned in Chapter 1, following their own research into new firm formation in Scotland, have launched their own strategy for improving the business birth rate in Scotland (15). The analysis of Keeble and Walker would suggest that the low population growth in Scotland and lack of home ownership will continue to limit new firm formation. Research by the author (16) with high technology small firms in the West Midlands and Scotland, illustrated that the gap between the two regions (that the strategy of Scottish Enterprise is trying to close) in new firm formation rates for new high technology small firms was quite daunting, with a very much smaller proportion of high technology small firms in Scotland formed in the five years 1990–5, than in the West Midlands. Recent evidence (17) on the effect of the continuing Scottish Enterprise Strategy, who have developed a 'Personal Enterprise Campaign' targeted at potential new start entrepreneurs, in conjunction with local innovative mentoring programmes of support for new firm formation, suggests that policy interventions can have an effect on start-up, performance and survival rates (this is discussed in more detail in Chapter 3). The apparent increase in new firm formation rates since the launch of the strategy (1993) may be due to natural growth of the local economy and further judgement will have to wait until a longer period has elapsed. Combining evidence from both Scotland and Northern Ireland suggests that co-ordinated intervention can make a difference to the formation rates of high quality growth firms.

The significance of home ownership as a means of providing collateral and equity is a theme that we will return to in Chapter 5. Home ownership can reduce the liquidity constraints that face entrepreneurs (18, 19) and influence the propensity to enter entrepreneurship. It is a constraint that has been identified as significant by Scottish Enterprise in its strategy.

CONCLUSIONS

We have concentrated on the importance of small firms in the UK economy. Historically, the UK's small firm sector, however defined, has been less important than in other developed nations which have enjoyed better economic performance and growth, notably Germany and Japan. Greater attention in the 1980s and through the 1990s has been paid to the small business sector for its potential in generating jobs and providing the engine for new economic growth. The result is that it is now received government policy that the small firm sector will provide the main vehicle for economic growth and development and will be the main provider of jobs into the new millennium.

Close examination of small firm statistics in the UK, however, reveals that the vast majority of small firms are not major job creators and 98 per cent will probably never employ more than 20 people. Much of the balance of evidence suggests that high growth small firms are very rare, perhaps only 3 or 4 for every 100 new firm starts. While the number of small firms has increased, especially micro firms employing less than 10 people, this pattern is very uneven throughout the UK with large regional (and sectoral) variations.

The decade of the 1980s may in future be called a decade of small firm growth in the UK. This is in both absolute and relative (as a proportion of employment) terms. However, it is often forgotten that it was a decade of high volatility in the small firm sector: high business birth rates were accompanied by high business death rates. Many people were encouraged to start their own business who did not have the management skills to survive, and so some new firms were doomed to failure in the first year of trading. The social costs were high, due to the personal tragedies that lay behind the bland statistics. In the 1970s losing your job did not mean losing your home; now a more frequent story can be loss of everything when the business fails, often putting intolerable strains on the small firm entrepreneur's family. In addition, the quality of many of the jobs created was questionable—often low paid, part-time and insecure. Secondary labour markets have expanded in line with the growth of small firms in the 1980s and 1990s.

Although the Government will claim that it fostered the successful growth of the small firms sector during this decade, a number of factors suggest that the growth would have occurred to some extent anyway, since small firms were better equipped to meet the rapidly changing demands of the late 1990s.

There are signs that we have learned some lessons from the 1980s decade of small firm growth. The emphasis in policy has switched to quality rather than quantity. Supportive policies in new firm formation, such as those in Scotland and Northern Ireland, are still selective; targeted at firms that have the potential to survive and grow. Germany has a more important SME sector, but new firm starts are likely to be higher quality than new firm starts in the UK. Policy is now focusing on quality, although we will see later that, as yet, few criteria have been developed to target fast growth firms.

Learning outcomes

Students should be able to:

1. Analyse the major trends in small firm creation in the UK.
2. Discuss the factors that account for these trends.
3. Evaluate the importance of new small firms for job creation.
4. Discuss different definitions of the small firm and SME sector.
5. Construct visual presentations of the resurgence in the importance of the SME sector.
6. Appreciate the volatility associated with the growth in the small firm sector.
7. Identify the social costs associated with small firm failures.
8. Suggest reasons why local and regional development agencies would develop new firm support policies.

Suggested assignments

1. Analyse and present data on new firm formation and the small business sector working in small groups.
2. Discuss reasons for differences in small firm formation rates in different regions in the UK as shown in Table 2.7. Why should the South perform better than the North?
3. Class or group discussion of the factors that affect business start-up, a topic which we will return to after examining in more detail the issues in business start-up and a case study start-up in the next chapter.

REFERENCES

1. THE EUROPEAN OBSERVATORY FOR SME, (1994) *Second Annual Report*, EIM Small Business Research and Consultancy, Netherlands.

2. H.M. GOVERNMENT (1971) *Report of The Committee of Inquiry on Small Firms (Bolton Report)*, HMSO, London.

3. EUROPEAN COMMISSION (1996) *Journal of the European Communities*, no. 107/6, Brussels.

4. CURRAN, J., BLACKBURN, R.A. AND WOODS, A. (1992) 'Profiles of the Small Enterprise in the Service Sector', paper presented to the 14th National Small Firms Policy and Research Conference, Blackpool, November.

5. CRESSY, R. AND STOREY, D.J. (1996) *New Firms and Their Bank*, Centre for SMEs, University of Warwick, Coventry.

6. WESTHEAD, P. AND BIRLEY, S. (1994) 'Environments for Business De-registrations in the UK, 1987–90', *Entrepreneurship and Regional Development*, vol. 6, no. 1, pp. 29–62.

7. BIRCH, D.L. (1979) 'The job generation process', *MIT study on neighbourhood and regional change*, MIT, Massachusetts, USA.

8. FOTHERGILL, S. AND GUDGIN, G. (1979) *The job generation process in Britain*, Centre for Environmental Studies. Leicester.

9. DALY, M., CAMPBELL, M., ROBSON, G. AND GALLAGHER, C. (1991) 'Job-creation 1987–89: the contributions of small and large firms', *Employment Gazette*, November, pp. 589–94.

10. RAM, M. AND HOLIDAY, R. (1993) 'Keeping it in the Family: Small Firms and Familial Culture', in Chittenden, F., Robertson, M. and Watkins, D. (eds) *Small Firms: Recession and Recovery*, Paul Chapman, London.

11. STOREY, D.J. (1994) *Understanding the Small Business Sector*, Routledge, London.

12. GALLAGHER, C. AND MILLER, P. (1991) 'New Fast Growing Companies Create Jobs', *Long Range Planning*, vol. 24, no. 1, pp. 96–101.

13. KEEBLE, D. AND WALKER, S. (1993) 'New Firms, Small Firms and Dead Firms: Spatial Patterns and Determinants in the UK', *Regional Studies*, vol. 28, no. 4, pp. 411–27.

14. BARKHAM, R., GUDGIN, G., HART, M. AND HANVEY, E. (1996) *The Determinants of Small Firm Growth: An Inter-regional Study in the UK 1986–90*, Jessica Kingsley Publishers, London and Regional Studies Association, London.

15. SCOTTISH ENTERPRISE (1993) *Improving the Business Birth Rate: A Strategy for Scotland*, Scottish Enterprise, Glasgow.

16. DEAKINS, D. AND PADDISON, A. (1995) *Risk Management and the Use of Insurance by High Technology-Based Entrepreneurs*, Paisley Enterprise Research Centre, University of Paisley.

17. DEAKINS, D., GRAHAM, L., SULLIVAN, R. AND WHITTAM, G. (1997) *New Venture Support: An Evaluation of Mentoring Support for New Entrepreneurs*, Paisley Enterprise Research Centre, University of Paisley.

18. EVANS, D. AND JOVANIVIC, B. (1989) 'An estimated model of Entrepreneurial Choice under Liquidity Constraints', *Journal of Political Economy*, vol. 97, no. 4, pp. 808–27.

19. BATSTONE, S. AND MANSFIELD, E. (1992) 'Births, Deaths and Turbulence in England and Wales', in Robertson, M., Chell, E. and Mason, C. (eds) *Towards the Twenty-first Century: the Challenge for Small Business*, Nadamal Books, Macclesfield, pp. 179–208.

RECOMMENDED READING

BANNOCK, G. AND DALY, M. (1990) 'Size distribution of UK firms', *Employment Gazette*, May, pp. 255–8.

BARKHAM, R., GUDGIN, G., HART, M. AND HANVEY, E. (1996) *The Determinants of Small Firm Growth: An Inter-regional Study in the UK 1986–90*, Jessica Kingsley Publishers, London and Regional Studies Association, London.

DALY, M., CAMPBELL, M., ROBSON, G. AND GALLAGHER, C. (1991) 'Job-creation 1987–89: the contributions of small and large firms', *Employment Gazette*, November, pp. 589–94.

DALY, M. AND MCCANN, A. (1992) 'How Many Small Firms?', *Employment Gazette*, April, pp. 47–51.

HM GOVERNMENT (1971) *Report of The Committee of Inquiry on Small Firms* (Bolton Report), HMSO, London.

3. Issues in Business Start-up

INTRODUCTION

This chapter returns to the process of entrepreneurship and explores in greater detail some of the start-up issues. It is worth bearing in mind that this start-up and development process can occur over a considerable period of time. Initial business ideas take time to formulate, research, raise funding, find partners and may be considerably refined before the launch of the business. The chapter also illustrates this process through the introduction of our first case study. Every business start-up is a unique event; circumstances that contribute to success are intangible and may be different for each individual entrepreneur. Thus we need to be careful about recommending 'paths to success'; what may work for one entrepreneur may not for another. However, we suggest that intervention and support still has a role in the start-up process. Later in this chapter, we examine research with start-up entrepreneurs on the impact of the provision of mentoring support and suggest that such intervention and support can achieve an impact on survival and performance of new business start-ups.

The business start-up process can be broken down into a number of stages: the formation of the idea, opportunity recognition, pre-start planning and preparation including pilot testing, entry into entrepreneurship, launch and subsequent development. Each of these stages have a number of factors that will impinge on the process. These may either encourage further development or have a negative influence, perhaps causing the individual nascent entrepreneur to terminate the process. These factors will include the nature of the local environment, culture, access to finance and enterprise support and encouragement. A representation and suggested paradigm of this process is illustrated in Fig. 3.1. For the sake of simplicity the representation abstracts from reality; in practice a host of factors may affect each stage, for example, the psychology of the individual entrepreneur, mental processes and personal characteristics such as tenacity and perseverance in overcoming obstacles and barriers. Some of these factors will be brought out in the case study that is included in this chapter (and other cases in other chapters of this book), but for this part of the chapter we discuss some of the more 'external' factors that can impinge upon the different stages. Again we don't attempt to capture all of these but some of the most important are represented in Fig. 3.1 and discussed below.

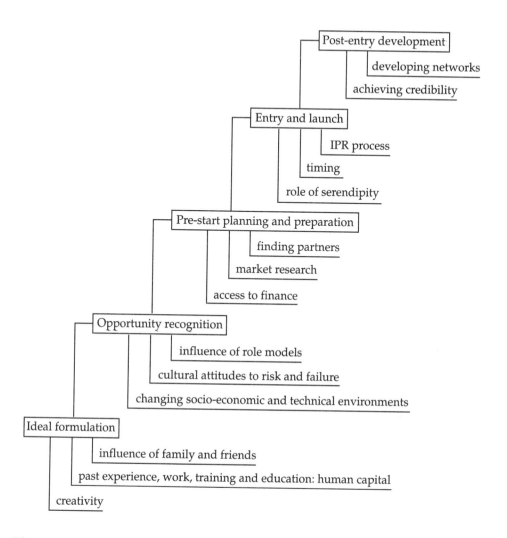

Figure 3.1   Business creation and the start-up process: a suggested paradigm

IDEA FORMULATION

The formation of business ideas will be affected by a nascent entrepreneur's past experience, training, education and skill development. This accumulation of knowledge, skills and experience is termed 'human capital'. A concept used particularly in the context of labour markets by economists following pioneering work of Gary Becker (1). Formulation of business ideas may be influenced by work experience, by individual training and recognition that a particular product or process 'could be done better'. Recognizing that a process or product could be done in a superior and different way has been the spur behind many new businesses. Later in this book we discuss the case of

Aquamotive—a case study concerned with innovation. The entrepreneurs in this case developed an innovative product after identifying a problem and realizing that they could provide a better solution. The majority of new business ventures are known to be in sectors or industries where the new business owners have had previous experience. For example, Cressy (2) has argued that human capital is an important determining factor in new business creation. The importance of human capital tends to be reinforced by external financial institutions, since our research has shown that bank mangers rate previous experience as an important factor in lending to new venture entrepreneurs (3).

For younger entrepreneurs, who will have limited human capital, it can be argued that education can have an important role in providing a conducive environment for idea formulation. It has been suggested that younger business owners (below 30) are under-represented in entrepreneurship because of limited personal capital and limited access to finance (4). The limited scope for idea formulation will also be a constraint, and the limited experience (or human capital) that potential entrepreneurs in this age range can draw upon will limit the scope of opportunities for developing ideas. Idea formulation here will be affected by educational experience and early training. It is arguable that education should provide scenarios that encourage creativity, lateral thinking and problem solving. However, there can be a conflict in providing sufficient scope within a curriculum for the development of such transferable and 'core' skills. There are indications that greater importance is being placed on 'enterprise' abilities including problem-solving, group work and ideas generation. In Scotland, as part of Birth Rate Strategy (mentioned in Chapter 1), a programme geared at all levels of education, *P1 to plc*, has been introduced into schools with some success (5). Other examples of attempts to widen the curriculum such as Young Enterprise (6) can, unfortunately, be 'add-ons' rather than developments that are embedded in the curriculum. Education systems are important in the development of creativity and idea formulation. For example Timmons (7) comments:

> The notion that creativity can be learned or enhanced holds important implications for entrepreneurs who need to be creative in their thinking. (p. 43)

Thus education is an important conditioning experience. Creative thinking can be enhanced or constrained by the education system and will affect the way we view opportunities, not just in our formative years but also later in life.

Figure 3.1 indicates that creativity will affect idea formulation. The process of creative thinking is now accepted as an important element in management. It has spawned a literature in its own right (8), so we can only recognize and comment on its importance here. Such literature suggests that obtaining the right environment and the right team of individuals is important for creative thinking and hence idea formulation (9).

Finally, it should be realized that idea formulation can take considerable time. The sudden breakthrough is comparatively rare. Ideas take time to refine;

they benefit from discussion with others, from research, from information gathering and from feedback. Thus being creative is only part of the process. Additional skills must be developed that can take basic ideas, then modify and refine them—perhaps involving considerable research—before they become viable business start-up ventures.

OPPORTUNITY RECOGNITION

Converting an idea into a business opportunity is the key element of the process of business creation. Moving from the idea stage to the exploitation of the opportunity requires many elements to be in place. The economic environment has to be conducive, the culture must be appropriate for risk taking and the nascent entrepreneur must have the confidence to take an idea suggested by opportunities through to fulfilment. Opportunities are generated by change. Change may be political, economic, social, demographic or technical. For example, economic change may be characterized by a period of economic growth and expanding demand, which may create opportunities for new business ideas that take advantage of increased affluence, leisure time and spending power of the population. The growth in the leisure industry has spawned many new developments and opened niche markets in areas such as sports, holidays and travel. The increased pace of technical change has created opportunities for new business ventures in new technologies, in new developments in information technology such as the Internet, in new applications in biotechnology. Social and demographic change may provide opportunities through changing attitudes or through creation of new markets in ageing population structures. These factors are the engines of change, but harnessing such change to create new business ventures requires new entrepreneurs to formulate ideas and fit them to the opportunity. It is this combination that is important. The idea has to be right for the opportunity. In a case which is examined later, Aquamotive, the entrepreneur recognized an opportunity to create a new fish farming application service, but the market required considerable development. It was not ready or receptive to the new technology. The correct timing of the idea with the opportunity created by forces of change is important.

Cultural attitudes to risk and failure can also impinge at this stage. It has been suggested that the UK has lower tolerance levels of failure than other nations such as the USA (10) and different attitudes to risk taking. Cultural factors are obviously intangible and difficult to gauge, but they help to determine whether the entrepreneur who has a business idea, who has recognized an opportunity, will be encouraged or discouraged from attempting to exploit that opportunity. If failure is heavily punished, as we suggest it is in the UK, then fear of failure may act as a significant constraint on this process (11). We suggest that the existence (or otherwise) of role models will also affect such a process. In Scotland a deliberate attempt has been made to provide more role models of new and recently successful entrepreneurs through the publication of the most important as *Local Heroes* (12). Other developments to provide more role models and 'surface' examples of under-represented groups have also been made in the UK, e.g., with successful black, female entrepreneurs (13). The purpose of such role models is to remove one of the stumbling blocks in the process of new business creation. Role models help to identify with success, with encouraging the next step of developing the business idea, and with identifying the right opportunity. Such role models should not be too successful; potential nascent entrepreneurs need to be able to identify with them, where they came from and how they were successful. More publications that help to identify entrepreneurs from many different ethnic and cultural backgrounds are needed as source material (13).

PRE-START PLANNING AND PREPARATION

A further combination of factors will be important to the eventual success of new business creation. Among the most important are research, obtaining information (to determine entry strategy) and raising sufficient finance. For obvious reasons, little research has been done on new business ventures that subsequently fail, but it is commonly asserted that one of the main reasons for the noted high failure rates (see Chapter 2) of such new ventures is under-capitalization (14). Researching the market and the competition is dealt with in more detail in Chapter 11, but search activity will also be required in raising finance.

The length and time of the search activity will depend on the opportunity and the characteristics of the new venture. If formal venture capital is required, raising such finance may take some time, because of due diligence procedures (12 months), as well as research and preparation. Recent research undertaken by the author (15) with entrepreneurs using non-executive directors, produced a number of cases where the entrepreneurs had spent some time researching opportunities in preparation for a management buy-in (MBI). In these cases the entrepreneurs had researched a large number of potential candidate companies (up to 100) as a target for an MBI. If informal, or business angel, finance is sought this will still involve a search and matching process by the entrepreneur before a suitable investor may be found (16). Even raising bank finance can entail a search procedure and time to find sufficient bank finance and the best terms and conditions (17).

Preparation means finding the right management team with complementary skills. Evidence on team starts (18) suggests that they have advantages over individual entrepreneurs because of the match of skills brought together within the team. However, the evidence is far from conclusive. Oakey (19) concluded that with new technology small firms the best performers were those with a single founder. Team starts have been the focus of policy 'best practice' (20), but it must be remembered that it is important to get the right 'mix' of skills in the proposed entrepreneurial team. Involving a friend who has been privy to the development of a new business idea may not work unless each person is able to bring knowledge or skill that is required in the business. Our research with entrepreneurs that had appointed non-executive directors demonstrated that the matching process was crucial to the success of the relationship and impact on the growth and performance of the firm (21).

ENTRY AND LAUNCH

As suggested above, the timing of entry is important. While advantages exist to first movers, moving too early can result in insufficient customers to make heavy investment worth while. The issue of timing becomes crucial if the protection of intellectual property rights (IPR) is involved. This is covered in more detail in Chapter 7, but the entrepreneur with a new product or process needs to decide whether and when to patent. Patents are expensive and time consuming but they may be a necessary prerequisite for formal or informal venture capital. Developing the entry strategy is an important part of the launch of the new business; attention will need to be paid to marketing, a factor that is sometimes neglected by a technology-based entrepreneur (22). The important relationship between marketing and entrepreneurship has been noted by a number of writers (23), but the concept of the development of the idea and formulating strategies has been explored by only a few writers. The issue of developing entry and early stage strategy is illustrated with a number of cases in this book and we also suggest an alternative paradigm for high technology-based firms, later in this chapter, based on some of our case study evidence.

The role of serendipity is often an underplayed factor in the start-up and business creation process. To the casual observer, the entrepreneurial and marketing strategies developed in the case study firms may appear to contain a strong element of chance, yet precursor developments can be highly important as preparation for exploitation of the business opportunity. With high technology-based ventures, non-high technology development beforehand, in different cases, was an important preparation for the entrepreneurial and marketing strategies concerned. The role of serendipity has scarcely been acknowledged, let alone researched, in entrepreneurial development and strategies (24), yet our evidence demonstrates that chance is only one element; the entrepreneur must be prepared to exploit opportunities, recognize and take advantage of them. The role of the non-technology phase of development lay in learning to deal with customers, to deal with suppliers, to deal with bank managers and in gaining general business experience.

POST-ENTRY DEVELOPMENT

Early stage development is a crucial phase for the novice entrepreneur. The entrepreneur is naive and must learn quickly to understand customers, suppliers, cash flow and how to deal with other stakeholders in the new business, which may include the bank manager or other financiers. For businesses in a team start, it is only the post-entry stage which leads to the testing of relationships between individuals, conformation of their role, and the value that each of them can bring. One of the most important issues that a new business faces is credibility. Being new, especially if markets are competitive, means that customers have to take quality on trust, that suppliers will be unwilling to give trade credit and that banks will be unwilling to extend significant credit facilities. One strategy that can overcome this lack of credibility is to include an experienced entrepreneur as a part-time director in early stage development. From our research with small companies that employed non-executive directors, we isolated a sub-sample of start-up companies only; in this sub-sample the most important reason for employing a non-executive director was to achieve credibility (25). Alternatively, the use of an experienced entrepreneur as a mentor may also lead to introductions to key customers, to achieving credibility with suppliers, and to bringing invaluable experience that overcomes the relative naiveté of the start-up entrepreneur. A discussion of the value of mentoring support is given later in this chapter.

In addition to achieving credibility, the establishment of early stage networks can be important in the development of new ventures. Part of the reason for bringing in experienced entrepreneurs, will be to access their extensive networks of contacts. Where this is not possible, new entrepreneurs need to establish their own network of contacts that may help them to break into new markets during the crucial early stage development of the new business. There is now an extensive literature on networks; as an example, Shaw (26) has provided evidence of the importance of networks in a competitive sector.

NEW TECHNOLOGY-BASED ENTREPRENEURS: A SPECIAL CASE?

It is generally accepted that start-up for a technology-based entrepreneur may not involve a product on the market during the post entry and early development stage. For example, such entrepreneurs can decide to start trading while still undertaking R&D, or still developing a prototype, perhaps being funded by grant aid to overcome negative cashflow. A standard paradigm for such a start-up is shown in Fig. 3.2 where the technology-based entrepreneur comes from one of two sources: a public sector research institution or the R&D department of a larger private-sector firm. For such entrepreneurs, obtaining patents (to secure markets and funding) may be more important than achieving credibility. Also, because the market may still have to be developed such entrepreneurs are generally seen to face special marketing problems (27).

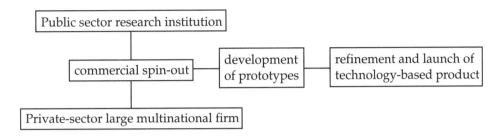

Figure 3.2   Technology-based start-up

NEW TECHNOLOGY-BASED ENTREPRENEURS: AN ALTERNATIVE PARADIGM

Figure 3.3 presents an alternative paradigm for early stage development of such entrepreneurs. Drawn from case study evidence, it suggests that high technology development can occur after an initial non-technical start-up. The non-technical start-up provides an important preparation for the entrepreneur through the learning experience, providing the basis for the development of more advanced strategies concerned with marketing, finance and risk management for the technology-based development. The importance of this preparation should not be underestimated. It provides the novice entrepreneur with a valuable window of development in which potential mistakes can be overcome, lessons can be learned, and contacts and networking can be developed. The entrepreneur, during this period, learns to recognize the importance of marketing strategies, while moving away from *ad hoc* developments. The traditional view normally sees the technology-based entrepreneur, in high technology environments, as a technical expert lacking commercial expertise. We suggest that an alternative paradigm can be presented; that a precursor non-technical period can be valuable and necessary in the preparation of entrepreneurial strategies for the technology-based development.

MANAGEMENT BUY-OUTS AND MANAGEMENT BUY-INS

Both management buy-outs (MBOs) and management buy-ins (MBIs) have not been regarded traditionally as examples of entrepreneurship and business creation. MBOs involve the buy-out of the equity of a company by the existing management team, often funded by a venture capital institution. Although this can lead to changes in management style and strategy, it can be argued that little new is created. MBIs involve an outside entrepreneur or management team buying into the equity of an existing company, again often funded by a venture

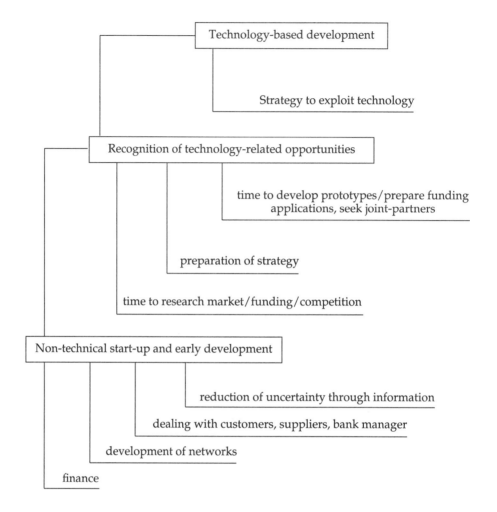

Figure 3.3 An alternative representation of start-up and early stage development in the high technology small firm

capital institution. As stated before, our research with small companies that employed non-executive directors, revealed MBIs where a single outside entrepreneur was often involved in the processes of new business creation; thus entailing considerable pre-MBI planning, research and search activity.

MBOs, by their nature, do not lead to new business creation *per se*, and have been regarded as very different from new start business creation. This may well be the case where an existing management team is given an opportunity to 'buyout' the equity of previous owners, a situation which does not lead to new business creation. However, some MBOs can be much closer to entrepreneurship, where either a team or an individual can virtually transform an old company and its associated way of doing business. In addition, where a MBO is undertaken by an individual rather than, say, the previous management team, this can be virtually equivalent to new business creation. The case study considered later in this chapter, Ace Cleaning (UK) Ltd, is an example of this type of transformation and 'new' business creation. Although it is not strictly a 'new business' creation, it does illustrate some of the management issues in early stage development and a management 'crisis'.

FRANCHISING

Another entry route, again not always associated with entrepreneurship, is to take on, or take over, a franchise. Franchising still involves new business creation and also, therefore, all the aspects of the process that have been identified in this chapter. The difference, of course, is that the franchisor rather than the franchisee undertakes much of this process, including idea formulation, opportunity recognition, pre-start planning and market research. Franchising has become a growth industry in its own right with 50 per cent of franchise systems being less than 5 years old (28) and, according to one estimate, one new franchise opening every 8 minutes (29). Although the large franchises are well known and are present on almost every high street, the vast majority are much smaller with 43 per cent having less than 10 outlets (30).

Buying a franchise, rather than undertaking *de novo* entrepreneurship, can have advantages as well as disadvantages for the individual. The main advantages can be listed as follows:

- the franchise is usually based on a proven and tested recipe for business success
- the franchisee can benefit from economies of scale, e.g., in marketing, advertising and buying supplies
- market research may be undertaken by the franchisor
- training is provided by the franchisor
- stationery and other business systems may be provided as part of the franchise package
- benefits from the strong brand name
- franchise systems are often favoured by banks due to established track record.

However, there are also disadvantages which are associated with the following factors:

- proven track records have their price—successful franchise systems require very large investments by the franchisee
- although you can sell on to someone taking over your role as franchisee, this will be less than you could achieve with *de novo* entrepreneurship
- trading is limited by geographical area and location, hence growth of the business will be finite and limited
- problems may exist in the relationship with the franchisor, leading to financial disputes.

Despite these considerable disadvantages arising from loss of control in a franchise, their popularity, as noted above, has mirrored the importance and growth of small firms in the economy as discussed in the previous chapter. The appeal of the reduced risk, while still retaining elements of entrepreneurship, has obviously been a powerful motivating factor for many people, and the growth of franchising seems likely to continue unabated into the new millennium.

SUPPORTING BUSINESS CREATION

In this section we examine some recent research undertaken with clients on a local area start-up programme that used experienced entrepreneurs as mentors for new venture client entrepreneurs. The support programme was local to the West of Scotland. The significant difference in this programme was that it used 'mentors' rather than professional 'advisers' to provide help and advice. To recruit the mentors, advertisements were placed in local media and previous or existing entrepreneurs were interviewed and recruited.

We discussed in Chapter 2 the high turbulence associated with business start-up and creation, a feature which tends to militate against intervention. For example, Storey (31) compared the provision of start-up support to 'a lottery in which the odds of winning are not good' (p. 16). The basis for this view was that the blanket coverage of start-up support programmes such as the Enterprise Allowance Scheme (EAS) did not result in a noticeable impact on the quality of firm starts and may have encouraged low-quality firm start-ups, even though Storey considered the EAS to be one of the 'better schemes'. The vast majority of new firm starts are known to be poor job creators (32). Thus it has been argued that the opportunity cost of such start-up support is high, since the careful targeting of public funds, in the form of enterprise support, at the small number of high-performing growth firms that are new starters, should result in a more cost effective way of supporting new venture development.

The research into the local area programme was conducted on an interview-basis with a sample of 45 new venture entrepreneurs who had been allocated a mentor as an adviser during the eighteen-month early stage development period. Profile data for these new entrepreneurs are shown in Tables 3.1–3.5. More important, and central to the present discussion, however, was the value of the intervention of the mentor. Table 3.6 indicates the perceived value by the new start entrepreneurs of the adviser/mentor's advice in the light of other sources of advice used.

Table 3.1   Personal profiles of the new start entrepreneurs

Gender	male 80%	female 20%
Average age	male 41 years	female 49 years
Prior employment status	employed 80%	unemployed 9%

Table 3.2 Business profiles

Business services	19 (42%)
Domestic/personal services	15 (33%)
Domestic and business services	4 (9%)
Retail/wholesale	3 (7%)
Manufacturing	2 (4.4%)
Financial services	1 (2.2%)
Forestry	1 (2.2%)
Total	45 (100%)

Table 3.3 Legal status

Sole trader	23 (51%)
Partnership	6 (13%)
Limited company	16 (36%)
Total	45

Table 3.4 Average projected turnover and employment

	Average	Std dev.
Turnover	£118 655	£179 526
Employment (FTEs)	3.6	8.94

Table 3.5 Sources of finance

	Mean score	Std. dev.
Personal sources, e.g., savings, redundancy etc.	4.16	1.38
EAS (first business grant)	2.91	2.13
Local authority grant	2.13	2.16
Trade credit	1.71	2.06
Bank overdraft	1.53	2.01
Other public sector source	1.24	1.97
Family/friends	1.07	1.91
Bank loan	0.93	1.76
Venture capital or business angel	0.24	0.96
PSYBT	N/A	N/A
Other specified source	0.24	0.98

Likert scale 0–5: $n = 60$ Likert scale 0–5 indicates not very important to very substantial, n = sample size

Table 3.6   Sources of advice

	Mean score	*Std dev.*
Business Adviser/Mentor	3.78	1.2
Accountant	2.47	1.8
Family	2.33	1.8
Bank Manager	1.98	1.7
Friends	1.49	1.8
Other	1.36	2.0

Likert scale 0–5: $n = 60$ Likert scale 0–5 indicates not very important to very substantial, n = sample size

The importance of the adviser/mentor was significantly higher than that of other sources of advice and demonstrated the importance of the mentor for short-term and general business advice. For more specific and specialized advice, the adviser/mentor was less important. For example, when asked who they would turn to for help in financial matters, 36 per cent of the entrepreneurs said the bank, 14 per cent their accountant, with only 22 per cent the business adviser. However, in terms of other or more general business advice, 62 per cent said the adviser, with only 4 per cent turning to either the bank manager or accountant.

The type of advice received, as expected, focused on general business start-up and construction and implementation of a business plan. Table 3.7 illustrates that a much smaller number of clients received advice that had a more strategic focus. The table confirms that for other categories of advice, the clients turned to more specialized providers.

Table 3.8, however, illustrates one of the key findings on the value and significance of the intervention and the key value of the mentoring support provision. When clients were asked to rank various criteria according to their

Table 3.7   Advice received

	Percentage of clients
Basic start-up including producing a business plan	44
General advice on running a small business	24
Strategic advice	27
Marketing strategy	13
Planning for growth	11
Other categories	2

Sample size: $n = 45$

Table 3.8 Significance of intervention

Difference made to	Rank order	Score
Achieving objectives	1	47
Ability to cope with problems	2	32
Ability to learn	3	31
Ability to manage	4	27
Ability to cope with change	5	26
Turnover	6	24
Profitability	7	19
Employment	8	17

Based on Likert scale, no difference to substantial difference (0 to 2).

significance, the softer and subjective criteria, such as the ability to cope with problems and even the ability to learn, rated more highly than differences made to 'hard' measures such as turnover, employment and profit. In terms of achieving objectives, 43 per cent reported that the mentoring relationship had made a substantial difference to their ability with this criterion. These objectives were concerned with short-term ability to cope with problems and general management. The abilities represented by Table 3.8 are relatively generic.

This study concluded that the most positive result was in terms of the value of intervention and the type of support. The support provided was highly valued by the new venture client entrepreneurs and encouragingly had more effect on managerial abilities and the ability of the new entrepreneurs to cope with change than with short-term outcomes. In principle, mentoring support, using previous entrepreneurs, should be effective in overcoming the crucial early stage learning period when new entrepreneurs have to learn how to handle change, crises and make strategic decisions. However, there is a balance. Such support should not be too interventionist and the findings indicated that training and case work by the team of mentors seemed to be encouraging the right balance. We suggested that this balance could easily be lost as the team of mentors grew, ironically partly because of the success of the programme.

THE ENVIRONMENT AND BUSINESS CREATION

Chapter 4 examines ethnic minority entrepreneurs, who have created new ventures in the inner city; by operating in ethnic enclaves, such entrepreneurs have achieved remarkable success in a difficult environment. Similarly, it is arguable that rural environments provide environmental problems associated with limited access and limited (or peripheral) markets and should be treated as a special case.

Business creation in a rural context

Clearly enterprise does not exist in a vacuum. Environments affect organizations through the process of making available or withholding resources and organizations can be ranked in terms of their efficacy in obtaining resources. The creation of new enterprise occurs within the context of an environment; the more supportive this environment, the greater the likelihood for micro enterprise. However, the efficacy and ability of the entrepreneur to draw on this supportive environment may play an important role in new venture creation. The nature of the environment may even affect the type of new ventures and the reasons for their creation. For example, the expansion of information technology creates a rich opportunity for new software businesses. The environment can therefore affect motivation. It also impacts upon venture survival and growth, so that the environmental resources which a firm controls play a key role in its success (33).

Environments are described as being abundant (i.e., munificent) or lacking (i.e., lean) in terms of critical resources associated with business creation (34). These resources have been argued to consist of a well developed infrastructure; human activity, power, influence, reputation, money and knowledge (35). Environments are dissimilar; each possesses distinct advantages and disadvantages and the entrepreneur has to engage with their environment to survive and prosper. This environmental dissimilarity is another reason why there is a wide variation in the kinds of new ventures. Since environments vary, different kinds of entrepreneurs exist and many influences may interact to cause a particular individual to form a particular business at any particular time and place (36). Two specific factors have been highlighted as determining the level of new business creation (37). Firstly, the *perception* of environmental munificence; that is, the extent to which the entrepreneur perceives the availability of critical resources. Secondly, resource acquisition self-efficacy; where the small business owner's ability to mobilize and gather the required resources from their environment becomes vital.

The rural environment is perceived as being disadvantaged, but it also offers the ideal circumstances in which to study business creation. Firstly, rural areas, by most definitions, are less concentrated in terms of business activity than urban areas and this means it is easier to trace out patterns of activities. Secondly, rural areas are viewed as being lean in terms of those resources associated with business start-up. They are portrayed as being distanced from main markets and main centres of business activity, have a lower and more dispersed population, a 'weaker' infrastructure, local markets are limited due to lower population, the cost of both obtaining and having raw materials delivered is higher due to the remoteness of location, and there may be shortages of skills within the local labour market. It is perceived to be scarce in terms of environmental munificence and the critical resources associated with the entrepreneurial process. Consequently, examining the process within the context of rurality is interesting, since it enables us to see how entrepreneurs overcome what could be viewed as potential difficulties and hindrances to growth and development. The following discussion, in the tutor's manual uses the rural context to investigate what entrepreneurs do and develops into a working definition and description of entrepreneurial actions.

Despite the apparent difficulties in starting up and running a rural business the number of such businesses has grown. In the example of the Scottish Highlands, an increase of 24 per cent occurred in self-employment between 1981 and 1991 (38). By 1997, the south-west of England, a predominantly rural area, relied on micro-sized firms to provide 40 per cent of all employment (39).

This level of growth has been attributed, at least partially, to the attraction of the quality of life which the countryside was perceived to provide, drawing people to rural areas who have set about providing their own jobs (40). These were often lifestyle businesses. It has also been suggested that the flexibility associated with rurality, the need to be more innovative and competitive has meant that the more dynamic expansionist firms have tended to be concentrated in smaller towns and rural areas (41).

Further discussion of the impact of rural environments is given in the tutor's manual, which also includes two case studies of business creation in a rural environment. Despite the problems of peripherality and limited local markets, these examples demonstrate that entrepreneurship associated with business creation in rural areas can be very successful. This supports known evidence that rural firms are more profitable and enjoy greater business growth (in certain size ranges) than their urban counterparts, possibly because rural environments have compensating factors such as a high quality and loyal labour force (42). Thus, although the environment may be a limiting factor, in practice if sufficient pre-start preparation, planning and research is undertaken, an opportunity for business creation can still be exploited successfully.

CONCLUSIONS

This chapter has considered the process of business creation, often regarded as the distinguishing feature of entrepreneurship. We have seen that the entrepreneur is required not just to generate ideas, but more importantly to recognize the correct opportunity for exploiting them. Although chance may be involved, pre-start preparation and planning is also crucial. For example, case evidence, drawn from research undertaken for this text, has demonstrated that precursor preparation before launching new technology-based products was an important period, allowing development of networks, learning and appropriate marketing strategies by the entrepreneurs concerned. This evidence was drawn from cases used later in this text including Alternative Publishing and Aquamotive. However, the last section of this text deals with one other case: Ace Cleaning Ltd.

It is arguable that intervention in the start-up and business creation process may not be valuable or productive. However, we have also examined recent research undertaken into a local area programme that seemed to indicate that the use of mentors (previous entrepreneurs) seemed to have some positive effects on the new start entrepreneurs' abilities to manage and to cope with a rapid period of change. Direct comments, by these entrepreneurs, have not been given in our brief review of this evidence, but largely testified to the benefit that such new start entrepreneurs gained and respect that they had for the mentors, the fact that such mentors had been in business recently was seen as contributing to the building of trust.

CASE STUDY

The first of our case studies, Ace Cleaning (UK) Ltd, concerns the creation and early stage development of the business. It has been included in this chapter because it takes the reader to a particular decision point faced by the entrepreneur, Mary Anderson. The case puts the reader in the position of the entrepreneur. You should decide what options are available and what you would do in the same situation. Student assignments are suggested after the case. What actually happened is detailed in the second part of the case, which is available in the tutor's manual that accompanies this text. Further discussion and tutor's notes are also available in the tutor's manual. It is also recommended that the reader should compare this case to another pre-start and early stage case, Alternative Publishing Ltd, at the end of the next chapter, which illustrates ethnic minority entrepreneurship.

ACE CLEANING (UK) LTD

Background

In 1991, after 14 years of continuous employment as contracts manager for a small/medium-sized cleaning company (ACE Ltd), Mary Anderson found herself without permanent employment and means of support. As a result of cumulative debts ACE Ltd had been forced into liquidation.

As a single parent, at the age of 52, the job market offered little prospect of re-employment. In particular, Mary had no hope of sustaining the moderate standard of living she enjoyed previously. Recognizing this dearth of opportunity and, in light of her previous experience, perceiving a potential within herself to successfully manage within this familiar market, Mary determined to investigate the concept of salvaging what contracts she could from ACE Ltd and starting her own company.

Start-up

The original ACE Ltd had gone into receivership with debts in excess of £80k. Mary, in acquiring their contracts list and goodwill, was required to take on board this debt. Although the debt referred specifically to leasing and purchasing agreements for equipment and stock, the low capital intensive and high labour intensive nature of the contract cleaning industry is such that a company's value can be measured to a greater extent by its contracts list and customer goodwill. Thus, such contract lists have a certain sale value. By taking responsibility for the £80k debt accrued by her previous employers, Mary ostensibly purchased the plant and equipment required to run the company. In fact, the principal lure in purchasing the company was the contracts list.

In addition to the £80k that it had cost to 'purchase' the contracts list from her previous employers the new company required working capital for wages and stock. The industry's staff are paid on a weekly basis, while invoice turnover and customer payment has a minimum cycle of 30 days. In addition, turnover on stocks has a lag period of between 4 and 8 months. As a result, though Mary required little finance for the purchase of capital equipment, the endeavour she proposed was not self-financing in the immediate term.

In effect, a nominal funding package in excess of £100k was required to finance the launch of ACE Cleaning (UK) Ltd. This figure was greater than any personal savings held by Mary. However, she was able to negotiate the phased payment of accrued debts by offering a 'director's guarantee' of future reimbursement. Thus, the outstanding £80k debt was to be repaid from monthly turnover over a period of 2–3 years. By this means Mary was able to waive the immediate requirement for such a substantial sum, albeit placing a continuing burden on cashflow and operating profits during the traditionally precarious stages of birth and early growth.

By offering this director's guarantee to creditors, Mary was also able to ensure the continuation of previous leasing and supply agreements. However, there still remained the requirement for operating capital in the region of £30–40k. On approaching the bank to request the provision of an overdraft facility for this purpose, Mary met with some initial resistance. Although she was in the position to invest £5k from private means, the shortfall she had hoped that the bank would provide in the form of an overdraft (£25k) would result in ACE Cleaning (UK) Ltd being relatively highly geared. By means of collateral, to compensate in some manner for the adverse gearing ratio, Mary was able to offer her house. The bank, in turn, would accept the collateral, valuing the house equity at £25k. However, there remained difficulties in obtaining the funding. ACE Cleaning (UK) Ltd were heavily in debt, had little or no tangible fixed assets/capital in the conventional manner and, while the contracts list inherited from the former ACE virtually amounted to guaranteed orders, the bank required assurances regarding cashflow and customer payment. Thus Mary was informed that provision of the overdraft facility would be contingent on the company securing an agreement for the factoring of its invoices.

Mary initially had difficulties in securing the factoring agreement. Many of the leading factoring companies were not prepared to accept the risk. An agreement was eventually reached with a factoring company whereby 100 per cent of her invoices would be factored at a cost of 4 per cent of total invoice value. Consequently the bank settled on the provision of a £25k overdraft facility. ACE Cleaning (UK) Ltd was now in a position to begin trading. However, the adequacy of the operating capital at Mary's disposal was marginal. The £5k of personal investment was immediately expended in covering wages for the first week's trading (£4.8k) and it became obvious that the probability of survival for the company during these early stages would itself be marginal.

Further, operating on this restrictive budget, the company had little scope when choosing premises at start-up and Mary chose to continue with the occupation of premises leased by the former ACE Cleaning. Although these were far from ideal, necessity dictated that they would suffice for initial trading purposes and they had the additional benefit of association. Since ACE Cleaning (UK) Ltd hoped to gain a majority of the custom enjoyed by the original ACE, the benefits of continued occupation, and hence visibility and ease of approach for previous customers, were obvious.

Marketing and Client Acquisition

ACE Cleaning (UK) Ltd began trading in August 1991. Although Mary was unable to secure the custom of all those firms with whom she had previously worked during her time as contracts manager at the original ACE, at start-up she had succeeded in regaining sufficient custom such that expected turnover on these contracts alone was in the region of £200k (75 per cent of which would be expended upon the associated wage bill). This custom had been gained primarily through going 'cap-in-hand' to former clients, offering security through perceived continuity. Further, as a result of her employment with ACE, Mary had been able to establish a considerable network of personal contacts within industry and client groups and her standing and visibility were high within the geographical confines of her immediate market.

No specific activities were undertaken with regards to the direct marketing of the company and its product. The distinctly low-tech nature of the service provided is such that throughout the industry there exists a degree of homogeneity of product. It was felt that since, prior to satisfactory completion of a contract, it was extremely difficult to compete on non-price factors (quality being the exception, but not demonstrable prior to sales) given the low profit margins involved making price competition more subtle, and appreciating the limitations of budget, a sophisticated marketing campaign would not prove to be either cost effective or, indeed, viable. This being the case, Mary continued the activities which had been employed in the early attempts to secure custom previously serviced by the original ACE—namely, direct personal approaches. As Mary became aware of the existence of a potential customer through industry contacts, or public information boards (e.g., newspapers, television, local authority contracts bulletins, etc.) she made direct speculative enquiries, offering free quotations to ensure that initial contact was gained.

A further operational practice, which can be viewed in some way as an extension of the marketing activities of Ace Cleaning (UK) Ltd, was the decision to undertake the contract cleaning of private dwellings. Profit margins in these cases were lower still than those for commercial cleaning contracts, to such an extent that the financial viability of undertaking this work was questionable. Yet Mary chose to pursue this type of work, utilizing it in a similar manner as 'loss leaders' are used by supermarkets. Carrying out this work increased the visibility of ACE Cleaning (UK) Ltd. Its vans could be seen out and about, and it could hope for the benefits of word-of-mouth and referral business, since those individuals who could afford the services of a contract cleaner were often in a position of relative authority within commerce.

As a result of these activities, shortly after commencing trading ACE Cleaning (UK) gained its first significant contract independent of the goodwill and contracts list associated with the original ACE. This contract, that of the Hilton Hotel at a major UK airport, represented £45k and provided the young company with a broader foundation from which to develop, whilst offering Mary confirmation about the sagacity of her investment and encouragement for the future.

Further, the addition of '(UK)' to the company name had not been simply an exercise in semantics. It had been a reflection of Mary's ambition to expand her company beyond its geographical market confines.

With regards to customer maintenance, or the securing of repeat custom, Mary appreciated that her business, in common with all service sector endeavours, required a strong customer orientation. From the outset customer care, quality and thoroughness were viewed as essential to success. She personally visited each individual corporate client to allow them to identify the managing force behind ACE Cleaning (UK) Ltd and make any complaints, or offer any suggestions, directly to the top.

At the end of the first year turnover had risen to over £350k and, through the activities described above, the company was beginning to enjoy the benefits of referral business. It had taken until this time for the business to become established and achieve a welcome degree of security.

Management Structure and Style

At start-up ACE Cleaning (UK) Ltd employed in the region of 70 staff. This figure was split into office staff (three, including Mary) and field staff (the number was growing steadily in line with client acquisition). The office staff, excluding Mary, were primarily concerned with administrative and clerical tasks and had no management responsibility *per se*. Of the field staff, there were two supervisors, while the rest of the company's relatively large staff were cleaners. Low profit margins, profits *per capita* employee, made it difficult for the company to employ essentially non-productive members of staff, in the form of supervisory or management positions.

The effect of this organizational structure, of Mary's desire to maintain a high degree of direct, personal and regular intercourse with clients and of the company's concern with customer orientation, resulted in a managerial style that was in some manner dictatorial or autocratic. The structure did not lend itself to the devolution of responsibility. There existed no middle-management with which to insulate or separate Mary from the line managers and in-field employees. Any empowerment which was exercised was limited to low-level, on-site tasks. As a result, Mary's time was concerned almost exclusively with the daily operational issues of her company, leaving little scope for strategic questions. Whilst business planning was undertaken, this was more often a mental activity on the part of Mary with little time available to establish a formal planning process.

Early Stage Growth

During the first two years' trading ACE Cleaning enjoyed steady, if unspectacular, growth. Turnover rose from £354 565, for the year until August 1992, to £380 772, for the trading year 1993 (an increase of 7.4 per cent). However, net profit fell from £12 925 in 1992 to a loss of £4 495 in 1993. During this period the personal drawings of Mary Anderson followed no formal path and were dependent on the capital needs of the company—when there arose a requirement for the purchase or maintenance of plant and machinery this affected Mary's salary. In effect she was paid, directly, what the company was able to afford.

This relative success over the first two years was as a result of increasing the client base from the approximate £200k turnover represented by clients salvaged from the original ACE. Although no formal marketing activities were undertaken to achieve this success, Mary felt that, in the absence of product differentiation capabilities, the vigour and determination of their direct approaches to potential customers played a significant role in gaining additional custom. Everything she owned was on the line, and as such, though superficially negative, her motivation to succeed was strong.

This initial growth was further reflected in the relocation of ACE Cleaning (UK) Ltd to new premises towards the end of the 1993 financial year. As mentioned earlier, through financial restrictions and the associated lack of opportunity, the company had been obliged to continue occupation of the original ACE premises. Necessity had obliged Mary to 'make do' with these premises, an arrangement which she had viewed as a temporary expedient. Through an advertisement in the local press Mary was made aware of the availability of alternative premises. The considerations normally associated with decisions regarding location (nearness to customers and/or suppliers, infrastructure, appropriately skilled workforce, etc.) were not of particular relevance in this instance. In addition, the new premises were considerably superior to those inhabited from start-up, and at a significantly reduced rate (the first three months of occupancy being rent free with the following three months at half rent). A further benefit gained through this move was the establishment of foundations for a working relationship with the local Enterprise Agency who were acting as agents in the leasing of the industrial estate.

The VAT Dilemma

After two years' trading with relative success the company may have reasonably expected to have gained a degree of security. However, at the end of the second year ACE Cleaning (UK) Ltd were suddenly faced with closure. As discussed, they had been trading and trading well, however they had been trading in the VAT. That is to say, the company had been charging clients the requisite 17½ per cent and, through naiveté, had been failing to transfer this revenue to the appropriate government body. In Mary's words the company had been over-trading. She had been under the mistaken impression that she would be able to pay the VAT owed by the company late and had been using all incoming revenue for prompt, and even early, payment of suppliers. As a result the company found themselves with a demand for £18 000 from the VAT Board and one week in which to pay in full. Although from a turnover in excess of £380k this may seem a small sum, the fact remained that, due to the nature of business costs, the money was not available. Further, no assets existed with which to raise the necessary finance and Mary Anderson stood to lose quite literally everything.

In retrospect, Mary believes that this situation forced her to 'face up to some home truths'. Until then she had been 'the Boss', enjoying the power without the responsibility. The shock of this crisis brought her to the realization that her role as managing director was to manage and direct the business, not 'to boss'. She had responsibilities to those who worked for her, to her creditors, and to her customers. After consideration she came to the conclusion that her business and those involved in it constituted an excellent venture which had suffered from *her* poor management, and she determined not to let others endure the consequences of her failings. Mary stood to lose everything but, more importantly to her, her staff (now in excess of 200) stood to lose their jobs.

FINANCIAL ACCOUNTS OF ACE CLEANING (UK) LTD

Profit and loss accounts for the year ended 31 August 1992	£	£
TURNOVER		354 565
Cost of sales		269 730
GROSS PROFIT		84 835
ADMINISTRATIVE EXPENSES		
Staff costs	15 813	
Depreciation	9 437	
Other operating charges	46 660	
		71 910
NET OPERATING PROFIT		12 925
Interest payable		1 603
PROFIT ON ORDINARY ACTIVITIES BEFORE TAX		11 322
Tax on ordinary activities		1 912
PROFIT ON ORDINARY ACTIVITIES AFTER TAX		9 410
STATEMENT OF RETAINED EARNINGS		
Retained profit for the year		9 410
RETAINED PROFIT CARRIED FORWARD		9 410

Balance sheet as at 31 August 1992	£	£
FIXED ASSETS		
Tangible assets		43 007
CURRENT ASSETS		
Stock and work in progress	10 090	
Debtors	31 286	
Cash at bank and in hand	783	
	42 159	
CREDITORS: amount falling due within 1 year	60 165	
NET CURRENT ASSETS		(18 006)
TOTAL ASSETS LESS CURRENT LIABILITIES		25 001
CREDITORS: amount falling due after 1 year		4 841
		20 160
CAPITAL AND RESERVES		
Share capital		10 750
Profit and loss account		9 410
		20 160

Profit and loss accounts for the year ended 31 August 1993	£	£
TURNOVER		380 772
Cost of sales		292 369
GROSS PROFIT		88 403
ADMINISTRATIVE EXPENSES		
Staff costs	20 346	
Depreciation	8 836	
Other operating charges	63 716	
		92 898
NET OPERATING PROFIT		(£4 495)
Interest payable		3 925
PROFIT ON ORDINARY ACTIVITIES BEFORE TAX		(£8 420)
Tax on ordinary activities		(£1 912)
PROFIT ON ORDINARY ACTIVITIES AFTER TAX		(£6 508)
STATEMENT OF RETAINED EARNINGS		
Retained profit for the year		9 410
RETAINED PROFIT CARRIED FORWARD		2 902

Balance sheet as at 31 August 1993	£	£
FIXED ASSETS		
Tangible assets		41 886
Goodwill		13 591
CURRENT ASSETS		
Stock and work in progress	10 412	
Debtors	39 641	
Cash at bank and in hand	8 832	
	58 885	
CREDITORS: amount falling due within 1 year	76 951	
NET CURRENT ASSETS		(£18 006)
TOTAL ASSETS LESS CURRENT LIABILITIES		37 411
CREDITORS: amount falling due after 1 year		8 509
		28 902
CAPITAL AND RESERVES		
Share capital		26 000
Profit and loss account		2 902
		28 902

Learning outcomes

At the end of this chapter you should be able to:

1. Discuss the importance of different factors that affect the business creation process.
2. Recognize the role and importance of education in creativity.
3. Understand the importance of developing, modifying and refining ideas over time.
4. Discuss the different paradigms involved with the start-up process in different types of new ventures.
5. Discuss the value of providing start-up support programmes with previous entrepreneurs as mentors.
6. Argue the case for and against state intervention in the start-up process.

Suggested assignments

1. Discuss the case of Ace Cleaning (UK) Ltd in a small group. Identify the options available to Mary Anderson and recommend and present a course of action.
2. Consider the case as consultants, discuss how Mary should change her management style and practices and make recommendations to Ace Cleaning (UK) Ltd.
3. Compare the Ace Cleaning case to the Alternative Publishing case (in Chapter 4). What are the similarities and differences between the two cases? From your knowledge of research findings and evidence on business start-ups, are the entrepreneurs concerned with each of these cases typical of new start-up entrepreneurs? How does the business creation process differ in each case?
4. Argue the case for and against intervention in the start-up process by public sector enterprise development agencies.
5. Why might the use of previous entrepreneurs as mentors to new start entrepreneurs be beneficial in terms of impact and development of such new start businesses?

REFERENCES

1. BECKER, G.S. (1962) 'Investment in Human Capital', *Journal of Political Economy*, vol. 70, pp. 9–49.
2. CRESSY, R. (1996) *Small Business Failure: Failure to Fund or Failure to Learn?*, Centre for SMEs, University of Warwick, Coventry.

3. DEAKINS, D. AND HUSSAIN, G. (1994) 'Risk Assessment with Asymmetric Information', *International Journal of Bank Marketing*, vol. 12, no. 1, pp. 24–31.

4. SCOTTISH ENTERPRISE (1993) *Scotland's Business Birth Rate: A National Enquiry*, Scottish Enterprise, Glasgow.

5. SCOTTISH ENTERPRISE (1995) *P1 to plc*, Scottish Enterprise, Glasgow.

6. GAVRON, R., COWLING, M., HOLTHAM, G. AND WESTALL, A. (1998) *The Entrepreneurial Society*, IPPR, London.

7. TIMMONS, J.A. (1994) *New Venture Creation: Entrepreneurship for the 21st Century*, 4th edn, Irwin, Illinois.

8. GOODMAN, M. (1995) *Creative Management*, Prentice Hall, London.

9. PROCTOR, T. (1998) *Creative Problem Solving for Managers*, Routledge, London.

10. BIRLEY, S. AND MACMILLAN, I. (eds) (1995) *International Entrepreneurship*, Routledge, London.

11. REYNOLDS, P. AND WHITE, S. (1997) *The Entrepreneurial Process: economic growth, men, women and minorities*, Quorum, Westport, USA.

12. SCOTTISH ENTERPRISE (1997) *Local Heroes*, Scottish Enterprise, Glasgow.

13. WANOGHO, E. (1997) *Black Women Taking Charge*, E.W. International, London.

14. CRESSY, R. (1996) *Small Business Failure: Failure to Fund or Failure to Learn?*, Centre for SMEs, University of Warwick, Coventry.

15. DEAKINS, D., MILEHAM, P. AND O'NEILL, E. (1998) 'The Role and Influence of Non-Executive Directors in Growing Small Firms', paper presented to Babson Entrepreneurship Research Conference, Ghent, Belgium.

16. MASON, C.M. AND HARRISON, R.T. (1995) 'Informal Venture Capital and the Financing of Small and Medium Sized Enterprises', *Small Enterprise Research*, vol. 3, no. 1, pp. 33–56.

17. DEAKINS, D. AND HUSSAIN, G. (1991) *Risk Assessment by Bank Managers*, Small Business Research Centre, University of Central England, Birmingham.

18. VYAKARNARAM, S., JACOBS, R. AND HANDLEBERG, J. (1997) 'The Formation and Development of Entrepreneurial Teams in Rapid Growth Businesses', paper presented to Babson Entrepreneurship Research Conference, Babson College, Boston.

19. OAKEY, R.P. (1995) *High Technology New Firms: Variable Barriers to Growth*, Paul Chapman Publishing, London.

20. DTI (1996) *Small Firms in Britain Report 1996*, DTI, London.

21. DEAKINS, D., MILEHAM, P. AND O'NEILL, E. (1998) 'The Role and Influence of Non-Executive Directors in Growing Small Firms', ACCA research report, ACCA, London.

22. OAKEY, R.P. (1995) *High Technology New Firms: Variable Barriers to Growth*, Paul Chapman Publishing, London.

23. For example, CARSON, D., CROMIE, S., McGOWAN, P. AND HILL, J. (1995) *Marketing and Entrepreneurship in SMEs: An Innovative Approach*, Prentice Hall, London.

24. MARTELLO, W.E. (1994) 'Developing Creative Business Insights: Serendipity and its Potential', *Entrepreneurship and Regional Development*, vol. 6, no. 2, pp. 239–58.

25. DEAKINS, D., MILEHAM, P. AND O'NEILL, E. (1998) 'The Role and Influence of Non-

Executive Directors in Growing Small Firms', ACCA research report, ACCA, London.

26. SHAW, E. (1997) 'The Real Networks of Small Firms' in Deakins, D., Jennings, P. and Mason, C. (eds) *Small Firms: Entrepreneurship in the Nineties*, Paul Chapman Publishing, London, pp. 7–17.

27. JONES-EVANS, D. (1997) 'Technology Entrepreneurship, Experience and the Management of Small Technology-Based Firms—exploratory evidence from the UK', *Entrepreneurship and Regional Development*, vol. 9, no. 1, pp. 65–90.

28. TIKOO, S. (1996) 'Assessing the Franchise Option', *Business Horizons*, vol. 9, no. 3, p. 78.

29. INTERNATIONAL FRANCHISING ASSOCIATION (1995) Franchising Industry Report, IFA, USA.

30. DICKIE, S. (1993) *Franchising in America: the development of a business method*, The University of North Carolina Press, North Carolina.

31. STOREY, D.J. (1993) 'Should We Abandon Support to Start-up Businesses?', in Chittenden, F. and Robertson, M. (eds), *Small Firms: Recession and Recovery*, Paul Chapman Publishing, London, pp. 1–26.

32. STOREY, D.J. (1994) *Understanding the Small Business Sector*, Routledge, London.

33. CHANDLER, G.N. AND HANKS, S.H. (1994) 'Market Attractiveness, Resource-Based Capabilities, Venture Strategies and Venture Performance', *Journal of Business Venturing*, vol. 9, no. 4, pp. 331–47.

34. JUDGE, W.Q. AND KRISHNAN, H. (1994) 'An Empirical Investigation of the Scope of a Firm's Enterprise Strategy', *Business and Society*, vol. 33, no. 2, pp. 167–90.

35. ALDRICH, H.E. (1979) *Organisations and Environments*, Prentice-Hall, Englewood Cliffs, NJ.

36. COOPER, A.C. AND DUNKELBERG, W.C. (1981) 'A New Look at Business Entry: Experiences of 1805 Entrepreneurs', in Vesper, K.H. (ed.) *Frontiers of Entrepreneurship Research*, Babson College, USA.

37. BROWN, T.E. AND KIRCHOFF, B.A. (1997) 'The Effects of Resource Availability and Entrepreneurial Orientation on Firm Growth', paper presented to the *17th Babson Entrepreneurship Research Conference*, Wellesley, MA, April.

38. ANDERSON, A.R. (1997) 'Entrepreneurial Marketing Patterns in a Rural Environment', paper presented to the *Special Interest Group Symposium on the Marketing and Entrepreneurship Interface*, Dublin, January.

39. DTI (1998) *Small and Medium Enterprise Statistics for the UK, 1997*, SME Statistics Unit, DTI, Sheffield.

40. CURRAN, J. AND STOREY, D. (1993) 'The Location of Small and Medium Enterprises: Are there Urban–Rural Differences?', in Curran, J. and Storey, D. (eds.) *Small Firms in Urban and Rural Locations*, Routledge, London.

41. ANDERSON, A.R. (1995) 'The Arcadian Enterprise: An Enquiry into the Nature and Conditions of Rural Small Business', unpublished PhD thesis, University of Stirling.

42. SMALLBONE, D., NORTH, D. AND KALANTARDIS, C. (1996) 'The Survival and Growth of Manufacturing SMEs in Remote Rural Areas in the 1990s', paper presented to the 19th ISBA National Small Firms Policy and Research Conference, Birmingham.

RECOMMENDED READING

MARTELLO, W.E. (1994) 'Developing Creative Business Insights: Serendipity and its Potential', *Entrepreneurship and Regional Development*, vol. 6, no. 2, pp. 239–58.

SHAW, E. (1997) 'The Real Networks of Small Firms', in Deakins, D., Jennings, P. and Mason, C. (eds) *Small Firms: Entrepreneurship in the Nineties*, Paul Chapman Publishing, London, pp. 7–17.

STOREY, D.J. (1993) 'Should We Abandon Support to Start-up Businesses', in Chittenden, F. and Robertson, M. (eds) *Small Firms: Recession and Recovery*, Paul Chapman Publishing, London, pp. 1–26.

STOREY, D.J. (1994) *Understanding the Small Business Sector*, Routledge, London.

TIMMONS, J.A. (1994) *New Venture Creation: Entrepreneurship for the 21st Century*, 4th edn, Irwin, Illinois.

4.   Ethnic Minority Entrepreneurship

INTRODUCTION

The predominance of ethnic minority entrepreneurship in some areas of Britain has led to attempts to explain this phenomenon. For example, writers have sought to explain the motivations of such entrepreneurs, and the issues they face, particularly the inherent characteristics of ethnic minority small firms and entrepreneurs who are often 'stereotyped' as concentrated in particular industrial sectors. The most notable stereotyping has been applied to Asian entrepreneurs who are often typecast as 'corner shop' retailers and seen as concentrated in the retailing, catering and clothing sectors. As we will see, this stereotypical and stylized view of the Asian entrepreneur is outdated. Ethnic minority entrepreneurs cannot be grouped into convenient categories based on industrial sector. In addition, the term 'Asian' now covers a wide range of distinct ethnic groups with their own characteristics such as Sikh, Muslim and Hindu entrepreneurs. Further, although Asian entrepreneurs are the most often described and discussed, there are of course many other ethnic minority groups in the UK with their own entrepreneurial characteristics. Those that have been studied include African-Caribbeans, Bangladeshis and Greek Cypriots. After a brief review, this chapter examines some of the issues that concern ethnic minority entrepreneurs and uses recent research evidence to discuss successful strategies adopted by them. It concludes with a case study of a start-up business drawn from this research.

In Britain's history, ethnic immigrants have traditionally been of crucial importance to economic development, a tradition that goes back to groups such as the Huguenots. These ethnic groups have been willing to accept new practices or bring new skills that facilitate significant economic developments. The tradition continues to be significant in the modern economy where Asian entrepreneurs were the first to open retail outlets on Sundays, predating a modern movement towards Sunday opening in most retail sectors. Ethnic entrepreneurs have also been willing to develop in areas which are shunned by 'mainstream' or white entrepreneurs, for example, economically marginal inner-city areas. The location in these inner-city areas has significant implications for ethnic minority entrepreneurs. Not only does the location often limit the available market to the ethnic enclave, it also makes the acquisition and availability of resources, especially finance and insurance, very difficult or (in the case of insurance) expensive.

To begin with, however, following the work of Blackburn (1), we review the state of ethnic enterprise in Britain. The potential of ethnic minorities in economic development has been highlighted by recent statistical analysis of census data by Ballard and Kalra (2), who show that one of the demographic features of ethnic minorities is their considerably younger age profile. For example, 33 per cent of the ethnic population is under 16 years of age compared with 19.3 per cent of the white population. This would seem crucial to the future economic development of Britain, especially in marginal inner-city areas which are still the predominant location for ethnic minority entrepreneurs.

THE PATTERN OF ETHNIC MINORITY ENTERPRISE IN BRITAIN

As Blackburn (1) points out, entry into self-employment is very uneven between ethnic minority groups. Table 4.1 shows that self-employment rates are among the highest in Pakistani and Bangladeshi groups and lowest in Black (West Indian and African) groups, with participation rates of 22.7 per cent compared to 6.7 per cent respectively. As Blackburn says: 'What is striking about the data is the relatively low proportion of the self-employed who are classified as Black who employ others' (p. 2). This indicates that not only are participation rates low among African-Caribbeans, but the size of African-Caribbean firms is likely to be much smaller than those owned by other ethnic groups. These observations are confirmed in our study of African-Caribbean entrepreneurs (3). We found that such businesses were typically small (average employment created was only three

Table 4.1 Key data on ethnic minorities in Great Britain (000)

	All	White	Ethnic minorities				
			All	Black	Indian	Paki-stani/ Bangla-deshi	Mixed/ other
Total population	54 860	51 843.9	3006.5	885.4	840.8	636.1	644.3
Total of working age	33 589.5	31 701.9	1887.6	582.1	547.1	344.9	413.6
Proportion self-employed	12.9	12.8	15.1	6.7	20.0	22.7	16.2
Proportion self-employed with employees as % of all self-employed	33.9	33.5	42.0	24.2	43.3	44.8	48.4

Source: Blackburn (1994)

full-time employees and average turnover was only £125 000) and young (the average age of the business being only four years). It should be noted, however, that given the young age of such African-Caribbean entrepreneurs and the location of the majority in the inner city, they have made significant progress and are probably catching up with other ethnic minority entrepreneurs in terms of enterprise development and the establishment of a significant presence in the inner city. African-Caribbean entrepreneurs are currently at a critical stage in their development and we have recommended special measures, such as specialized units, to ensure that African-Caribbean entrepreneurs can achieve success. Wanogho (4) has also demonstrated that black female entrepreneurs can achieve successful growth businesses in such inner-city environments.

The potential contribution of ethnic minority entrepreneurs to the regeneration of inner-city areas is confirmed by national data which illustrate the concentration of ethnic minorities in the traditional conurbations. Ram and Jones (5) have reviewed the literature on ethnic minorities in business and confirm their dependency on their ethnic communities. The limited economic wealth and high unemployment of such communities often limits ethnic minority entrepreneurs in terms of enterprise development.

ETHNIC MINORITY ENTREPRENEURSHIP LITERATURE

The literature on ethnic minority enterprise development has focused on three main issues: *accessing resources*, notably finance and labour; *accessing markets*, and *motivation*. Earlier literature focused on the cultural and additional forces that led early-stage immigrant labour into self-employment and high rates of participation in entrepreneurship. For example, Light (6) stressed the importance of cultural minority status which produced a strong sense of social solidarity in immigrant and ethnic enterprise in North America. Bonacich *et al.*'s study (7) of Koreans in Los Angeles identified access to resources and informal support networks as two of the key factors that accounted for the success of this ethnic minority group in entrepreneurship. Some writers have pointed to the success of ethnic groups despite difficult trading conditions, with survival achieved through piecing together a living from semi-legal activities (8, 9). Light (6) identified particularly the difficulties of black entrepreneurs in North America due to limited access to resources. Models of such ethnic enterprise development, as for example those of Waldinger (10, 11), reflect these issues and focus on how the entrepreneurial attributes of different ethnic groups determine the ability to access resources and markets to achieve entrepreneurial success (12, 13).

Accessing Resources

The first of the three issues has concerned the ability of ethnic minority entrepreneurs to generate or access resources. In some cases, writers have claimed that informal networks have given ethnic minorities in business an advantage due to their access to sources of finance and family labour (14, 15, 16). Waldinger (10) also pointed to the importance of informal networks as a key factor in successful entrepreneurial development of ethnic immigrants in New York. More recently, their relationship with banks has attracted research. Curran and Blackburn's study (17) of Bangladeshis, Greek-Cypriots and African-Caribbeans in the UK highlighted the problems of the latter ethnic group in accessing bank finance, which they considered was due to poorly prepared business plans. However, our research with Asian entrepreneurs in the West Midlands, and commercial banks (18), revealed that there was much variety in practice in the importance of financial constraints. For example, in some cases, good practice by bank managers had led to involvement in the Asian community and improved ability of Asian entrepreneurs to access bank loans. This practice, however, was very uneven and was often disrupted by the tendency of bank managers to move from one branch to another, and by changing strategies and staffing policies. Thus, generalizations about accessing resources cannot easily be made, even across one ethnic minority community. Further research with African-Caribbean entrepreneurs (3) revealed that this group were disadvantaged by their low profile in some cities and had distinct problems that could not be attributed to all ethnic minority entrepreneurs and small firms. Curran and Blackburn (17) have also shown that there are a variety of development issues that face different ethnic minority entrepreneurs.

The importance to ethnic businesses of the use of family and co-ethnic labour has been highlighted by writers such as Wilson and Portes (19), whose study of Cubans in Miami pointed to the importance of ethnic preferences in hiring labour which allowed this group to thrive where native whites did not; even where the native population had superior access to resources.

Finance

Curran and Blackburn confirm much of the author's previous research (18, 27), which shows that small firms owned by ethnic minority entrepreneurs are no different from white-owned small firms in being heavily dependent on the banks for external finance. However, they find that reliance on bank finance was much less significant for African-Caribbeans; a finding also confirmed by the author's research (3).

As Curran and Blackburn suggest, this could be due either to reluctance to deal with banks because of perceived discrimination, or to differences in approach by the banks to different minority groups. Curran and Blackburn suggest that the variations between the groups in the use of bank finance can be accounted for by different business problems (rather than different treatment by the financial institutions). For example, Blackburn (1) states:

> However, although the results show a relative disadvantage in securing finance by the Afro-Caribbeans, it is not as bleak as suggested by others. . . . Many of the problems expressed by the business owners were *business* problems rather than race-related. . . . (p. 29)

However, our research with African-Caribbean entrepreneurs revealed that the quality of their information was at least as good as that of other minority groups. For example, we found that bank managers were often of the opinion that the poorest prepared business proposals came from Muslim groups and in such circumstances they would rely on recommendation and introductions. We found that one of the problems that African-Caribbeans faced was that bank managers did not have much experience in dealing with those groups (because of their relatively low representation in the business population), whereas they were often experienced in dealing with proposals from Asian entrepreneurs. The practice and experience of bank officers also varied considerably. We found evidence of good practice, but bank policies of moving on staff often militated against building up good relationships with ethnic minority groups. As we comment later, there is still much that the banks could do to improve the potential of ethnic minority groups through developing best practice, such as involvement in the local ethnic community. It is not surprising that the experience of African-Caribbeans was considerably different from that of other minority groups.

Accessing Markets

The second issue has stressed the reliance of ethnic minorities in business on co-ethnic markets (20, 21). While this may be a deliberate strategy (11), Light (6) has argued that, in the case of black Americans, their concentration in ethnic enclaves traps them in a potentially disadvantaged cycle from which it is difficult to break into the mainstream of officially registered businesses. UK studies have stressed the importance of the need for successful break-out into mainstream white-dominated markets (22, 23), an issue that we would expect to be more important where markets are limited and peripheral. The related issue of location and the geographical characteristic of concentration of ethnic businesses in inner-city areas has further highlighted problems of break-out.

In the UK, the success of ethnic minority entrepreneurs has been officially recognized in the past, for example, with the reports from the Ethnic Minority Business Initiative (EMBI) (24), but the constraints that such entrepreneurs have overcome have not always received the same recognition. Their success has been achieved in marginal economic environments of the inner city and with limited access to either resources or mainstream markets. Debate on developing the need for break-out, following the EMBI Report, led to the view that ethnic minority businesses can only be secured through the development of more diversification into different sectors with discussion about the best way to secure strategies to move away from dependence on ethnic market niches (17, 23). The ability of ethnic firms to achieve successful break-out has been shown by Ram and Hillin (25) to depend on successful integration of a holistic strategy involving marketing, finance, human resources and 'key' contacts with mainstream markets.

Motivation

Attempts in the literature to explain the importance of ethnic minority entrepreneurs concentrate on the relative primacy of 'negative' or 'positive' factors in the motivations and development of ethnic minority small-firm owners, for example, Ward and Jenkins (12). The debate surrounds whether or not discrimination faced by ethnic minorities in the labour market was the predominant motivating factor in business ownership and entrepreneurship or whether positive factors such as a group's background experience of business ownership were more important in the motivation decision. Although Curran and Blackburn (17) have indicated that motivational factors such as 'independence' were significant in entry to entrepreneurship, there is little doubt that a history of disadvantage and discrimination has led to the concentration of ethnic minority firms and entrepreneurs in marginal areas of economic activity.

Curran and Blackburn (17) surveyed 76 ethnic minority entrepreneurs from three groups in three different localities. As indicated before, the three groups were African-Caribbeans, Bangladeshis and Greek-Cypriots and were selected from London, Sheffield and Leeds. On motivation, perhaps surprisingly, they found that positive factors associated with the desire to be independent were higher than expected and they claim that this was on similar levels to white-owned businesses. To some extent, the strong motivational factors were confirmed by our research with African-Caribbean entrepreneurs and (later) with Asian entrepreneurs in Scotland (3, 26). Over 80 per cent of African-Caribbean and Asian entrepreneurs agreed with positive statements concerning ambition and control of their environment. Yet, for a significant minority, negative factors associated with the lack of opportunity elsewhere were also important. Over 40 per cent (for both these groups) agreed that they had faced discrimination in previous employment. In such circumstances, discrimination and the lack of opportunities in the labour market are significant 'push' factors. Evidence from these studies showed that such entrepreneurs were often more highly qualified than equivalent white entrepreneurs. Analysis on motivation factors with African-Caribbean entrepreneurs showed that a 'mix' of positive and negative factors were important in start-up and motivation. Negative factors include the lack of employment opportunities (although this may also be a significant factor for white entrepreneurs) and the lack of career opportunities when in employment. It may be that African-Caribbean entrepreneurs have the characteristics that we would expect for white entrepreneurs. However, evidence of discrimination and frustrated career ambitions was found to be a factor for some of the African-Caribbean entrepreneurs.

Although a number of issues remain unresolved in motivation, such as the low participation rate of African-Caribbeans in entrepreneurship, attention has shifted from start-up to enterprise development issues. For example, ethnic minority entrepreneurs are perceived to be located in ethnic niche markets, such as Asian clothing firms supplying the needs of the Asian community or African-Caribbean hairdressers supplying a service that meets the needs of their community. The issue of 'break-out' from this reliance upon niche markets has come to the fore and has been recognized as a policy issue for ethnic minority entrepreneurs. For example, the EMBI Report pointed to the need for ethnic minority entrepreneurs to become accepted into the 'mainstream'.

The next section concentrates on the development of successful entrepreneurial strategies drawing on in-depth case work and the experience of ethnic minority entrepreneurs in Scotland (28). Such experience can of course be applied in other areas of the UK, and to other groups of entrepreneurs, but it is also possible to argue that ethnic minority entrepreneurs faced special issues and problems that have been discussed above.

SUCCESSFUL ENTREPRENEURIAL STRATEGIES

The research involved 40 interviews and a number of re-interviews to develop case material of successful entrepreneurial development. One of these cases, Alternative Publishing Ltd, has been developed and discussed at the end of this chapter. Cases for the study were chosen on the basis of several criteria including successful diversification and breaking into close-knit and mainstream markets. Our case study entrepreneurial firms had achieved success notwithstanding their limited access to finance, problems in accessing markets and successfully diversifying, 'despite the odds' of being trapped in sectors that had declining market shares. Ethnic minorities in business, throughout many areas of the UK, have previously been successful in traditional sectors such as retailing, wholesaling and clothing manufacturing, yet they are increasingly facing declining market share and need to achieve successful diversification and break-out from ethnic market niches if they are continue to be successful in the future. We examine some of the key success factors involved in the study firms and draw lessons that can be applied in other areas of the UK. These factors are identified under five headings: *accessing markets, accessing finance, networking, diversification strategies* and *empowering the community through entrepreneurship*.

Accessing Markets

One of the key success factors was marketing strategy. Although we found a high proportion of sales to white customers (63 per cent), it is likely that successful future development will be in market niches that depend on high quality of service and product, where the entrepreneurs concerned can use their abilities to react quickly to changes. For example, the owner of a specialized computing and software supplier commented: 'For us it was important to be focused in a certain area, to have a niche product and to control credit and product development'.

In common with other entrepreneurs that had successfully diversified, gaining the initial break was seen by a successful retailer who had diversified into manufacturing as important: '(Important issues were) . . . initially gaining premises, machinery, staffing and trying to get into the big boys, the large chain shops, breaking into the market'. For any small firm, breaking into new markets is crucial. For ethnic minority entrepreneurs, overcoming this hurdle was seen as particularly daunting since barriers were overlain and reinforced by issues of race. These factors need to be dealt with sympathetically by support agencies, perhaps through the use of specialists and intermediaries.

A majority of the entrepreneurs recognized the need to innovate, to manage change and to respond quickly to market conditions. It was generally accepted that part of successful development lay in the need to break into new markets. However, barriers were identified that prevented successful exploitation of niche markets. For example, a food manufacturer when trying to break into a new market commented on difficulty experienced in the following terms:

> We think it is our colour. We have tried to knock on the door of these supermarkets to no avail. We think that discrimination plays a part, but also, we don't offer anything new. They chop and change suppliers regularly but they are not giving us a chance at all.

Dealing with racial bias requires a strategy; it requires persistence, resources and emphasis on quality. As illustrated by our case study publishing firm, diversification may mean pioneering activity in sectors or areas that have seen no previous ethnic minority firms and as a consequence such activity encounters inherent bias. One entrepreneur commented: 'We overcame this (prejudice) by sheer perseverance'.

Accessing Finance

As discussed before, Asian entrepreneurs have been identified with a competitive advantage arising from their ability to finance business start-up and development from informal sources within their own community (12). While this was still significant in some cases, a characteristic which might lead to less reliance on bank finance, in general we have found that access to bank finance was not seen as an important issue in Scotland. There were, however, one or two important issues concerning how ethnic minority entrepreneurs can be helped to realize their potential.

We have mentioned that banks require well presented information through carefully prepared business plans, and points were made which supported further development work with entrepreneurs to improve presentation skills. In addition, for business development, a majority of entrepreneurs said that they would consider equity investments from business angels. Business angels are individuals who are prepared to invest long-term risk capital, but who have individual preferences for certain sectors or firms. More could be done to develop this source of capital, perhaps by placing informal networking and finance on a more formal footing such as the establishment of a 'capital matching agency' by support agencies.

Small Firms' Loan Guarantee Scheme (SFLGS)

The potential role of the SFLGS has been a 'thorny' issue, since the inner-city location of much ethnic minority enterprise would lead us to expect that take-up rates of the SFLGS would be significant. However, we know that take-up rates generally on this scheme, and particularly in Scotland, have been low (29). Less than 10 per cent of our sample were involved with the SFLGS. Its potential needs to be harnessed much more successfully in the inner-city areas, where take-up should be high. As with other studies we found that the problem lies in one of *engagement*. Awareness rates are often high, as with other inner-city schemes, but with ethnic minority entrepreneurs there are also relevance problems to be overcome. Achieving relevance means working with banks and ethnic communities to ensure that appropriate communication is used and means bank managers working with appropriate people in the community.

Networking

One of the keys to successful marketing strategies lies in establishing effective networks of contacts. The case study of the publishing firm illustrates the importance of networks. The two founding entrepreneurs brought in a third director to help with their marketing strategy, but as one of the entrepreneurs commented:

> We brought in . . . because of his contacts, he had a network of contacts in the industry. The (desk-top publishing) industry is close-knit and you have to fight hard to establish your reputation.

A network of contacts was often the key to market entry in sectors, particularly when the firm is relatively new. The case study firm was able to solve the problem of successful entry by bringing an established person with existing contacts. There may be a potential role for similar 'brokers' who are able to provide market access, or broker resources such as finance. Successful enterprise development strategies may depend upon the identification of 'brokers' who can bring the right contacts to the firm.

Networking must be with the full business community, not just within the ethnic community. As a result, it can involve a bilateral strategy, one branch connecting to the full business community and the second branch concentrated on building and gaining advantage from the existing ethnic network of business contacts. One way to develop effective networking with the wider community is through the development of business/enterprise forums that involve the full enterprise community.

Business and Enterprise Forums

The establishment of business forums can enhance the effectiveness of networks. To be effective, they must be relevant to the ethnic community but also to involve mainstream entrepreneurs and communities. A comment from a well respected leader of the Asian community recognized the need to involve all groups to make the forum effective:

> We have taken the first step . . . and it has taken us a long time to persuade all the different ethnic minority groups (Sikhs, Muslims, Hindus) to come together because they all want to form their own business club . . . and it will be open to everyone.

Diversification Strategies

Diversification strategies are closely tied into marketing and may be addressed as part of an overall marketing strategy. Successful diversification requires careful research, perhaps through a feasibility exercise. It requires, firstly, recognition that there is a need to change and a focused strategy for development. This process had been successfully carried out by one entrepreneur who had broken into the marketing of flowers. He comments on the process as follows:

> It is very hard break away from the traditional wholesaler or importer, we had to do something different, something unique. We tried to get products in that nobody else had. Because of the nature of the market we had to constantly innovate. A fairly big obstacle for us was peoples' reluctance to buy from a coloured person. I wouldn't call it discrimination, more bias.

And in developing a strategy: 'We had to hire a consultant who was here for about 6 months'.

The need for diversification is exemplified by the rapidly changing nature of the retail trade. A large cash and carry wholesaler predicted:

> In December 1993 the independent sector had 9 per cent via the corner shop, I predicted in the year 2,000 they are only going to be left with 6% . . . we are going to lose 40 per cent of the business from that sector.

Of course, translating the need for diversification into a workable strategy requires considerable thought and planning. It also requires education and training of existing shop owners if economic decline for the Asian community is to be avoided. As one entrepreneur commented:

> There is scepticism, there still is and independent shopkeepers they do tend to put the cart before the horse really (they need to) accept that they need to change (and) accept that there has been a lack of planning.

Empowering the Community through Entrepreneurship

Empowerment was found to be an important factor in motivation and enterprise development in our case study at the end of this chapter. It concerned a publishing bureau started by two young Asian entrepreneurs. As an example of a start-up in Scotland it was atypical. Both entrepreneurs were young (under 25), highly qualified, had professional careers and their decision to enter entrepreneurship represented a high opportunity cost. One of them had been working as a doctor and could look forward to a career leading to a position as a consultant. Motivation for him lay with empowering himself to achieve his goal of working and helping his local community. Commenting on the reasons for starting the business he stated:

> I had a decision to empower myself. Working as a doctor, you do not have time to commit yourself to working in the community. You are working at the cutting edge of a caring profession—you think you are in a position to help them (socially), but you cannot simply because of your position.

Although the entrepreneurs had different backgrounds, their uniting objective was to work and help their community. They identified entrepreneurship merely as a means to achieving this objective. This was carried forward to the establishment of a fund at some future date that could channel profits (from their business) to help the community: 'We would like to set up a charitable fund at some point in the future to spin off some of the profits'. The business was operated virtually as a community enterprise. Where possible they brought in workers from the community. They commented: 'We would help by having people working with us from time to time as well'. The two entrepreneurs took the entry decision knowing that it was going to adversely affect their standing in the Asian community. Again they commented: 'Our status within the community changed drastically when we gave up our professional career'.

This particular case study, along with others, illustrated how successful enterprise development was achieved from the specialization in expanding niche markets. Innovation was introduced either through the introduction of a new service or product. Two of the cases represented niche software firms, but in both of them a strong desire to achieve was reinforced by the empowerment principle.

CONCLUSIONS

This chapter has examined issues in ethnic minority enterprise development. The literature is now well established and has indicated, in North America and in the UK, the potential importance of ethnic minority entrepreneurs in the revitalization of the inner city. More recent literature has studied the maintenance of successful ethnic minority entrepreneurship through accessing mainstream markets. Constraints in the past have been perceived to be concerned with accessing resources, especially finance and with accessing new markets. However, apart from highlighting these issues and problems that characterize ethnic minority enterprise development, there has been little in the way of positive suggestions for overcoming these constraints and developing successful entrepreneurial strategies.

Our research with ethnic minority entrepreneurs in Scotland confirmed the importance of accessing finance and the crucial need to develop diversification strategies that tackle the reality of the business environment in which they operate. Successful strategies hinged upon the development of effective marketing and networks, appropriate support when required and the availability of financing instruments that met the need of the community. The diversity of ethnic minority enterprise development emerged from the research, a point which has been made by other writers (30). Yet initiatives designed to help the ethnic minority entrepreneurs overcome the constraints associated with the inner-city environment and limited access to capital are often generic and ignore the diversity of such enterprise and entrepreneurial activity.

Issues, constraints and barriers have long been recognized, yet the take-up of initiatives designed to overcome these barriers has been woefully low. Ethnic enterprise development has succeeded largely outside mainstream support and largely without access to special support. In Scotland, success has been achieved through entrepreneurs and other community leaders taking individual action and setting up their own initiatives, using ethnic minority literature to ensure that firms and entrepreneurs are engaged. As one Asian entrepreneur commented:

> One thing that the agencies have got to start doing is to market effectively to ethnic minority businesses, for example, Scottish Power . . . wanted to reach the black and ethnic communities . . . they designed a leaflet in different ethnic languages and then took their message to the temples and mosques—and they had a lot of success.

The diversity of ethnic minority enterprise is increasing. Generational issues have not been explored in this chapter, yet new young Asian and other ethnic minority entrepreneurs are entering entrepreneurship from very different backgrounds from their parents and grandparents. While the family experience and tradition is still important in the Asian community, many of these new young entrepreneurs may have a family background that does not have the tradition of business ownership. It is these new entrepreneurs that are forging the future of ethnic minority enterprise development in the UK. They have different expectations are often highly educated and enter entrepreneurship against a background of high family expectations not to follow a career in self-employment. Policies continue to defy this experience.

This diversity of enterprise development needs to be addressed through policies which are more flexible and responsive to the needs of individual ethnic minority entrepreneurs and their firms. In Scotland, *Enterprise Forums* have been established by individual Asian community leaders, who have recognized the need to widen the contacts of the Asian (and other) business communities and to develop them with mainstream businesses and agencies. These initiatives from within ethnic minority communities need encouragement and support. Best practice means working with the infrastructure and community links that already exist. Developing completely new policies is not only wasteful of resources, but also likely to be demoralizing to community leaders who have already invested considerable effort and resources to establish links.

One way forward should be through the establishment of more flexible 'expert' team arrangements such as a *task force*. The principle involves the setting up of a team that may consist of ethnic community leaders, business and marketing expertise and be capable of drawing on additional expertise in response to the individual needs of ethnic minority firms. This type of support has a number of advantages which include: flexibility, relevance to the ethnic community, responsiveness to changing needs of firms and entrepreneurs and the ability to use appropriate advertising and other media that will be recognized as relevant by ethnic minority entrepreneurs and small firm owners. It should also overcome, in a flexible and cost effective way, the problems of low engagement in support that have been discussed in this chapter.

Accessing finance remains a crucial constraint for ethnic minority entrepreneurs. Policies to overcome this constraint have focused on special funding and incentives geared to the needs of firms in the inner city, for example, through special incentives for take-up, as exist with the SFLGS. Inner-city Glasgow appears to be little different from other inner-city areas with low participation rates on such schemes. More such schemes are *not* required, rather what are needed, are *mechanisms* to achieve greater take-up. Developing effective forums/networks that can *promote* these funding schemes can be the challenge to the team-based *task force*. It is a challenge that has to be met if successful future enterprise development in the inner city is to be achieved.

CASE STUDY

This chapter concludes with the discussion of the start-up part of a case study of a firm started by two young Asian entrepreneurs, Alternative Publishing Ltd. Additional material can be obtained from the tutor's manual on the subsequent business development of the case which illustrates some of the strategies of ethnic minority entrepreneurs discussed in this chapter. It can also be used to illustrate some of the issues in start-up for any business (see Chapter 3). The purpose is to provide the student with a pre-entry and start-up situation and the associated decision making. (The first part of the case, written with Andrew Paddison, has been included. The tutor's manual contains further material, written by Linda Graham, on what happened with this business subsequently.)

ALTERNATIVE PUBLISHING LTD (Part A)

Background

Alternative Publishing Ltd was started in 1992 by two young entrepreneurs, Majid Anwar and Suhail Rehman. The firm focused on business services in desk-top publishing and associated computer services such as software development. It was established in a major UK city centre.

Both entrepreneurs were in their early twenties when their idea of starting in business was first thought of. They were British born, but of Asian background. Apart from this characteristic they both had very different histories. Majid was from a medical family and had himself followed this path after leaving school. Suhail was the same age, but had studied avionics at university and his position differed in that his family had a predominantly business background. Both entrepreneurs finished university with good degree qualifications.

They met through one of their extra-curricular study activities—community work—to which they both allotted significant amounts of time. They viewed this as a worthwhile and rewarding task since it afforded an opportunity to put something of human value back into the community that they had been brought up in and so help young people from an inner-city environment. Both had a desire to help their ethnic community.

After leaving university they found professional jobs with strong career structures. Majid started as a junior doctor working in various hospitals, whilst Suhail worked as a software engineer with GEC Ferranti.

Motivating Factors leading to Business Start-Up

Putting Profits Into Community Projects

The entrepreneurs' main motivating factor was the wish to put something back into their ethnic community. They had also devoted a lot of time to voluntary work. The plan was to skim off, in the future, some of the profits and put them into a charitable fund which would benefit and enable others within the ethnic community to realize their aims (and also enter business).

The Desire To Empower Themselves

Apart from this very distinctive plan, there were other factors which motivated both entrepreneurs to decide to go into business. Majid had a strong desire to empower himself. This had emanated from his career as a junior doctor with the NHS, where the high pressure of his position meant that he could not help the community—over and above his normal duties—even when he wanted to. Starting a business was one way in which he could take his own decisions about every aspect of his life. This wish to empower himself was not an easy option. He wanted to be able to influence the decisions regarding the course of his life and had to justify them to himself, his family and members of his ethnic community that had supported his career.

Family Background

Suhail's reasons for going into business were broadly similar, though his family involvement in business gave him an additional motivation to take this course. He had always had an inclination to go into business from an early age, though he felt that due to a lack of work experience it would have been unwise to do so straight after leaving university. Thus he had followed the plan that he had set himself, of going to work for a few years for a large company in order to gain the necessary corporate skills, and had deliberately delayed the starting up of a business until he was experienced enough.

Barriers To Entry

The Influence Of The Ethnic Community

The strength of both entrepreneurs, and their determination to succeed, was accompanied at the same time by certain forces which could be considered to be barriers to entering business. They experienced much cumulative pressure to continue with a professional career. In the Asian community a lot of emphasis is placed upon the younger generation achieving a professional career, in contrast to their parents who may not have had the same educational and career opportunities. Therefore they both faced much opposition from members of the ethnic community who were not able to appreciate why they were motivated to start a business. Also, because of the value placed upon a professional career, to leave their jobs meant a consequent loss in status which resulted in a narrowing of their marriage prospects.

Loss Of Professional Status

The other factor which might be seen to mitigate against a business start-up was that their professional careers offered them relative security with the prospect of high salaries in the future.

Planning And Implementing The Business Start-Up

The Choice Of Business

The founders possessed a strong interest in publishing and printing from their days of voluntary work where knowledge of publishing had been acquired. Secondly, they were interested in computing from their extra-curricular activities and, in Suhail's case, from his previous job as a software engineer which had provided him with much expertise in this area.

Finally, both partners recognized that future technological changes were going to make computing skills and knowledge even more crucial for a publishing career and their interests as mentioned already fitted this trend. From the outset both of them knew there was a gap in the market which had yet to be satisfied, though precise quantitative information on the market did not exist. Initial market research had established the feasibility of business entry.

Planning And Initial Phase

Even though they had identified publishing as a route to take, both founders were only in the early stages of planning. They realized that market research had to be done before any business could be started. In the initial phase they had to do a lot of the marketing themselves. They discovered that the building they were located in was actually the hub of the printing industry in the city centre. This was a feature that had not been known, but it proved fortuitous since it provided plenty of opportunities for networking. Majid and Suhail were able to use the location as the basis for forging contacts and creating a network of links within the sector.

The marketing skills required for desk-top publishing were different from those of more traditional printing. As mentioned above, the importance of networking soon become apparent as well as the need to forge contacts. Therefore they decided to bring in another partner and recruited Imran as a third director. Imran was considerably older than the other two founders. They reckoned that his greater experience would be useful to them in making contacts and conducting successful networking.

In the pre-start phase the team had to decide what business functions each was to be responsible for. Since both of them were anxious for a smooth start-up it was important to define this clearly. In the end a clear structure was devised. Notwithstanding Imran, it was decided that Majid should be responsible for the creative side with the design and artwork, whilst Suhail would deal with sales, marketing and administrative duties.

Customers And Competition

They had to make various decisions about how to deal with customers and elicit business. The path taken was to listen to the requirements and specifications of the customer for the job. From this the directors would then go back to them with a price for the job and a sample.

Majid and Suhail estimated that the public sector was the chief market that they wanted to develop. They recognized that there were many projects emanating from these authorities which would require new skills and expertise. In the initial phase they encountered two features of this sector: firstly, that the culture was generally less competitive and demanding; secondly, that the sector was generally difficult to break into, or as Majid put it, 'business tends to go round in circles'.

By contrast, the competitive market was variable. For example, in some areas, such as traditional printing, trading patterns were vertical with some competition, whereas in new areas there was little or no competition. In these new areas of desk-top publishing and 'printing with technology' the entrepreneurs found that it was possible to choose their price. This was where they were offering specialized services and in these cases it was possible to dictate to the market the price. In areas where there was a lot of competition, there was little customer loyalty and they were compelled to negotiate prices each time. As a result, both directors felt that to get themselves established in such a market took a lot longer than in some of their more specialized niche markets.

Included with this part of the case are financial extracts and forecasts from the business plan for the first year.

Financial Projections for Alternative Publishing Ltd, Year 1

Expenditure   £
    Insurance, electricity, rent and rates   6 000
    Wages   4 800
    Telephone/postage   1 500
    Subscriptions (journals, etc.)   100
    Consumables   1 500
    Legal and professional fees   500
    Advertising/publicity   2 000
    Equipment   5 500

    TOTAL   21 900

Income
    TOTAL from directors/investors   15 600

Sales
    Turnover for first year   25 000

Assets
    As equipment less 20 per cent depreciation

Liabilities
    VAT
    Directors' loans

TOTAL EXPENDITURE   21 900
TOTAL income   40 600
NET profit before tax   18 700
NET profit margin   43%

Alternative Publishing Ltd Cashflow forecast

	Oct M1	Nov M2	Dec M3	Jan M4	Feb M5	Mar M6	Apr M7	May M8	Jun M9	Jul M10	Aug M11	Sep M12	TOTALS £
Expenditure													
Insurance, electricity, rent and rates	1500	0	0	500	500	500	500	500	500	500	500	500	6000
Wages	400	400	400	400	400	400	400	400	400	400	400	400	4800
Telephone/postage			375			375			375			375	1500
Subscriptions (journals etc.)	75			25									100
Consumables	100	20	20	50	150	160	160	160	160	170	170	180	1500
Legal and professional fees		500											500
Advertising/publicity	400	150	150	300	125	125	125	125	125	125	125	125	2000
Equipment	700	200	200	4000			400						5500
TOTAL	3175	1270	1145	5275	1175	1560	1585	1185	1560	1195	1195	1580	**21900**
Income													
Directors/investors	12300	300	300	300	300	300	300	300	300	300	300	300	15600
Sales		500	1000	1000	1500	2000	2000	3000	3000	3000	4000	4000	25000
TOTAL income	12300	800	1300	1300	1800	2300	2300	3300	3300	3300	4300	4300	**40600**
Cash flow	9125	−470	155	−3975	625	740	715	2115	1740	2105	3105	2720	**18700**
Opening Balance	12300	9125	8655	8810	4835	5460	6200	6915	9030	10770	12875	15980	
Closing Balance	9125	8655	8810	4835	5460	6200	6915	9030	10770	12875	15980	18700	

Learning outcomes

At the end of this chapter you should be able to:

1. Describe the importance of ethnic minority entrepreneurs for the continued local economic development in the UK, especially the inner-city areas.
2. Identify the importance of Asian and African-Caribbean entrepreneurs.
3. Describe the untapped potential of development that still exists with black entrepreneurs.
4. Explain why ethnic minority entrepreneurs are dependent on bank finance.
5. Explain why the issue of 'break-out' has become important for the future development of ethnic minority entrepreneurs.
6. Discuss policy measures that could be taken to encourage this future development.

Suggested assignments

1. Consider the case of Alternative Publishing Ltd. Should Majid and Suhail start the business? In your answer, consider the advantages and disadvantages for these two ethnic minority entrepreneurs.
2. There has been considerable research into understanding characteristics of ethnic minority entrepreneurs, the issues they face, and their potential in economic regeneration and recovery. Using material from this chapter discuss the reasons for this attention with Asian ethnic minority entrepreneurs.
3. Why should African-Caribbean entrepreneurs have been neglected as a focus of research on ethnic minorities?

REFERENCES

1. BLACKBURN, R. (1994) 'Ethnic Enterprise in Britain', paper presented to the Ethnic Minority Small Firms Seminar, University of Central England, Birmingham.
2. BALLARD, R. AND KALRA, V.S. (1994) *Ethnic Dimensions of the 1991 Census*, University of Manchester, Manchester.
3. RAM, M. AND DEAKINS, D. (1995) *African-Caribbean Entrepreneurship in Britain*, University of Central England, Birmingham.

4. WANOGHO E. (1997) *Black Women Taking Charge*, EW Publishing, London.

5. RAM, M. AND JONES, T. (1998) *Ethnic Minorities in Business*, Small Business Research Trust, Milton Keynes.

6. LIGHT, I. (1984) 'Immigrants and Ethnic Enterprise in North America', *Immigrants and Ethnic Enterprise in North America*, vol. 7, no. 2.

7. BONACICH, E., LIGHT, I. AND WONG, C. (1977) 'Koreans in Business', in *Society*, vol. 14, pp. 54–9.

8. LIGHT, I. (1980) 'Asian Enterprise in America', in Cummings, S. (ed.) *Self-Help in Urban America*, Kennikat Press, New York, pp. 33–57.

9. GLASGOW, D. (1980) *The Black Underclass*, Josey-Bass, San Francisco.

10. WALDINGER, R. (1988) 'The Ethnic Division of Labour Transformed: Native Minorities and New Immigrants in Post-industrial New York', *New Community*, vol. 14, no. 3.

11. WALDINGER, R., ALDRICH, H., WARD, R. AND ASSOCIATES (eds) (1990) *Ethnic Entrepreneurs*, Sage, London.

12. WARD, R. AND JENKINS, R. (eds) (1984) *Ethnic Communities in Business*, Cambridge, London.

13. WALDINGER, R., ALDRICH, H., WARD, R. AND ASSOCIATES (1990) *Ethnic Entrepreneurs*, Sage, London.

14. LIGHT, I. AND BONACICH, E. (1988) *Immigrant Entrepreneurs*, California University Press, Berkley.

15. WERBNER, P. (1990) 'Renewing an Industrial Past: British Pakistani Entrepreneurship in Manchester', *Migration*, vol. 8, pp. 7–41.

16. WARD, R. (1991) 'Economic Development and Ethnic Business', in Curran, J. and Blackburn, R. (eds) *Paths of Enterprise*, Routledge, London.

17. CURRAN, J. AND BLACKBURN, R. (1993) *Ethnic Enterprise and the High St Bank*, Kingston Small Business Research Centre, Kingston University.

18. DEAKINS, D., HUSSAIN, G. AND RAM, M. (1993) *The Finance of Ethnic Minority Entrepreneurs*, University of Central England, Birmingham.

19. WILSON, K.L. AND PORTES, A. (1980) 'Immigrant Enclaves: An analysis of the labour market experiences of Cubans in Miami', *American Journal of Sociology*, vol. 86, pp. 295–319.

20. REEVES, F. AND WARD, R. (1984) 'West Indian Business in Britain', in Ward, R. and Jenkins, R. (eds) *Ethnic Communities in Business*, Cambridge, London.

21. JONES, T., McEVOY, D. AND BARRETT, J. (1992) 'Raising Capital for the Ethnic Minority Small Business', paper presented for the ESRC Small Business Research Initiative, University of Warwick, September.

22. RAM, M. (1993) *Managing to Survive: Working Lives in Small Firms*, Routledge, London.

23. RAM, M. AND HILLIN, G. (1994) 'Achieving Break-Out: Developing a Strategy for the Ethnic Minority Firm in the Inner-City', paper presented to the Ethnic Minority Small Firms Seminar, UCE, Birmingham, March.

24. ETHNIC MINORITY BUSINESS DEVELOPMENT INITIATIVE (EMBI) (1991) *Final Report*, Home Office, London.

25. RAM, M. AND HILLIN, G. (1994) 'Achieving Break-Out: Developing Mainstream

Ethnic Minority Businesses', *Small Business and Enterprise Development*, vol. 1, no. 2, pp. 15–21.

26. DEAKINS, D., MAJMUDAR, M. AND PADDISON, A. (1995) *Ethnic Minority Enterprise in the West of Scotland*, Paisley Enterprise Research Centre, University of Paisley.

27. DEAKINS, D., HUSSAIN, G. AND RAM, M. (1994) *Ethnic Entrepreneurs and the Commercial Banks: Untapped Potential*, University of Central England, Birmingham.

28. DEAKINS, D., MAJMUDAR, M. AND PADDISON, A. (1997) 'Developing Success Strategies for Ethnic Minorities in Business: Evidence from Scotland', *New Community*, vol. 23, no. 3, pp. 325–42.

29. SCOTTISH ENTERPRISE (1993) *Scotland's Business Birth Rate: A National Enquiry*, Scottish Enterprise, Glasgow.

30. RAM, M. AND SPARROW, J. (1993) 'Minority Firms, Racism and Economic Development', *Local Economy*, vol. 8, no. 3, pp. 117–29.

RECOMMENDED READING

CURRAN, J. AND BLACKBURN, R. (1993) *Ethnic Enterprise and the High St Bank*, Kingston Small Business Research Centre, Kingston University.

ETHNIC MINORITY BUSINESS DEVELOPMENT INITIATIVE (EMBI) (1991) *Final Report*, Home Office, London.

RAM, M. AND JONES, T. (1998) *Ethnic Minorities in Business*, Small Business Research Trust, Milton Keynes.

WALDINGER, R., ALDRICH, H., WARD, R. AND ASSOCIATES (1990) *Ethnic Entrepreneurs*, Sage, London.

5. Sources of Finance: Overview of Issues and Debt Finance

INTRODUCTION

This chapter will be concerned predominantly with sources of finance for entrepreneurs and small and medium-sized enterprises (SMEs), taking definitions of SMEs as given in Chapter 2. Thus for many small firms certain sources of finance are not available due to entry barriers. For example, many entrepreneurs and SMEs are automatically excluded from financial sources such as the Stock Exchange, and face difficulties raising types of finance such as long-term loans because of the automatically higher risk associated with firms who have little equity in the form of share capital. In the majority of cases the only equity is that of the proprietors. This chapter will give an overview of the sources of finance, but the focus is on debt finance. The following chapter will examine sources of equity finance. Some time will be spent examining theoretical issues which provide the foundation for an examination of this important area. This chapter is linked to a case study, Peters and Co., which gives a practical example of a start-up proposition that is seeking finance. There are a number of possible assignments that can be set based upon the case study.

It is worth making a distinction between the theoretical basis of entrepreneurs' and SMEs' finance and what we know about the sources of finance that they actually use. It is easy to hypothesize, from what has been said above, about the difficulties facing entrepreneurs and small firms; that they are likely to rely heavily on personal savings and equity for long-term finance, and perhaps trade credit for short-term finance. However, these hypotheses need to be balanced with what actually happens, i.e., the empirical evidence. We will consider each in turn.

There are a variety of sources of finance available to the entrepreneur and small- and medium-sized firm. These can be classified as internal and external. Internal sources include the personal equity of the entrepreneur, usually in the form of savings, re-mortgages, or perhaps money raised from family and friends. After the initial start-up of the firm, retained profits and earnings provide internal capital. Usually within a SME it is normal for internal sources to provide the major proportion of the firm's capital and financial structure. External finance can be drawn from a number of sources. The principal sources for the SME and entrepreneur are advances from banks, equity from venture capitalists and informal investors, and short-term trade credit. Other external sources may include leasing, hire purchase and factoring. In the UK the small firm entrepreneur may also qualify for grants or 'soft loans' from government bodies such as the DTI (e.g., Regional Selective Assistance—RSA) or for other schemes such as the Small Firms' Loan Guarantee Scheme (SFLGS). Local government may also provide loans and grants, and there are a number of agencies that have attempted to set up their own financing schemes for small firms. These may include venture capital and loans from enterprise agencies, Training and Enterprise Councils (TECs), or in Scotland the Local Enterprise Companies (LECs), development agencies, enterprise boards and Inner City Task Force Funding.

Whether SMEs and entrepreneurs face real difficulties in raising external finance can be disputed; but the concern of policy makers with this area has given rise to a barrage of assistance that is now available to small firms and entrepreneurs. Whether these schemes are effective is an issue which we touch upon later, but they have arisen at least in part because of theoretical concerns that small firm entrepreneurs will be at a disadvantage in raising finance compared to large firms. In particular concern has centred on whether SMEs and entrepreneurs face finance gaps, because the supply of relatively small amounts of finance that small firms require, less than £200 000, can be uneconomic to provide and subsequently monitor by financial institutions (especially when considering sources of equity capital). We turn to consider these issues in more detail.

ISSUES FOR SMEs AND ENTREPRENEURS

1. Finance Gaps

If gaps arise they do so because of mismatches between supply and demand. The existence of a finance gap will arise because demand from small firms is greater than the willingness of financial institutions to supply at current market conditions. For finance such as bank loans these gaps may be termed credit rationing. A gap may exist such as that illustrated by Fig. 5.1, where demand exceeds the available supply at current market rates of interest.

In Fig. 5.1 total advances that small firms would like to take up are given by ob. However, the amount that banks are willing to supply is given by oa. Hence the existence of a debt gap given by the distance ab. Governments can attempt to close this gap by shifting the supply curve of (debt) finance to the right by the introduction of schemes such as the Small Firms' Loan Guarantee Scheme (SFLGS).

The discussion so far is an over-simplification of the market for small firm entrepreneurs' finance. For example, we are assuming that all propositions from small firms that banks receive are homogeneous. This will, patently, not be the case and we would expect some propositions to be treated more favourably than others. An equally important point arises about whether the 'good' propositions receive finance and whether the 'poor' propositions do not. This is the problem of adverse selection which is discussed in more detail below.

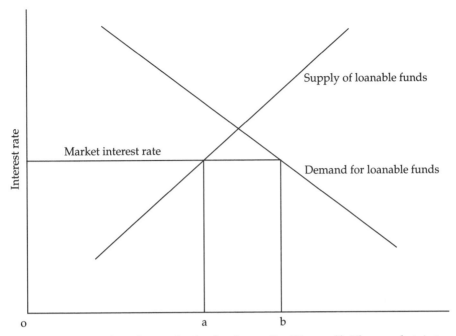

Figure 5.1 Demand and supply for bank credit. Notes: (i) The market interest rate is likely to be established below the equilibrium level due to state and Bank of England regulation. (ii) The demand for loanable funds is assumed to consist of homogeneous and 'good' propositions seeking bank finance implying a 'gap' which could be met by rationing.

Finance gaps have been recognized for over 60 years. They were first highlighted by the Macmillan Report of 1931 (1), and subsequently termed the 'Macmillan gap'. Macmillan found, at the time, that small businesses and entrepreneurs would have difficulty in raising amounts of less than £200 000, equivalent to £4m today. The Stock Exchange required a minimum figure of this amount to allow the trading of equity capital in a firm. There is little doubt that this gap has been substantially narrowed with the development of the venture capital industry in the UK. However, various official reports and other researchers have pointed to the continued existence of an equity gap in the UK. For example, it has been mentioned by the Bolton Report in 1971 (2), the Wilson Report in 1979 (3) and for a more recent study see Mason *et al.* 1991 (4). There is general consensus that there is still a gap for raising equity of amounts below £250 000, although as discussed in the next chapter there have been important recent developments in the promotion of sources of informal venture capital and alternative stock markets. This equity gap for SMEs and entrepreneurs still exists because of the following reasons:

1. It is not economic to issue shares for relatively small amounts of equity on the Stock Exchange (e.g., commission costs are high for small issues of less than £1m).

2. Difficulties can exist in getting a listing on the Stock Exchange. This became easier with the development of the Unlisted Securities Market (USM) and the Third and Over The Counter (OTC) markets, but the need for a trading record of at least three years is a barrier to many small firms. The demise of the USM in 1993 was a testimony both to the problems of entrepreneurs and small firms in the raising of equity and to the problems of providers in the administration of markets for relatively small amounts of equity capital. The launch of an Alternative Investment Market (AiM) appears, initially, to be successful and is discussed in the following chapter, but it still remains to be seen, however, whether it will be any more successful than previous alternative stock exchanges.

3. It is not economic for venture capitalists to provide relatively small amounts of equity capital. The reasons for this are that venture capital companies will want to monitor the performance of the company closely, because they supply equity not debt capital and are consequently not guaranteed a return. Furthermore, the costs of arranging the finance and the appraisal of propositions are generally fixed costs (5).

4. Following on from point 3, venture capitalists require high rates of return because they are assuming higher risks than the banks. Only certain high performing entrepreneurs and firms, the high growth firms, will be able to achieve the high rates of return required by venture capitalists who have in turn to satisfy the requirements of the shareholders in the venture capital fund. As a consequence of this, venture capitalists tend to concentrate on certain sectors of the economy only, or on certain types of finance such as Management Buy-Outs (MBOs). For a consideration of these issues see Dixon (6). Recent figures on the formal venture capital industry show that the majority of the sector's funds are invested in MBOs and Management Buy-Ins (MBIs) (7), so that the importance of this sector for the finance of SMEs and entrepreneurs is limited. For example, in 1995 65 per cent of all venture capital in the UK went into MBOs and MBIs (8).

5. Venture capitalists will apply a 'due diligence' procedure to any proposition that is being considered for investment. This will take a considerable period of time and only a small proportion of applications eventually receive funding after the due diligence procedure. Less than 5 per cent of applications for such formal venture capital will receive funding from this sector.

6. Venture capitalists will also require an exit route for the sale of their shareholding after a period of time with their investment in the entrepreneurial concern. The normal method of seeking an exit route for such a holding will be to seek an initial public offering (IPO) on the Stock Exchange or AiM. Thus venture capitalists will seek high growth entrepreneurial concerns that can be turned within a short period (say five years) into public companies and provide an IPO as an exit route for their holding and their funds.

7. Venture capitalists will also seek to take an active part in the management of the company to safeguard their investment. They will seek to add value to their investment through an active role in the management and use their networking capabilities to open up additional opportunities for the growth of the

entrepreneurial concern. The extent to which venture capitalists can add value has been one of the concerns in the venture capital sector.

Informal venture capital, which has seen important developments in recent years, has considerable potential to reduce equity gaps for small firms, and is discussed in more detail in the following chapter.

2. Finance and the Banks

The problems that exist theoretically can be analysed using theory from the economics of information. When conditions of uncertainty combine with asymmetric information (where providers and borrowers have different sets of information), we get two problems for the banks:

- Adverse selection
- Moral hazard.

Adverse selection occurs when the bank either provides finance for a venture that subsequently fails or refuses finance for a venture that would have been successful. It may occur because the bank does not have all the available information or the information is imperfect. The difficulty here is that the information required by the bank to assess perfectly the risk of the proposition is not costless to obtain. However, it can be argued that banks should reduce the mistakes they make, since they should have the skills and resources necessary to increase the frequency of correct decisions.

Moral hazard is more difficult for the bank to control. Once an entrepreneur has raised the bank loan, there is no guarantee that they will act in the best interests of the bank. In theoretical terms this is an example of a principal–agent situation; the bank as principal engages the borrower as agent to undertake the proposition, resulting in a profit for both sides. Therefore moral hazard is a monitoring problem and for relatively small amounts of finance it is not economic for banks to monitor performance closely. For this reason banks will usually require security, yet this contributes to the problems facing entrepreneurs. Those entrepreneurs without substantial equity and insufficient security will fall into the debt gap.

We have argued that bank assessments of small firm applications for loan finance are examples of decision making under uncertainty, incorporating asymmetric information for the provider and the client. The foundations of analysis of possible mismatches between supply and demand which can occur under these conditions have been laid down by Akerlof's seminal 1970 paper (9). Writers have developed the significance of these conditions for finance theory using a principal–agent framework (10, 11, 12). The relevance of these insights is limited when considering the finance of entrepreneurs and small firms who have restricted access to financial markets. Concepts of moral hazard and adverse selection, however, are still important and have been further refined by later writers (13, 14, 15).

Stiglitz and Weiss (16) have shown that the problems of moral hazard and adverse selection are likely to produce credit rationing, insufficient credit available for all sound propositions. It is possible to argue that these problems can lead to a credit glut (17) and a report by Aston University suggested that growing firms who wished to expand and were sound propositions were able to raise finance when they needed to (18). However, comprehensive surveys by Binks *et al.* in the UK, 1988–97 (19, 20) have revealed the expected mismatches between providers (the commercial banks) and clients suggested by the theoretical papers.

Research by the author and Hussain (21, 22) and the author and Philpott (23) has revealed that adverse selection certainly occurs in the UK and that risk assessment practices of UK bank managers are considerably different from their counterparts in Germany and Holland. The argument is that criteria used in Germany and Holland for risk assessment are different and less likely to lead to adverse selection. Deakins and Hussain took on the role of entrepreneurs seeking a funding proposition from 30 bank officers in the UK for a new venture. They hypothesized that banks would require financial and managerial information in risk assessment of propositions from new entrepreneurs. They expected bank officers to place more importance on the abilities and experience of the entrepreneur, since financial information which might appear as financial projections of income and costs in the cashflow forecast will be subject to uncertainty and treated with caution. Of course, with new propositions there is no financial track record of profitability and other criteria which may be used to assess existing propositions such as liquidity, sales growth, debtors and other measures of financial performance. If the new entrepreneur involves an application of new technology, we have the added factor of technological uncertainty. For these propositions they expected the banks to develop networking methods with outside institutions that can provide information on the assessment of the technology and the technical abilities of the entrepreneur that would help to reduce the more acute problem of asymmetric information.

We found that, of the 30 bank officers, 50 per cent would have backed the proposition and 50 per cent would not, but that there was also considerable variation in the approach of different officers. They also noticed that there was a bias in approach to financial criteria whereas important management criteria were discounted. Table 5.1 illustrates the importance of different information for their proposition. We can see from this table that only 10 per cent of managers considered small business experience and enterprise ability to be important. Further research by the author and Philpott (23) with German bank officers revealed much greater importance in Germany placed on managerial information.

This research has been extended by Fletcher (24) with 38 Scottish bank managers. Taking the same proposition as used in the Deakins and Hussain study, but with modifications to allow for slightly different economic conditions and the Scottish environment, Fletcher found a number of significant differences between the Scottish bank managers and the findings of the author's study. A greater proportion of Scottish bank managers (68 per cent) were prepared to back the proposition and some Scottish bank officers were prepared to back the proposition without security, despite the relative high gearing of the proposition. Some of the differences are illustrated in Table 5.2. Fletcher attempts to account for them by

Table 5.1   Criteria used or sought on the proposition

Information	Percentage of managers
Gearing	83
Entrepreneurs' personal financial position	73
Forecasted balance sheet and P&L account	66
Entrepreneurs' drawings	63
Entrepreneurs' contacts in industry	60
Timing of income payments	60
Contingency plans	57
Entrepreneurs' personal collateral	50
Market research	50
Entrepreneurs' qualifications and careers	43
Cashflow assumptions	40
Entrepreneurs starting separately	37
Role of IT consultant	33
IT development costs	27
Business/managerial strategy	13
Enterprise and small business experience	10

Notes:
(i) $n = 30$.
(ii) These are selective criteria.

Source: Deakins and Hussain (22).

Table 5.2   English v. Scottish bank managers' decisions

Score out of 10	Number of officers	
	English	Scottish
0	1	1
1	4	3
2	4	1
3	3	2
4	3	5
5	1	1
6	3	4
7	10	13
8	1	7
9	0	1
10	0	0
Total	30	38

Source: Deakins and Hussain (22) and Fletcher (24).

reference to the different banking structure and relationships in Scotland. The three Scottish banks, the Royal Bank of Scotland, the Bank of Scotland and the Clydesdale Bank, operate with closer relationships to their business customers than the main English clearing banks. This, coupled with the different environment (e.g., there is less owner-occupied housing in Scotland), might account for some of the differences found in practice between English and Scottish bank managers, with Scottish bank managers closer to the German approach where greater emphasis was placed on the entrepreneurs' abilities and managerial experience.

3. The Role of Security

We can also hypothesize that bank officers will stipulate requirements on the small business owner which may involve frequent monitoring of information to reduce moral hazard. However, a cost minimization approach will also include using methods that ensure commitment on the part of the entrepreneur. We would expect collateral to have an important role because it can ensure commitment and also provides a fail-safe method for the bank to recover losses in the case of the form of adverse selection that involves selecting a business failure. In conditions of uncertainty, signalling is obviously important and following Spence (25), a number of writers have developed theoretical implications of the importance of signalling (26, 27, 28). The importance of signalling commitment has also been recognized (29). Thus liquidity constraints and uncertainty combine to encourage the provider of finance to require security when this is available. Also Chan and Kannatas have pointed out that the type of security provided by the entrepreneur can provide information for the provider (30).

Collateral, however, is not without costs and its own problems, e.g., there are valuation problems, there might be depreciation to consider; and it might be necessary to revalue collateral at intervals. The taking of collateral, then, needs to be balanced against the costs of management for the bank. Also the taking of collateral does nothing to reduce adverse selection. It merely provides a method for the bank to recover (some) potential losses where it considers risks to be high. However, if we assume that bank managers are risk averse, we can expect that collateral will be required where risks are perceived to be high, e.g., with new technology entrepreneurs or with propositions which have high gearing.

Table 5.3. shows the importance of general criteria from the study with English bank managers. While security requirements do not appear to be of high importance, in practice they will often be critical requirements where risk is perceived to be high, such as our proposition that was discussed with 30 bank managers. For example, of those that would have backed the proposition all required security. The importance generally of gearing (the ratio of debt to equity) as a criterion is reflected in Table 5.3, which reinforces the view that financial information such as the gearing level is a critical factor for bank managers in the UK.

Theoretically, adverse selection should not occur if the bank has perfect information and can rely with certainty on cashflow predictions. Following

Table 5.3   Importance of criteria used to assess lending propositions

Criteria	Rank order	Mean score	Std deviation
Trading experience	1	4.43	0.5
Projected income	2	4.37	0.85
Existing profitability	3	4.3	0.6
Equity stake	4	4.18	0.69
Repayment of previous loans	5	4.12	0.76
Gearing	6	3.82	0.9
Client an existing customer	7	3.78	0.76
Net profit to sales	8	3.75	0.89
Previous loans	=9	3.73	0.69
Personal guarantees	=9	3.73	0.69
CVs of clients	11	3.7	0.76
Trade debtors	12	3.65	0.71
Liquidity ratios	=13	3.62	0.85
Gross profit to sales	=13	3.62	0.85
Trade creditors	15	3.57	0.85
Charge on personal assets	16	3.55	0.65
Fixed charge on business assets	17	3.52	0.91
Floating charge	18	3.00	1.07

Note: 6 point scale used from 0 to 5.

Altman (31), we have argued that it is necessary to define two different categories of adverse selection. Firstly, the bank officer could approve a proposition that turns out to be a business failure. Secondly, the bank could refuse to accept a proposition that turns out to be a business success. We define these categories as Type II and Type I errors respectively. (The reader should note that this reverses the Altman classification.) We consider that bank officers are overly concerned with avoiding Type II errors (partly because Type I errors will not be discovered) and that this contributes to adverse selection.

Systems that control for Type II errors may minimize risk, but they also miss business propositions that might contain higher risk but provide profitable opportunities for growth in the business of the bank. These hypotheses provide theoretical explanations of why bank officers may turn away small firm propositions that have high potential for growth and profitability.

4. Some Empirical Evidence

In terms of empirical research, it is known from various sources that entrepreneurs and small firms are highly dependent on internal sources of finance, as might be expected to follow from our discussion above. Research by Cambridge University's ESRC Centre for Business Research (CBR) 1992–8 (32, 33, 34) indicated that bank finance was by far the most important source of finance for entrepreneurs and SMEs. Table 5.4 gives their figures for sources of finance received in the period 1995–7. In 1998, the CBR study found that 41 per cent of their sample of 1520 SMEs and entrepreneurs had attempted to raise finance from external sources in the previous three years. This figure represents a considerable improvement on the 26 per cent found by the Bolton Report (1971) but it still represents some degree of introspection by small firms and entrepreneurs in seeking finance. It may also represent the existence of barriers to obtaining finance. This may have two identifiable consequences:

1. It will affect the speed and growth of their development and confirms that few firms are high growth performers.
2. It raises the question of whether sufficient entrepreneurs and small firms are available that are actively seeking equity finance to make matching schemes for business angels and entrepreneurs worth while.

Table 5.4   External sources of finance from a sample of 2520 small firms 1995–7

	Percentage of respondents receiving some finance from:
Banks	68.7
Venture capital	5.2
Hire purchase/leasing	49.5
Factoring	13.4
Trade credit	5.3
Partners/working shareholders	14.4
Other private individuals	7.4
Other sources	6.3

Source: ESRC Centre for Business Research (34).

It is likely that internal sources and the entrepreneur's equity will be very important for start-up finance. For comparative purposes, using our study of start-up small firms discussed in Chapter 3 (35), we report the results in terms of importance or sources of finance in Table 5.5. Although it shows that a high proportion of start-ups do use bank finance, a more significant feature is the comparative importance of personal savings as a source of finance which are rated significantly higher than bank finance.

Table 5.5   Start-up finance for a sample of 60 entrepreneurs in Scotland

Source	Percentage of respondents	Importance (mean score)
Personal sources	80	4.2
Enterprise Allowance Scheme*	66	2.9
Local govt grant	50	2.1
Trade credit	44	1.7
Bank overdraft	37	1.5
Other public sector	29	1.2
Family and friends	20	1.1
Bank loan	22	0.9
Venture capital	7	0.2
PSYBT**	12	4.86
Other source	7	0.2

Notes: *The importance of the EAS is accounted for by the large majority of respondents trading for less than one year.

**Prince's Scottish Youth Business Trust (applies to young entrepreneurs only; less than 26 years old).

Source: Deakins *et al.* (35).

———————— *Question for discussion* ————————

Do female entrepreneurs face disadvantages when raising finance compared to male entrepreneurs?

It has been suggested that if entrepreneurs and small firms face problems in raising finance and are faced by finance gaps, then female entrepreneurs and small business owners face more acute problems since their propositions may not be taken (as) seriously by funders or they may face disadvantages through lack of equity, security and possibly support from their spouse. It is only recently that systematic and careful research has been carried out on this important topic. Three studies have adopted careful research methodology which overcomes some of the limitations of previous (more *ad hoc*) attempts to research this issue.

Firstly, Read (36) has examined the question of whether bank managers have any preference for lending to men rather than women. She examined matched samples of 40 pairs of male and female entrepreneurs and found 'more similarities than differences' in their relationships with the bank and their use of overdrafts and loans. However, she did find some evidence of patronizing treatment of a minority of the female entrepreneurs by the bank and some differences in the relationship suggesting that women adopt a different strategy when dealing with the bank manager.

Secondly, Rosa *et al.* (37) have also made a careful study of the differences between male and female entrepreneurs. They found that differences in terms of capitalization and economic performance between male and female entrepreneurs are complex, but women significantly are likely to have lower levels of capitalization and hence levels of external finance. However, as they comment, given that female entrepreneurs have started from a much lower base, they conclude that the performance of female-owned businesses has been quite remarkable and that they are 'catching up fast' with male-owned businesses.

Thirdly, Chell and Baines (38) have examined the differences between male and female business owners in their study of micro-firms in the business services sector. In terms of financial performance they found 'no significant differences'. Although, unfortunately, they do not include data on external finance, they conclude that we should treat stereotypical views of either male- or female-owned businesses with extreme caution. This perhaps indicates that if women do face disadvantages in raising finance, these are likely to be quite subtle; e.g., anecdotal evidence suggests that women may be asked different questions by potential funders compared to men with similar propositions.

RELATIONSHIPS BETWEEN ENTREPRENEURS/SMALL FIRMS AND THE BANKS

Work on the relationship between the entrepreneur/small business owner and their bank has been carried out in the comprehensive surveys by Binks *et al.* (20, 39, 40) for the Forum of Private Business. Bank charges, although frequently cited in the press, may not be of most concern to small business owners and entrepreneurs; but Binks *et al.* did find that only 26 per cent of respondents thought that bank charges were good value for money. There have been improvements by the banks, particularly in staff training and developing specific posts such as 'Enterprise Managers', but entrepreneurs do have genuine grievances if charges are not itemized and the bank operates a hands off-policy. This is something that the banks have tried to correct with their Small Business Charters. However, Binks considers that: 'Bank charges, interest rates and the banks' demand for collateral remain important constraints on small firms' (41).

Over time the relationships between entrepreneurs and the banks seem to have improved, although the surveys carried out for the FPB indicate that the extent of this improvement varies between the different commercial banks (40). For example, there has been an overall improvement in the relationships, but individual commercial banks have made efforts to improve their relationships with small business customers. The authors comment: 'The overall improvement in bank performance may reflect more positive trading conditions for businesses and banks but also genuine substantive improvements in bank service quality' (p. 1152).

CONCLUSIONS

In this chapter we have taken an overview of the important issues in the finance of SMEs and entrepreneurs. Much of this discussion has centred on finance gaps and their implications for entrepreneurs and small firms. We have tried to show, theoretically, why these gaps might emerge given problems of uncertainty and asymmetric information.

We have shown that entrepreneurs and SMEs continue to be dependent on banks for external finance despite schemes that attempt to improve the availability of equity capital. We have shown that entrepreneurs also face problems in raising bank finance, that UK bank practices of risk assessment can be variable and that adverse selection (where potentially viable projects are not receiving finance) is higher than it needs to be.

By now you should be able to discuss the advantages and disadvantages of the most important of these sources. You should also have an understanding of why small firms and entrepreneurs are at a disadvantage compared to larger firms in financial markets and also have an appreciation of the problems that face providers of finance.

This chapter has focused on debt finance; the following chapter will examine in more detail sources of equity finance (including formal and informal venture finance) and some of the issues in raising equity. Alternative sources of finance, some publicly provided, are also discussed.

CASE STUDY

The remaining section of the chapter is concerned with our next case study, Peters and Co. The case concerns a start-up proposition and business plan involving three entrepreneurs seeking to raise bank finance. It is designed for use with students to illustrate some of the issues in raising bank finance. Suggested assignments are given at the end of the chapter and further information is available in the tutor's manual.

PETERS AND CO.

Introduction and Background

The following information is based on a real business. The names of the three entrepreneurs concerned have been changed, but otherwise all information is based on their actual business, including financial costings and research. The information provided is for a start-up venture which is seeking to raise finance from a bank. You are provided with the following sets of information:

1. Summary of the proposition.
2. Business plan for the following 3 years for Peters and Co.

3. Information on the three entrepreneurs who are to be equal directors in the concern.

The Three Proprietors

The three proprietors are all qualified chartered quantity surveyors (QS). Two of them are working for a major QS partnership which has offices throughout the UK. Noel Peters, who is to be the managing director for Peters and Co., has nine years' experience with local authorities and seven years' experience with the UK QS practice; his qualifications include a BSc in QS. He has been rapidly promoted and is a senior partner. He has worked on schemes up to £100m in value. Graham Davis is a colleague of Noel Peters with 20 years' experience in the QS industry. He heads up the cost planning unit at the UK practice. Tony Franks has been a chief QS with a local authority and cost centre manager before leaving to be managing director of a company in private practice. He has 30 years' experience in QS and the construction industry. More details are provided on the individual proprietors later.

The Service

The business will offer traditional cost and auditing control of QS through, for example, billing of quantities, which is the traditional costing service of QS. It will also use its experience to offer project and facility management. Experience in project management means that the business can draw on the skills and expertise of the proprietors to offer this service. The business also hopes to offer an integrated IT construction service. This marks a difference from the standard traditional QS costing and auditing service. The business will offer a bespoke service by applying CAD techniques to the design, construction and costing of projects. This use of information technology offers exciting opportunities to break the mould of traditional QS. A project could be designed, costed and controlled using information technology applications that allow the customer to vary specifications and produce different costings as part of the service.

To develop this service the business will employ an 'automization director', Joe Wilcot. He has worked with Noel Peters before on developing CAD techniques in the QS industry and the present employers of Peters and Davis, Gleeds. A section of the business plan is devoted to a 'strategy for growth' which concentrates on the role of IT and new technology in the construction industry. If the business is successful it is likely that Joe Wilcot will be brought in as a full director. The directors are excited about the development of a revolutionary housing product developed by Joe. If this takes off then they have been promised a good percentage of the QS work which will result.

In the first six months that the business is in operation, the proprietors have identified a further service that could offer potential for growth, particularly for local authority housing departments and housing associations—the provision and targeting of an energy auditing service.

The Market

Potential clients are to be drawn from both the private and public sectors. Obviously the nature of the recovery means that the business will have to market for clients actively. However, there are some areas which have major growth potential as construction projects, e.g., in hotels and leisure. The development of housing associations also offers great potential. The proprietors believe that the flexibility of a small firm could be used to their advantage in the recovery. This ability of a small firm to control costs, react quickly to opportunities, and to be flexible is likely to be an important factor in the success of this proposition.

The Role of the Dutch Company

A section of the business plan is devoted to the association with a company in the Netherlands that has developed the application of IT and new technological developments to the construction industry on the continent. A number of options are under discussion at the present time. The proprietors have had several meetings with representatives of this company and have secured agreement for some investment by it, but the deal still has yet to be ratified. The options at present include cash injection in return for an equity stake, a fee arrangement, or a more loose association with the business using software and technology developed by the Dutch company.

The Business Rationale

Both Noel and Graham have been frustrated for some time while working for Gleeds at their inflexibility and slow progress in adopting new integrated CAD techniques and new technology. They both feel that they have achieved as much as they can within their present environment and that the time is right, despite the fragile nature of the recovery in construction, to launch their own business. They are bringing Tony in because he has contacts in the construction industry and also has experience of running a small company himself. They are hopeful that they will be able to take some customers with them when they leave to start up the business. In addition, the role of the automization director will be significant as new technology is adopted in the construction industry. Joe Wilcot has developed a revolutionary housing product which is currently being patented and has generated a lot of interest. Peters and Co. will receive a great deal of work as a result if this new technology and product is adopted in the construction industry. The potential could be huge since the product is ideally suited to the needs of housing associations for low cost housing. Housing associations now have the majority of state funding that is devoted to housing construction.

Business Plan

Strictly confidential
No contact to be made with present employers under any circumstances

Summary of Proposals

Peters and Co. is being established to provide cost control and management services to the construction industry. The company will focus on four principal areas of service:

- Cost control
- Project management
- Facility management
- Construction information technology.

These areas will form the basis for the growth and expansion of the business where our expertise in cost control and project management will be the main activity in the initial stages. From this base, growth will develop into the other areas which will then provide a comprehensive construction and property service to clients.

Although the directors are chartered quantity surveyors (QS) by training, they all acquired specialized skills during their careers to respond to the changing demands and needs of their clients. Peters and Co. bring these people together to form a partnership that will be unfettered by QS tradition.

A strong association with a Dutch company, the Brink Groep, will widen business opportunities for both parties and will also provide advantages for technical development and joint initiatives in other markets.

The Directors

The directors are chartered quantity surveyors as follows:

Noel Peters BSc, FRICS
Currently a partner with a national QS practice. He will be managing director with principal responsibility for policy and future business direction.
Graham Davis ARICS
Currently an associate with a national QS practice. He will be the technical director with specific responsibilities for cost control and the integration and expansion of the business in IT areas for both the partnership and the clients.
Tony Franks
Currently employed as managing director of a specialist construction company. He will be responsible for financial matters within the firm and provide expert contractual advice to clients.

All three directors have excellent experience and knowledge of the UK construction and QS industry and have gained a wide range of business contacts.

Business Philosophy

The company will offer an exceptional personal service based upon the knowledge, expertise and involvement of the directors. Experience has proved that a commitment to use and develop the most up-to-date computer technology, including the integration of CAD systems with cost control techniques, will provide the firm with a major advantage over its competitors.

To maintain this philosophy we aim to provide:

1. An expertise that encompasses costing, planning and management, ranging over all aspects of property and construction-related activities.
2. The establishment of a working environment which can provide security for all members of the organization and which will manifest itself into the service we reflect towards our clients.

The firm is envisaged as presenting an image which combines quality of service and personal attention with particular emphasis on standards of presentation. To enhance this image we intend to establish a permanent presence in Bath with easy access to all road and rail links. We are currently negotiating a lease for an office with a prestigious city centre location.

Strategy for Growth

The problem with traditional QS service

The standard QS appointment provides for a cost monitoring role. This is reactive and not acceptable as it will not be good enough to cope with the demands of clients who want security and certainty of price in their dealings with the construction industry. Clients' concerns are reflected primarily in the growth of the 'Design and Build' sector of the market where over 20 per cent of commercial work is executed in this way. In this area the traditional QS service has a limited role to play.

We also believe that the presence in the UK of European clients and investors from other countries seeking a marketing foothold in Europe has already affected the attitude and approach of the UK construction industry; the Single European Market has accelerated the pace of this change.

Cost control

We will concentrate on cost control by restructuring the fee arrangement to allow us to maximize the service in areas of value management, project planning and risk avoidance.

Our clients will see budgetary control that will seek to reduce the risk of major cost/time over-runs which are the hallmarks of the UK construction process.

Project management

Because project management is difficult to achieve, the current trend is to appoint a project manager with no direct responsibilities. We believe good project management should be cost linked so that the time frame is viewed at every turn in regard to the cost effects. This requires us to be involved in the auditing of the design process, including the programming of the design input, as well as the more traditional aspects of project management.

Facility management

There is much evidence that many consultant firms are seeking to diversify as the market changes and workload declines. Our growth and expansion into facility management is calculated to maximize our market share and provide a wider base from which to operate and so stabilize our fee income.

This work will provide an extension to our role to form a more general property management service. Facility management provides the opportunity to be appointed for work where major new build schemes are envisaged—this being a natural progression from the facility management role.

IT in the construction industry

Peters and Co. believes that there is a dearth of data with which to make key decisions that affect the building process. Thus the key procedure in all the above areas is to capture, analyse and store all pertinent information on computer databases. This will be structured in a way that will allow the data to be transferred throughout the cost control and construction process. It is intended to offer this service to clients by expanding into a support role for bespoke applications.

The growth of the firm will see an automization director, previously identified (Joe Wilcot), who will take a consultancy role in the interim while the market is established. The link with the Brink Groep will also help to support this strategy.

Summary

This range of operations will see a mixture of professional disciplines employed within the firm. The strategy seeks to provide an embracing cost control service to guide clients at any point in their dealings with construction and property.

The potential market is extensive, being in the order of £1500–2000m of fee income in the UK. We believe that we can establish a share of this market that will see us as a 30-strong practice within eight years with a turnover of at least £2.5m.

The Potential Market

We are confident that our contacts will provide suitable commissions in the following areas:

1. Private sector
   (a) commercial (offices and retail)
   (b) industrial
   (c) hotels
   (d) leisure.
2. Public sector
   (a) housing associations
   (b) state schools
   (c) local authorities
   (d) central government agencies.

We fully recognize the difficulty in launching a new firm and to help us in the launch period we have negotiated agreements with two contacts who will actively market on our behalf. One of these contacts has a detailed involvement with educational establishments where he has extensive contacts both at local and national levels. The other contact already provides general marketing for other organizations and has a proven track record. These people will act on the basis of commission.

Assumptions on Cashflow

Due to the limited recovery in the UK construction market we expect to receive minimal fee income in the initial seven months of trading. We hope to secure one medium-sized contract and several smaller contracts in the first six months.

As we become more established and recovery takes place, we anticipate an increase in our market share in line with that recovery. At the peak of the fourth year of trading we anticipate an income per month of £45 000 and to have secured approximately £22m worth of work (five or six medium-sized jobs). The cashflow shows a consequent increase in staffing levels for this growth.

It should be noted that we expect all directors to achieve an earnings capacity of £75 000 per head per annum.

The figures take no account of reinvestment to fund other areas of growth such as facility management and the expected increase in automization.

Proposed Start Date

The provisional start date is set for 1 January, Year 1. This would mean the funding would need to be in place by 1 December.

One or more of the directors intends to start earlier than this date in order to concentrate on matters in connection with a business start-up and to establish some of the basic procedures needed to allow the firm to run efficiently from the launch date.

Proposals for an association with the Brink Groep, Holland

There are several options that we consider might be of interest to the parties and we outline them as follows:

1. A venture stake in the firm where the Brink Groep becomes a shareholder. We believe that we have much to offer Brink Groep in new areas of research such as value engineering and risk management. With this closer relationship we would be able to mould a professional service for a European operation using the Brink Groep marketing identity. This would assist the Brink Groep to establish a network of European offices.

   This degree of involvement would heavily encourage the Brink Groep to market Dutch clients who may wish to work in the UK and would create a stronger drive to establish an automization arm earlier than would otherwise be possible. Under this scenario the suggested cash involvement of Brink Groep would be £40 000 in return for a 20 per cent shareholding.
2. The Brink Groep to secure fee-earning work for Peters and Co. A pre-agreed commission rate for this work would be paid by Peters and Co. in the form of a shareholding up to an agreed maximum with cash arrangements thereafter.
3. The Brink Groep becomes a minority shareholder of Peters and Co. with, say, a 5 per cent share of the equity for a direct capital injection of £10 000.
4. A more loose association with Peters and Co. promoting the software of the Brink Groep, with us providing general or bespoke databases to be used in conjunction with such software.

Generally

We are currently arranging our finance for the venture through major banks or venture capital companies.

The proprietors are also injecting £30 000 into the business and accepting the risk of leaving well-paid jobs to set up this venture.

The Three Directors

Noel Peters

Experience

1968–69   Trainee, Worcester County Council

1969–73	Four-year sandwich course, BSc in QS
1973–77	Assistant QS with QS partnership
1977–81	QS and cost planner, Gloucester County Council
1981–85	Cost Planning Group Leader, Hackney Borough Council
1985 to date	Partner with Gleeds, one of UK's major QS partnerships

In the last five years Noel has been rapidly promoted at Gleeds. He has been prepared to take on and develop IT applications in the QS field. He has enjoyed direct managerial responsibility for the securing and execution of major commercial work, working on schemes ranging in value from £1m to £100m. He deals with the main clients at both local and national level.

He is married with two teenage sons and he owns his own property, currently valued at £150 000 with a mortgage of £50 000.

He is well paid at Gleeds with an annual salary in excess of £40 000 excluding expenses and perks. Thus he is giving up well-paid, secure employment to take the risk of launching this company. He believes that the only way to make further progress in the application of IT is to develop applications with his own business.

Graham Davis

Experience

1969–79	QS with three firms in private professional practice
1979–85	Senior QS
1985 to date	Associate partner at Gleeds

Graham currently heads the cost planning unit at Gleeds and has concentrated in recent years on developing fast-track contractual procedures in the commercial sector, together with computerized systems to reflect the changing climate of the industry and to assist in the preparation of cost control and tender documentation. Graham has good contact with both local and national clients and has generated a high fee income in recent years. His current salary is in excess of £30 000 excluding perks.

Graham has worked closely with Noel on projects to develop IT applications and both have been involved in a number of demonstrations to important clients.

He is married with two teenage daughters and owns his own property, valued at £120 000 with a mortgage of £30 000.

Tony Franks

Experience

1959–67	Junior partner in family building company
1967–73	Commercial manager with masonry subcontractor
1973–76	Senior QS with QS partnership

1976–90   Chief QS, Dorset County Council
1990 to date MD of private construction company

Tony is a regular lecturer in law to the industry and also at Bath University. He has extensive practical site management experience and a wide circle of public sector contacts. He was for many years responsible for strategic and project cost planning advice. As chief QS and cost centre manager he assumed responsibility for the whole range of QS functions as well as fee accountability for the department. He was responsible for selection and vetting of contractors and consultants.

Tony has close links, professionally, with Noel and Graham and has worked on a number of contracts with them. He has some very good administrative and small business experience and understands company and commercial law.

He built the bungalow that he presently lives in some 20 years ago and has paid off any outstanding debts. The bungalow has been valued at £120 000.

CASHFLOW PROJECTIONS

(Note: base rates at the time were 12 per cent p.a.; interest charges were based on +3 per cent over base rate.)

PETERS AND CO.—CASHFLOW PROJECTIONS YEAR 1

19XX	JAN	FEB	MAR	APRIL	MAY	JUNE	JULY	AUGUST	SEPT	OCT	NOV	DEC	TOTALS
INCOME	0	0	1000	2000	3000	3000	3000	8000	8000	8000	12000	12000	60000
CAPITAL	30000	0	0	0	0	0	0	0	0	0	0	0	30000
TOTAL INCOME	30000	0	1000	2000	3000	3000	3000	8000	8000	8000	12000	12000	90000
EXPENSES													
DRAWINGS	6000	6000	6000	6000	6000	6000	6000	6000	6000	6000	6000	6000	72000
HEALTH INSURANCE	90	90	90	90	90	90	90	90	90	90	90	90	1080
NHI PAYMENTS	677	677	677	677	677	677	677	677	677	677	677	677	8124
STAFF COSTS	0	0	0	0	0	0	0	0	0	0	0	0	0
OVERHEADS	1142	1142	1142	1142	1142	1142	1142	1142	1142	1142	1142	1142	13704
RENTAL ITEMS	3963	0	0	3963	0	0	3963	0	0	3963	0	0	15852
FURNITURE	2000	0	0	0	0	0	0	0	0	0	0	0	2000
CARS	1000	1000	1000	1000	1000	1000	1000	1000	1000	1000	1000	1000	12000
TRAVEL	333	333	333	333	333	333	333	333	333	333	333	333	3996
HARDWARE	270	270	270	270	270	270	270	270	270	270	270	270	3240
SOFTWARE	608	608	608	608	608	608	608	608	608	608	608	608	7296
PI COVER	4500	0	0	0	0	0	0	0	0	0	0	0	4500
MARKETING	333	333	333	333	333	333	333	333	333	333	333	333	3996
BROCHURE	1500	0	0	0	0	0	0	0	0	0	0	0	1500
VAT (REBATE)	0	0	0	-4029	0	0	-2629	0	0	-2629	0	0	-9287
INTEREST/CHARGES	0	-303	0	0	467	0	0	1449	0	0	2055	0	3668
TOTAL PAYMENTS	22416	10150	10453	10387	10920	10453	11787	11902	10453	11787	12508	10453	143669
NET CASH FLOW	7584	-10150	-9453	-8387	-7920	-7453	-8787	-3902	-2453	-3787	-508	1547	
OPENING BALANCE	0	7584	-2566	-12019	-20406	-28326	-35779	-44566	-48468	-50921	-54708	-55216	
CLOSING BALANCE	7584	-2566	-12019	-20406	-28326	-35779	-44566	-48468	-50921	-54708	-55216	-53669	

PETERS AND CO.—CASHFLOW PROJECTIONS YEAR 2

19XX	JAN	FEB	MAR	APRIL	MAY	JUNE	JULY	AUGUST	SEPT	OCT	NOV	DEC	TOTALS
INCOME	13000	13000	15000	17000	17000	17000	21000	21000	21000	18000	16000	16000	205000
CAPITAL	0	0	0	0	0	0	0	0	0	0	0	0	0
TOTAL INCOME	13000	13000	15000	17000	17000	17000	21000	21000	21000	18000	16000	16000	205000
EXPENSES													
DRAWINGS	6000	6000	6000	6000	6000	6000	6000	6000	6000	6000	6000	6000	72000
HEALTH INSURANCE	90	90	90	90	90	90	90	90	90	90	90	90	1080
NHI PAYMENTS	677	677	677	677	677	677	677	677	677	677	677	677	8124
STAFF COSTS	0	0	0	2318	2318	2318	2318	2318	2318	2318	2318	2318	20862
OVERHEADS	558	558	558	558	558	558	558	558	558	558	558	558	6696
RENTAL ITEMS	4988	0	0	4988	0	0	4988	0	0	4988	0	0	19952
FURNITURE	0	0	0	0	0	0	0	0	0	0	0	0	0
CARS	1250	1250	1250	1250	1250	1250	1250	1250	1250	1250	1250	1250	15000
TRAVEL	500	500	500	500	500	500	500	500	500	500	500	500	6000
HARDWARE	513	513	513	513	513	513	513	513	513	513	513	513	6156
SOFTWARE	454	454	454	454	454	454	454	454	454	454	454	454	5448
PI COVER	4500	0	0	0	0	0	0	0	0	0	0	0	4500
MARKETING	417	417	417	417	417	417	417	417	417	417	417	417	5004
BROCHURE	0	0	0	0	0	0	0	0	0	0	0	0	0
VAT (REBATE)	-2629	0	0	-3599	0	0	-2811	0	0	-2811	0	0	-11850
INTEREST/CHARGES	0	2225	0	0	2148	0	0	1736	0	0	999	0	7108
TOTAL PAYMENTS	17318	12684	10459	14166	14925	12777	14954	14513	12777	14954	13776	12777	166080
NET CASH FLOW	-4318	316	4541	2834	2075	4223	6046	6487	8223	3046	2224	3223	
OPENING BALANCE	-53669	-57987	-57671	-53130	-50296	-48221	-43998	-37952	-31465	-23242	-20196	-17972	
CLOSING BALANCE	-57987	-57671	-53130	-50296	-48221	-43998	-37952	-31465	-23242	-20196	-17972	-14749	

PETERS AND CO.—CASHFLOW PROJECTIONS YEAR 3

19XX	JAN	FEB	MAR	APRIL	MAY	JUNE	JULY	AUGUST	SEPT	OCT	NOV	DEC	TOTALS
INCOME	26000	26000	26000	30000	30000	30000	38000	38000	38000	38000	40000	40000	400000
CAPITAL	0	0	0	0	0	0	0	0	0	0	0	0	0
TOTAL INCOME	26000	26000	26000	30000	30000	30000	38000	38000	38000	38000	40000	40000	400000
EXPENSES													
DRAWINGS	6000	6000	6000	6000	6000	6000	6000	6000	6000	6000	6000	6000	72000
HEALTH INSURANCE	90	90	90	90	90	90	90	90	90	90	90	90	1080
NHI PAYMENTS	677	677	677	677	677	677	677	677	677	677	677	677	8124
STAFF COSTS	6956	6956	6956	6956	6956	6956	6956	6956	6956	6956	6956	6956	83472
OVERHEADS	729	729	729	729	729	729	729	729	729	729	729	729	8748
RENTAL ITEMS	6050	0	0	6050	0	0	6050	0	0	6050	0	0	24200
FURNITURE	2000	0	0	0	0	0	0	0	0	0	0	0	2000
CARS	1250	1250	1250	1250	1250	1250	1250	1250	1250	1250	1250	1250	15000
TRAVEL	500	500	500	500	500	500	500	500	500	500	500	500	6000
HARDWARE	697	697	697	697	697	697	697	697	697	697	697	697	8364
SOFTWARE	575	575	575	575	575	575	575	575	575	575	575	575	6900
PI COVER	5000	0	0	0	0	0	0	0	0	0	0	0	5000
MARKETING	500	500	500	500	500	500	500	500	500	500	500	500	6000
BROCHURE	0	0	0	0	0	0	0	0	0	0	0	0	0
VAT (REBATE)	-2811	0	0	-4472	0	0	-3247	0	0	-3247	0	0	-13777
INTEREST/CHARGES	0	662	0	0	21	0	0	-1405	0	0	-3655	0	-4377
TOTAL PAYMENTS	28213	18636	17974	19552	17995	17974	20777	16569	17974	20777	14319	17974	228734
NET CASH FLOW	-2213	7364	8026	10448	12005	12026	17223	21431	20026	17223	25681	22026	
OPENING BALANCE	-14749	-16962	-9598	-1572	8876	20881	32907	50130	71561	91587	108810	134491	
CLOSING BALANCE	-16962	-9598	-1572	8876	20881	32907	50130	71561	91587	108810	134491	156517	

Learning outcomes

At the end of this chapter students should be able to:

1. Discuss the importance of alternative sources of finance for entrepreneurs and small- and medium-sized enterprises.
2. Describe why entrepreneurs and SMEs are at a disadvantage compared with large firms in financial markets.
3. Appreciate some of the problems that face the providers of finance to the SME sector.
4. Compare survey results and known national characteristics on the importance of sources of finance for start-up entrepreneurs and existing ventures.
5. Describe research findings comparing risk assessment practices of English and Scottish bank managers and be able to indicate the main differences in these practices.

After the case study and associated assignments you should be able to:

6. Discuss how this case differs from the majority of small firms and typical start-ups as shown by Chapters 3 and 4.
7. Describe the roles and main functions of the three entrepreneurs and discuss how these match the concepts of entrepreneurs discussed in Chapter 1.
8. Understand some of the financial constraints involved in a non-standard start-up.
9. Appreciate and account for the importance of bank finance as a source of external finance for entrepreneurs and small firm owners.
10. Be prepared to answer questions from bank managers on any start-up proposition for a new firm, including that of your own business.
11. Describe the advantages of a 'team start' as opposed to an individual start-up.

Suggested assignments

1. Role play assignment

Students are required to:

1. Familiarize yourself with information on the venture.
2. Prepare for a role-play exercise by taking the role of one of the entrepreneurs which will be allocated to you by agreement.
3. Research additional information on sources of finance and risk assessment by financial institutions (see References and Recommended reading at the end of this chapter).
4. Carry out role-play exercise by arranging interview with bank manager (member of staff).
5. Complete an individual project report on 'Issues in Start-up of SMEs and Finance for Start-up Entrepreneurs'.

Assessment criteria

1. Knowledge of material and additional research.
2. Confident and persuasive presentation.
3. Appreciation of the strengths and weaknesses of the businesses.
4. Evidence of preparation for specific questions on financial information such as knowledge of gearing, profit and forecasted financial information.
5. Students work in groups of three but will be expected to answer questions individually and will be assessed individually. This will account for 30 per cent of the assessment.
6. Completion of individual report on issues in start-up and sources of finance for new entrepreneurs using role-play information and additional literature references. This will account for the remaining 70 per cent of the assessment.

Suggested assessment weighting

Role play interview: 30 per cent (note: students can be allocated individual marks although they will prepare for the interview in groups).
Written report: 70 per cent.

2. Case study analysis and report

Students analyse the case study as bank manager.

You are required to analyse the start-up proposition of Peters and Co. and give a funding decision on whether or not you would provide the required finance.

You are required to justify your decision by bringing in concepts concerning finance and other issues in the start-up of firms.

Produce a written report giving your decision, including financial analysis of the projections in the business plan. You may qualify your answer, for example, that you do or do not require security to fund the proposition.

3. Role play

Students divide the role of the bank manager and proprietors between them, working in groups of four where possible.

Additional reports are required from the students on sources of finance for small firms with particular emphasis on sources for start-up entrepreneurs.

Assessment criteria as above.

REFERENCES

1. H.M. GOVERNMENT (1931) *Report of The Committee on Finance and Industry* (Macmillan Report), CMND 3897, HMSO.

2. H.M. GOVERNMENT (1971) *Report of The Committee of Inquiry on Small Firms* (Bolton Report), CMND 4811, HMSO.

3. H.M. GOVERNMENT (1979) *Interim report on The Financing of Small Firms* (Wilson report), CMND 7503, HMSO.

4. MASON, C., HARRISON, R. AND CHALONER, J. (1991) *Informal Risk Capital in the UK*, Venture Finance Research Project, Working Paper no. 2, University of Southampton.

5. HARRISON, R. AND MASON, C. (1991) 'Informal Investment Networks: A Case Study from the UK', *Entrepreneurship and Regional Development*, vol. 3, no. 2, pp. 269–79.

6. DIXON, R. (1991) 'Venture Capitalists and the Appraisal of Investments', *OMEGA*, vol. 19, no. 5.

7. MURRAY, G. AND ROBBIE, K. (1992) 'Venture Capital in the UK', *International Journal of Bank Marketing*, vol. 10, no. 5, pp. 32–40.

8. BVCA (1997) 'Venture Capital in the UK': Annual Report, British Venture Capital Association, London.

9. AKERLOF, G. (1970) 'The Market for Lemons: qualitative uncertainty and the market mechanism', *Quarterly Journal of Economics*, vol. 89, pp. 488–500.

10. MIRRLEES, J.A. (1974) 'Notes on Welfare Economics, Information and Uncertainty', in Balch, M., McFadden, D. and Wu, S. (eds) *Essays in Economic Behaviour Under Uncertainty*, North Holland.

11. MIRRLEES, J.A. (1975) *The Theory of Moral Hazard and Unobservable Behaviour*, Nuffield College, Oxford.

12. JENSEN, M.C. AND MECKLING, W.H. (1976) 'Theory of the Firm: Managerial

Behaviour, Agency Costs and Ownership Structure', *Journal of Financial Economics*, vol. 3, pp. 305–60.

13. HARRIS, M. AND TOWNSEND, R.M. (1981) 'Resource allocation under asymmetric information', *Econometrica*, vol. 49, pp. 33–64.

14. HELLWIG, M. (1987) 'Some recent developments in the theory of competition in markets with adverse selection', *European Economic Review*, vol. 31, pp. 319–25.

15. MAGILL, M. and SHAFER, W. (1991) 'Incomplete markets', in Hildenbrand, W. and Sonneschein, H. (eds) *The Handbook of Mathematical Economics*, vol. IV, North Holland.

16. STIGLITZ, J. AND WEISS, A. (1981) 'Credit rationing in markets with imperfect information', *American Economic Review*, vol. 71, pp. 393–410.

17. DE MEZA, D. AND WEBB, D. (1987) 'Too much investment: a problem of asymmetric information', *Quarterly Journal of Economics*, vol. 102, pp. 281–92.

18. ASTON BUSINESS SCHOOL (1991) *Constraints on the Growth of Small Firms*, DTI, HMSO.

19. BINKS, M., ENNEW, C. AND REED, G. (1988) 'The Survey by the Forum of Private Business on Banks and Small Firms', in Bannock, G. and Morgan, V. (eds) *Banks and Small Businesses: A Two Nation Perspective*, Forum of Private Business, Knutsford.

20. FORUM OF PRIVATE BUSINESS SURVEY (1993) *Small Businesses and Their Banks*, Forum of Private Business, Knutsford.

21. DEAKINS, D. AND HUSSAIN, G. (1991) *Risk Assessment By Bank Managers*, Birmingham Polytechnic Business School, Birmingham.

22. DEAKINS, D. AND HUSSAIN, G. (1992) 'Overcoming the Adverse Selection Problem', paper presented to the 15th National Small Firms Policy and Research Conference, Southampton, November.

23. DEAKINS, D. AND PHILPOTT, T. (1993) *Comparative European Practices in the Finance of Small Firms: UK, Germany and Holland*, University of Central England Business School, Birmingham.

24. FLETCHER, M. (1994) 'Decision making by Scottish bank managers', *International Journal of Entrepreneurship Behaviour and Research*, vol. 1, no. 2, pp. 37–53.

25. SPENCE, A.M. (1974) *Market Signalling*, Harvard University Press.

26. CRAWFORD, V. AND SOBELL, J. (1982) 'Strategic information transmission', *Econometrica*, vol. 50, pp. 1431–51.

27. QUINZII, M. AND ROCHET, J.C. (1985) 'Multidimensional signalling', *Journal of Mathematical Economics*, vol. 14, pp. 261–84.

28. CHO, I-K. AND KREPS, D. (1987) 'Signalling games and stable equilibria', *Quarterly Journal of Economics*, vol. 102, pp. 179–221.

29. MILGROM, P. AND ROBERTS, J. (1982) 'Limit pricing and entry under incomplete information: an equilibrium analysis', *Econometrica*, vol. 50, pp. 443–59.

30. CHAN, Y. AND KANNATAS, G. (1985) 'Asymmetric valuations and the role of collateral in loan agreements', *Journal of Money, Credit and Banking*, vol. 17, no. 1, 1985, pp. 84–95.

31. ALTMAN, E.I. (1971) *Corporate Bankruptcy in America*, Heath Lexington.

32. ESRC CENTRE FOR BUSINESS RESEARCH (1992) *The State of British Enterprise*, Department of Applied Economics, University of Cambridge.

33. ESRC CENTRE FOR BUSINESS RESEARCH (1996) *The State of British Enterprise-Up-date*, Department of Applied Economics, University of Cambridge.
34. ESRC CENTRE FOR BUSINESS RESEARCH (1998) *The State of British Enterprise-Up-date*, Department of Applied Economics, University of Cambridge.
35. DEAKINS, D., GRAHAM, L., SULLIVAN, R. AND WHITTAM, G. (1997) *New Venture Support: An analysis of mentoring provision for new entrepreneurs*, Paisley Enterprise Research Centre, University of Paisley.
36. READ, L. (1994) *Raising Bank Finance: A comparative study of the experiences of male and female business owners*, Venture Finance Working Paper, no. 11, University of Southampton.
37. ROSA, P., CARTER, S. AND HAMILTON, D. (1994) 'Gender and Determinants of Small Business Performance: Preliminary insights from a British study', paper presented to the 17th National Small Firms Policy and Research Conference, Sheffield, November.
38. CHELL, E. AND BAINES, S. (1998) 'Does gender affect business performance? A study of microbusinesses in business services in the UK', *Entrepreneurship and Regional Development*, vol. 10, no. 2, pp. 117–36.
39. BINKS, M. AND ENNEW, C. (1996) *Private Businesses and Their Banks*, Forum of Private Business, Knutsford.
40. BINKS, M. AND ENNEW, C. (1991) 'The changing relationship between banks and their small business customers in the UK', paper presented to the 20th National Small Firms Policy and Research Conference, Belfast, November.
41. BINKS, M. (1993) *Financial Times*, 19 January.

RECOMMENDED READING

ACOST (1990) *The Enterprise Challenge: overcoming barriers to growth in small firms*, HMSO, London.
BANNOCK, G. (1991) *Venture Capital and The Equity Gap*, National Westminster Bank, London.
DEAKINS, D. AND HUSSAIN, G. (1991) *Risk Assessment By Bank Managers*, Birmingham Polytechnic Business School, Birmingham.
STANWORTH, J. AND GRAY, C. (eds) (1991) *Bolton 20 Years On*, Paul Chapman, London (Chapters 4 and 6).
WALKER, D. (1989) 'Financing The Small Firm', *Small Business Economics*, vol. 1, no. 1, pp. 285–96.

6. Sources of Finance: Equity, Venture Capital and Alternative Sources

INTRODUCTION

Raising equity finance causes two problems for the entrepreneur that do not exist with bank finance: firstly, it involves a search procedure of some description; and secondly, seeking outside investors automatically involves dilution of the entrepreneur's equity which may affect willingness to raise such finance and the subsequent behaviour of the entrepreneur.

Small firm entrepreneurs can also run into problems. Knowledge of both sources and procedures can be a barrier. Despite the growth in centres of business advice, such as the Business Links in the UK (which might provide such information), it is much easier for the small firm entrepreneur to approach the local bank manager. Just the act of starting a new venture (normally) requires a business bank account. By comparison, a decision to raise equity finance immediately requires a search procedure that is not necessary with bank finance due the prominence of commercial banks in the high street.

Theoretically entrepreneurs may be reluctant to raise equity, let alone engage in any search procedure, due to dilution of personal resources involved. The pecking order hypothesis (POH) associated with Myers (1), suggests that external sources of equity are only approached by entrepreneurs as a last resort (after personal sources and debt are exhausted). Michaelos (2), in a study of financing structures with small firms, suggests that the gearing (ratio of debt to equity finance) of small companies varies with their age and size, but more notably, that gearing declines (the ratio of debt finance decreases) as firms' profitability increases. This may indicate that higher levels of profit are required to raise equity.

Having made these introductory remarks, however, sources of external equity are potentially important, since they are sources of risk capital. Equity providers take an element of entrepreneurial risk and for this reason the levels of activity in such sources are sometimes seen as associated with levels of entrepreneurial activity in society. Access to risk capital is seen as a prerequisite of an entrepreneurial society (3). The most important sources for entrepreneurs are formal and informal venture capital. We review developments in these sources before examining alternative sources of (equity and non-equity) finance.

FORMAL VENTURE CAPITAL

The UK has the most developed formal venture capital sector of any European country. For example, according to a recent European report (4) the UK venture capital industry accounts for 44 per cent of the EU venture capital funds. However, it is still the case that only a small proportion of these funds go into early-stage investments; the majority, 65 per cent, go into either Management Buy-Outs (MBOs) or Management Buy-Ins (MBIs) (5). Although the European venture capital industry has been considered to be on a par with that of the USA (6), the low proportion of deals concerned with early-stage investments is in marked contrast to the USA, where venture capitalists are more prepared to consider high risk investments in early-stage and technology-based entrepreneurial firms, that have the potential for high growth/high returns. As Murray (7) has commented: 'The magnitude of the trend away from start-up and early stage investments has most clearly been seen in the UK industry' (p. 98).

An overview of the main issues concerning the finance of small firms was given in the previous chapter, in which we discussed some of the problems faced by formal venture capital companies when assessing risk of new ventures. Two of these problems—project risk (or adverse selection) and the uneconomic size of venture deals—have been highlighted by Murray as the main factors causing a retreat from early-stage financing in the UK venture capital industry (7). The real financing problem facing venture capitalists lies as much *ex post* the investment decision as *ex ante*. This moral hazard, or monitoring problem, means that the venture capitalist will want to be much more involved in the management of the venture than was the case with bank finance.

Adding Value

Formal venture capital companies seek investment opportunities with ventures that have the potential to achieve substantial growth, so that their original investment can be liquidated through an exit route, normally in a five-to-seven-year period. Exit routes do not have to be through initial public offerings (IPOs), but may involve a trade sale or some other sale of their shareholding. The objective then of venture capitalists will be to ensure that there is sufficient *added value* from their investment in the company. Thus one of the issues that they may be concerned with is the quality of the management team. For example, a venture capitalist considering an investment in a new technology-based firm may be concerned if there is insufficient commercial expertise to grow the company to a substantial operation. One method by which a venture capitalist attempts to add value, and monitor growth and performance, is through the appointment of a non-executive director (NED) to the board of the investee company.

Theoretically, the role of non-executive directors (NEDs) in the development process of growing small companies can be important, especially with respect to the relationship between the key entrepreneur(s) and the NED(s). NEDs may bring contacts, discipline, planning skills and a number of other intangible skills to the growing small firm. This intervention may be crucial in the development of such companies. The NED should be able to build a long-term relationship with the key or founding entrepreneur and bring their own network of contacts to aid the growth process. However, in the field of entrepreneurial research we have little evidence on the nature and impact of such relationships and also on the impacting factors (recruitment, payment, power sharing) on such relationships. This apparent neglect of the potential role of NEDs in small unquoted companies has been noted by a number of writers (8, 9) and is surprising. Much attention has been given to their role in large, quoted companies in the UK, due to their enhanced prominence in corporate governance recommended by the Cadbury Report (10).

A research study into the role of NEDs, carried out by the author and colleagues from Paisley (11), with small growth companies in Scotland found that they were characterized by complexity and variety. However, the findings also showed that there was an important impact on strategic planning. Other roles that were seen as important included using past experience to give advice and using constructive criticism. Rather surprisingly, although there were variations in perceived importance, the networking role of NEDs was not rated as highly. It has been claimed that NEDs bring contacts that might enable growing small firms to access new markets, perhaps resources and/or information (12). While this role was seen as important for some firms, our findings, at best, only partly bear out this hypothesis. For example, only 47 per cent of entrepreneurs agreed that the NED had an important networking role and an impact on the contacts used.

Entrepreneurs that seek venture capital must be prepared for a lengthy 'due diligence' procedure, as well as a willingness to accept a nominated member of the board from the venture capitalist company as a NED. However, raising venture capital may not be as daunting for entrepreneurs with the potential high growth that a venture capitalist would seek. Also, as demonstrated by our findings (11), considerable flexibility is allowed in the appointment of a NED by venture capital companies, with choice of nominated candidates and the ability to change the appointment if there is a subsequent problem with the entrepreneur–NED relationship. If allowances are made for these factors, then seeking formal venture capital can be a viable option for an entrepreneur that has a venture with high growth potential. Indeed in some cases, venture capital may be the only route of funding for new starts that require considerable early-stage investment of, say, greater than £200 000. Indeed it is a common lament of such investors that there is no shortage of venture capital funds, merely a shortage of suitable propositions for investment (13).

Assessment criteria used by venture capitalists

We discussed in the previous chapter assessment criteria used by bank managers who focused on financial statements and security rather than the management team. Studies with venture capitalists have shown that important criteria include the entrepreneurial team and the importance of entrepreneurial skills (14, 15). One such study of a regional venture capital fund in the UK (16) revealed the importance of a unique selling point (USP) at the initial screening stage and the overriding importance of the management team at the various stages of 'due diligence'.

Implications for entrepreneurs seeking venture capital are that there must be a USP associated with the product/service of the proposition; there must be a good management team with complementary skills; there must be growth potential (probably in global markets), and the entrepreneurial team must be prepared to go through a lengthy due diligence procedure which may take at least a year (although with the right preparation this can be considerably shortened).

Although there has been the noted growth in the formal venture capital sector in the UK, and in other advanced industrial nations, difficulties for the vast majority of entrepreneurs (that do not have high growth ventures that venture capitalists require) in the appropriateness of formal venture capital have meant that there has been greater attention focused on the potential of the informal venture capital sector for providing equity for small firm entrepreneurs.

INFORMAL VENTURE CAPITAL

Informal risk capital, provided by informal investors or 'business angels', has attracted attention as a means of providing small amounts of equity capital to small firms to close the equity gap. The main work in this area in the UK has been completed by Mason and Harrison (17, 18). They argue that the informal venture capital sector has enormous potential for closing the equity gap. They estimate that the total venture capital available, if properly tapped, would be in the order of £4–5 billion, which places it potentially on a par with the formal venture capital sector. However, the significance for small firms is far greater because, according to Mason and Harrison, business angels would be more patient than the formal sector, less likely to want to be directly involved in the firm and be willing to invest small amounts of capital in line with needs of entrepreneurs and the owners of small firms. Estimates of active UK business angels put the number at approximately 18 000, who have around £500 million invested in 3500 firms (19).

Mason and Harrison have shown that the informal venture capital sector is well developed in the USA and claim the following advantages:

- Business angels are willing to invest small sums of perhaps less than £50 000 that will meet the needs of start-up entrepreneurs and existing small firms.
- The time spent in analysing propositions is much shorter than the formal venture capital sector where the due diligence procedure can take many months.
- Business angels are less likely to seek quick exit routes and will be more patient than the formal venture capital sector.
- Business angels will be satisfied with lower returns since there is no need to satisfy shareholders of a venture capital company. They may invest because they have an interest in the industry or

business sector and they can bring their own expertise (however, they will not have the same network of contacts as venture capitalists).

- Business angels may be more suited to high technology-based entrepreneurs and small firms who have special seed capital requirements in order to finance the research and development process. It can be argued that business angels have the patience and the expertise necessary in order to invest in high technology-based entrepreneurs.

While it is unquestionable that the informal venture capital sector does have great potential for closing the SME and entrepreneurial equity gap, there remain, nevertheless, some disadvantages with business angels associated with the administration of any scheme to link angels with entrepreneurs that need finance. These disadvantages include:

- There is no formal matching procedure established. Not only are business angels difficult to find, they have to be matched to suitable entrepreneurs that they are interested in funding. Such search costs are difficult to adequately finance and administer.
- There may be limited expertise that the business angel can provide to the entrepreneur. Hence value-added may be problematical and business angels will not be able to tap into extensive networks of contacts that are well established by venture capitalists (to help the growth potential of entrepreneurs). These matching problems include search costs for both suitable entrepreneurs with suitable propositions for investments and suitable business angels that can match funding and preferences to the proposition.
- It has been claimed that many entrepreneurs and small firm owners do not want external equity holders since the loss of control and dilution of equity takes away some of their independence and decision-making ability—an independence that may have been a prime motivating factor in start-up.

The major problems in this sector concern the search costs for investors and firms who have to match each others' requirements, since business angels will have their own preferences for different types of firms and investments. In order to overcome these problems Mason and Harrison have suggested that non-profit making agencies, such as Training and Enterprise Councils (TECs) and Local Enterprise Companies (LECs), should set up matching services (20). Their work has been influential in encouraging the Government to promote a service with the TECs, known as LINC (Local Investment Networking Company) to provide a match for business angels and entrepreneurs. LINC Scotland has also developed a Scottish version of this matching service (21).

A study by Lengel and Gulliford (22) of business angels and their investee firms with LINC confirmed the importance of business angel finance to early growth and business development; 71 per cent of the sample businesses were under three years old with investments in a wide range of industrial sectors. In this study, the key investment criteria cited were the attributes of the entrepreneur, with 20 per cent citing personal chemistry as important; the market with quality of product/service and the growth potential highly rated; and the product itself, with 66 per cent of investments made in sectors with which the investor was familiar.

There are indications that syndication of deals is becoming more important. For example, the LINC study found that 57 per cent of deals involved single investors, with the remaining 43 per cent involving syndicates. Half of those involved friends or associates of the LINC investor, while the remainder involved unrelated smaller investors. In comparison to the 1994 results, this represented a 15 per cent increase in the level of syndication. The study suggested that LINC investors were keen to syndicate once they had evaluated the total funding needs of the investee business and it highlighted the need for organization which can cut across regional boundaries and offer access to a wider range of opportunities within the investor's preferred criteria. This study also found that the median size of investment, including LINC and non-LINC co-investors, was approximately £57 000; almost twice the 1994 figure.

Policy in this area has also tried to promote the development of business angel networks (BANs) as one way of enabling business angels to channel financial resources and hands-on expertise to small firms by removing the financial constraint which has handicapped matchmaking initiatives. In an evaluation study of a DTI initiative, Mason and Harrison (23) reviewed five projects, which by the time of the final review, March 1995, had over 260 investors registered. While most were private individuals, most of the projects had some professional intermediaries registered on behalf of clients. There was, however, a significant degree of churn in the market and over the life of the projects almost 350 investors had been involved at some time.

Mason and Harrison estimated that over £26 million was available over the five projects for investment and more than 500 investment opportunities had been promoted. They confirmed that opportunities were weighted to start-up and early-stage investments. 'Typical' investment sought was between £50 000 and £100 000. They claimed that (in comparison to small venture capital funds) the performance of the projects was impressive in terms of client numbers and deal flow, with the five projects facilitating a total of 64 investments worth £3.7 million. (By comparison, the Midland Bank Enterprise Fund, which operates via 11 regional funds, averages 2.3 deals per fund per year with an average investment size of £100 000.) The projects average over five per annum at £50 000 per investment. The authors of this evaluation also claimed that further benefits occurred such as leverage effects, the unlocking of finance from banks, including loan guarantee scheme and other equity investors; additional networking opportunities to investors and entrepreneurs via investor clubs and seminars widening the influence beyond those registered with the BAN; and further commercial benefits were gained via the introduction service in terms of sales development, technology licensing and acquisition opportunities.

Value Added and Business Angels

It can be expected that business angels will have a close involvement after the investment decision, but be much more hands-on than formal venture capital. We have noted that formal venture capital companies are likely to appoint NEDs as intermediaries. With informal venture capital investment it is the business angel that is likely to take on the NED role directly. Indications here are again positive. For example, the LINC study (22) found that investors adopted a hands-on role in just over 80 per cent of the cases examined, providing strategic advice, specialized help in marketing, finance and accounting and networking benefits which were rated highly. Mason and Harrison's evaluation of BAN projects (23) also showed that, where business angels take a hands-on role, they can promote a broadening and strengthening of the management skill base in the firm enabling full development potential to be realized.

However, it is also likely that the extent of value added will be affected by the matching process, which will be especially important in the case of business angel investment. For example, the author's study of NEDs (11) involved a small number that were business angel investors. There was mixture of effects and relationships which were not all positive, indicating a high degree of variety in the extent of value added.

Assessment criteria used by business angels

In contrast to formal venture capital, angel venture finance can be secured much more quickly, involving merely an initial screening and assessment by the angel (or syndicate of angels) of a proposition. We might expect business angels to have particular industry and product preferences and be more concerned about the business characteristics than entrepreneurial characteristics. A recent study by Harrison and Mason (24), however, found that entrepreneurial characteristics were more important.

For entrepreneurs seeking business angel finance, there are still major search problems involved, although commercial vehicles do exist, such as the *Venture Capital Report*, to advertise propositions to potential investors. However, it must be remembered that business angels will want an active role in the firm after the investment and may insist on control as a result of their investment.

Recent research has also highlighted the under-utilized potential of *corporate venturing* for developing sources of equity and venture capital for entrepreneurs and small firms. According to McNally (25) there is under-utilized scope for corporate venturing particularly for high technology concerns where corporations can contribute to specialized venture capital funds and contribute expertise to improve the available networking skills from venture capitalists.

Secondary Equity Markets: the Alternative Investment Market

In recent years there has been the development of secondary or 'junior' stock exchanges that are intended to enable small companies to raise equity. The most important of these secondary stock markets is the Alternative Investment Market (AiM).

AiM provides a market for small companies that do not wish to go through the full procedure involved with a listing on the London Stock Exchange and as a result there are fewer regulations and requirements to gain an AiM listing. AiM was established in the summer of 1995 and although activity quickly grew to a record 294 companies trading by 1997 (26), recently the amount of activity and new business has been affected by the failure of some firms that were registered on AiM but expanded too fast (27). Lately the growth in AiM has slowed down significantly and the cost of flotation, even on such secondary markets, is still a barrier for small firms.

GOVERNMENT SCHEMES

The recognition that the availability of finance is a major constraint for the start-up and growth of entrepreneurs and small firms, coupled with the need to have a strong SME sector in the economy, has led to the introduction of a number of state schemes designed to relieve some of the aspects of these constraints and the difficulties that face small firms which have been discussed in the previous chapter. These are outlined briefly below.

1. Enterprise allowance scheme (EAS)

Now phased out, this scheme was originally designed to encourage unemployed people to start up their own business. It provided a grant designed to tide over the new business during the first year of operation. The actual level of grant varied depending on the region, since the scheme was operated by the Training and Enterprise Councils (TECs) and Local Enterprise Companies (LECs), but was approximately £2000 or £40 per week in the first year of trading. Under the TECs and LECs the qualifications for the scheme varied; for example, you did not have to be unemployed, but normally had to demonstrate a viable business plan. In some TECs and LECs capital input was required from the entrant to the scheme. The use of the EAS was phased out due to concerns about the effectiveness of such a blanket coverage scheme. It was a less than optimal use of state resources because it:

- Created businesses that were not viable
- Subsidized inefficient businesses
- Created unemployment (or displacement) when other businesses were forced to stop trading by 'unfair competition', since EAS businesses were subsidized.

Despite these criticisms one evaluation study has claimed remarkably high survival rates of 75 per cent after the first year of trading (28).

Research by the author and colleagues in the West of Scotland (29), with local new start entrepreneurs, found a high degree of variance in the value of the local equivalent of the EAS, before this version of the scheme was withdrawn. With up to half of those in receipt of the grant the value of the finance was either negligible or of low importance, indicating a high level of deadweight for such publicly-funded schemes. Making the EAS more selectively targeted was always going to be very difficult, since it is not easy to determine pre-start which new businesses would actually need the grant. In the face of high levels of deadweight, defending such public intervention is difficult and the EAS has been effectively phased out (although in some areas similar schemes may still operate funded by European money).

2. Small Firms' Loan Guarantee Scheme (SFLGS)

The SFLGS was designed as a scheme of last resort lending for entrepreneurs who have limited security. A major problem with the scheme is that financing propositions have to be put forward to the DTI by the banks to qualify for support and the banks have not been enthusiastic supporters. Sometimes the banks have pushed forward marginal and high-risk ventures onto the scheme. These factors have contributed to a low take-up of the scheme.

The scheme was made more attractive in 1993 by increasing the proportion of the state guarantee (from 70 to 80 per cent) and reducing the premium interest rate which the scheme employs. Since then, applications under the scheme have increased, but the numbers and value of loans are still relatively small compared to similar guarantee schemes in other countries. The government part of the scheme is also expensive, since the interest rate is subject to a premium above the usual rate charged to small firms by banks. This premium is charged to make the scheme self-financing and to cover the losses incurred where there are defaulters. The premium charged also depends on the nature of the loan. At the time of writing, a loan with a fixed rate of interest is subject to a 0.5 per cent premium, and the variable rate loans are subject to 1.5 per cent. The problem with the premium is that it reduces the retained earnings of the firm, which may affect the business development. Again this is a possible reason for the low take-up rates of the scheme. The amount borrowed under the scheme can be up to a maximum of £250 000 over a period of seven years.

3. Enterprise Investment Scheme

The Enterprise Investment Scheme has gradually replaced the Business Expansion Scheme (BES), since the 1992 Finance Act announced the abolition of the latter owing to the fact that it was failing to meet the needs of entrepreneurs. The scheme operated by giving tax breaks to investors prepared to take an equity stake in a business. These schemes were intended to fill the equity gap. Unfortunately, under the BES, much of the investment capital raised went into property companies in the south-east of the UK. The scheme, therefore, became a housing policy instrument and part of the tax avoidance industry. The EIS has attempted to revive interest in making small amounts of equity available, but interest in these schemes by investors has remained low (30).

4. Venture Capital Trusts (VCTs)

Venture Capital Trusts were established by the 1995 Finance Act to encourage small investors to invest in equity through specially created trusts. According to figures given by the Bank of England (30), over the two-year period to 1997, £360 million was raised by eighteen VCTs, of which £90 million was invested. It is likely that much of this would be invested through 'junior' stock markets such as AiM.

5. Other Schemes

There are a variety of state schemes which are available to help the entrepreneur and small firm. These are often in the form of grants or awards. The main grants available come under Regional Selective Assistance which is intended to assist entrepreneurs and small firms in designated areas of the UK which have been targeted, and are often given for the purchase of manufacturing premises. The Enterprise Initiative was also in the form of a grant and enabled the SME owner and entrepreneur to purchase the time of a management consultant to improve the operation of the firm.

Awards are also available to high technology entrepreneurs and firms under the Small Firms Merit Award for Research and Technology (SMART) and Small Firms Award for Projects Under Research (SPUR). Both schemes are part of the DTI's assistance to high-technology based firms that may have difficulty in raising funding for innovative products. Although these schemes may give small firms and entrepreneurs much needed assistance, their effectiveness can be questioned, mainly because of their small scale. The SMART scheme is a competition that rewards winners in two stages: Stage I provides a grant to cover 75 per cent of project costs up to £45 000; Stage II awards a further grant of 50 per cent of eligible costs up to £60 000. From 1997, Stage II was absorbed into SPUR which can give 50 per cent of eligible costs up to £105 000. By comparison the equivalent scheme in the USA (Small Business Innovation Research programme) provides up to £480 000 (31).

Although SMART and SPUR were meant to help small firm entrepreneurs that are having difficulty attracting finance to develop products, the competitive nature of the schemes means that only a small proportion of applications are funded by the DTI. For example, the Bank of England's research on the finance of technology-based firms found that only 15 per cent had qualified for a SMART (32). However, those that did have awards found them effective (32). Problems centred on the timing of the awards, rather than the effectiveness of the grant.

MUTUAL GUARANTEE SCHEMES

Considerable attention has focused recently on the potential of Mutual Guarantee Schemes (MGSs) for reducing funding gaps, especially for existing firms that are seeking finance to expand. It remains the case that MGSs have been successfully established in European countries such as Spain, France and Germany, yet at the time of writing there are only a limited number of pilot MGSs established in the

UK (33), despite the fact that the European Commission has made funds available for this purpose.

Mutual Guarantee Schemes have been established on the European mainland for some time, most notably in France, Germany, Italy and Spain, although their importance, individual sizes and number vary considerably from one EU country to another. For example, there are 125 MGSs in France with an average guaranteed fund value of 26m ECUs, compared to 24 MGSs in Germany with an average guaranteed fund value of 141m ECUs (34). Their importance has been established for some time in these EU countries. For example, the first French MGSs date from the 1930s (35). Theoretically they provide an additional source of debt finance for small and medium-sized enterprises (SMEs) who are members of an individual MGS. An individual MGS represents a co-operative arrangement between member SMEs who undertake to guarantee any default by members who borrow from the fund's bankers; a fund which is established with each individual MGS. Usually the fund is able to negotiate with a major commercial bank or other financial institution; member firms enjoy greater borrowing facilities and are supported by the MGS in loan applications. In EU countries there can be considerable differences in the way that individual MGSs are established, operate and administer their fund (36).

In principle, the member firms of individual MGSs should be able to borrow at below 'normal' SME market rates from the fund's commercial bank; it is also claimed by the National Association of Mutual Guarantee Societies (NAMGS) that members will enjoy lower bank charges (33). Banks have the attraction of the mutual guarantee of the member firms, which reduces risk of lending to SMEs, but in addition the claimed better managerial practices and financial discipline for SME members of the MGS, means that banks should have greater confidence in managerial abilities of SME members. For example, MGSs are claimed to have additional advantages for member SMEs in terms of improving management competencies of owner-managers, and other managers in the member SMEs, creating greater financial discipline and increasing the extent of strategic planning (33). It is has been argued that because of the co-operative nature of MGSs, pressure will be placed on members to participate in training and other management development schemes targeted at SMEs. Thus MGSs may be particularly attractive as a policy development for the SME sector, because it is more likely that members will participate in targeted training, awareness or other initiatives, such as the Information Society Initiative (ISI), or in benchmarking schemes such as Investors in People (IIP). In the UK, if the introduction of an MGS can be co-ordinated with a lead agency such as a TEC or Business Link, it can be expected that there will be spin-off benefits through increased participation in services, targeted at SMEs, and delivered by the lead agency (37).

In the UK, MGSs are in their infancy and have been established only very recently through the initiative and support of the NAMGS. At the time of writing eight 'pilot' schemes have been established, of which seven have been established within the last year (1997–98). The NAMGS operates in the UK to assist societies or lead agencies to start-up, develop and establish individual MGSs. It provides advice, expertise and experience and detailed procedural guidelines for the establishment of the MGS and its associated fund (38). Establishing an MGS presents considerable legal and procedural barriers since precise rules governing the relationship between member firms, the bank and the society are required. In the UK, the eight pilot societies have been established as industrial and provident societies within the appropriate legal framework for these societies. Thus, the focus on the operation and procedures of the eight existing pilot schemes, their main funders (banks), lead agencies, procedural advice and support from the NAMGS all differ in practice.

Benefits from co-operation

Closer co-operation and networking has been advocated as a way for SMEs to increase their competitiveness and performance. Networking and co-operation by SMEs can be undertaken in spatially specific forms such as practised in industrial districts, or non-spatially specific designs such as advocated by the EU, by supporting participation by SMEs in 'enterprise networks' (39). By co-operating SMEs can achieve various economies of scale namely: internal economies, pecuniary or competitive external economies, technological or exogenous external economies and collective external economies (40). Collective external economies arise when firms co-operate over input activities such as finance. These economies are external to the firm but internal to the group or network of participating firms. Co-operation emerges through repeated economic interaction which can be reinforced by institutional and cultural environments which encourage co-operation and trust. Furthermore, unco-operative behaviour which could jeopardize loan guarantee schemes, for example, can be restricted by exclusion. Firms have to belong, and abide by the rules of the network, to take advantage of the potential benefits which arise from co-operation and networking activities.

In theory the co-operative principles of MGSs should heighten awareness of SME owner-managers to support and advice schemes, including counselling, advice and management support, perhaps making them more willing to draw upon specialized consultancy, export advice and other technical support. However, there are costs associated with MGSs, since an individual MGS must be administered, rules for membership must be agreed, terms and conditions of membership need to be laid down. Evidence in Europe suggests that problems can arise with the administration of individual societies and with ensuring the agreement of members (36). Agency theory suggests that peer pressure can make members more willing to adhere to norms laid down by peers, but potential for disagreement also exists. Some members of the MGS may undertake improvements in their own competitiveness, while others may be tempted to 'free-ride', enjoying reduced interest rates and/or reduced bank charges.

Impact on Management Competencies

The impact of membership of the MGS on managerial competencies will take time to evolve and may exist in a number of subtle forms; for example, through increased awareness of events, increased awareness of initiatives, increased sharing of knowledge and dissemination of information, reduction of uncertainty for growth firms. The extent of impact will depend on the composition and make up of the membership of the MGS, for example, the mix between mature, developing and start-up firms. Membership of an MGS may yield particular benefits to new and emergent growth firms, by enabling them to draw upon the experience available with the wider membership.

Membership

In the UK the eight pilot MGSs have been established on a regional or local, as opposed to an industrial sector, basis. In theory, there are arguments for the membership of the MGS to be cross-sectional in terms of age, size and sector for different firms. However, this may reduce the extent to which the provision of targeted schemes (e.g., support services such as technical counsellors) are likely to be disseminated and taken up within the MGS. According to NAMGS, the target size of firm for membership is 5 to 100 employees (38), but large firm participation (but not membership), for example through sponsorship, is expected and encouraged (33). NAMGS also claims that member firms are likely to take advantage of the cross-sectional nature of the membership to inter-trade, a claimed added value to members (33).

Financial Benefits

Although there are claimed benefits for member SMEs in terms of additional loan finance, the principle of MGS membership requires an expectation that members will save into the Guarantee Loan Fund; only some members will borrow. The larger the fund the more likely that there will be associated financial benefits such as higher interest rates on savings. In addition, greater financial discipline on members, such as requirements to keep management accounts, will lead to enhanced SME performance.

Because of the pilot nature of the funds it is only very recently that any member firm in the UK has borrowed from a fund. However, according to a recent NAMGS newsletter, the first loan was made to a member of the Lancashire MGS in 1998 (41).

CONCLUSIONS

Despite official attempts to promote venture capital and alternative sources of equity, such as secondary stock markets, entrepreneurs still face difficulties in raising such risk finance. There are considerable search and matching costs with informal venture capital; and with formal venture capital there will be a lengthy due diligence or preparation required before a deal is completed. The operation of venture capital markets in the USA is sometimes held up as a desirable model for the UK to emulate (42). Different cultures of risk taking by investors mean that it is easier for American entrepreneurs to raise early-stage risk capital; yet it is also worth remembering that bank relationships are different in the USA. For example, evidence suggests that American entrepreneurs change their bank much more frequently than do European entrepreneurs and there is a greater level of dissatisfaction with the bank manager–entrepreneur relationship (43). We need to remember that improving supply-side sources of finance may not match the desired type of finance, whether debt or equity, by entrepreneurs. However, there seems to be scope for intervention by agencies in improvement of the accepted low take-up in the UK on sources of venture finance. This may be in educating and induction as much as in facilitating.

The pilot MGSs that exist in the UK provide an interesting alternative method of raising finance for entrepreneurs. However, the funds created as a result, do not in themselves provide an extra source of finance, but should reduce the cost of bank finance. These MGSs may well turn out to be attractive alternative to sources of venture and equity finance.

Learning outcomes

At the end of this chapter you should be able to:

1. Understand the difficulties facing an entrepreneur seeking to raise venture capital.
2. Distinguish between informal and formal sources of venture capital.
3. Describe the advantages of business angel finance (over formal sources of venture finance) for entrepreneurs and discuss some of the problems for agencies in promoting this type of finance.
4. Identify alternative sources of equity through the secondary stock markets and VCTs.
5. Recommend and advise an entrepreneur on how to prepare for raising venture finance.
6. Describe the importance of funding that may be raised by technology-based entrepreneurs through Government-sponsored schemes such as SMART and SPUR.
7. Discuss the potential of MGSs as an alternative source of finance.

REFERENCES

1. MYERS, S.C. (1984) 'The Capital Structure Puzzle', *Journal of Finance*, vol. 34, no. 3, pp. 575–92.
2. MICHAELOS, N. (1997) 'Firm Characteristics and Capital Structure Choice in Small Privately Held Firms: some new evidence', paper presented to the ESRC Finance of Small Firms Group, Manchester, April.
3. DTI CONFERENCE (1998) 'The Entrepreneurial Society', London.

4. EUROPEAN COMMISSION (1998) *Report on Venture Capital in the EU*, EU, Brussels.
5. BVCA (1997) *Annual Report*, BVCA, London.
6. MURRAY, G. (1995) 'Evolution and Change: an analysis of the first decade of the UK venture capital industry', *Journal of Business Finance and Accounting*, vol. 22, no. 8, pp. 1077–107.
7. MURRAY, G. (1998) 'Modelling the Economic Viability of an Early Stage, Technology Focused, Venture Capital Fund', in Oakey, R.P. and During, W. (eds) *New Technology Based Firms in the 1990s*, vol. 5, Paul Chapman Publishing, London, pp. 97–121.
8. WESTHEAD, P. (1997) 'Factors Associated with the Employment of Non-Executive Directors by Independent Unquoted Companies', unpublished working paper, University of Stirling.
9. MILEHAM, P. (1996) 'Boardroom Leadership: do small and medium companies need non-executive directors?', *Journal of General Management*, vol. 22, no. 1, pp. 14–27.
10. CADBURY REPORT (1992) *Report on the Financial Aspects of Corporate Governance*, HMSO, London.
11. DEAKINS, D., MILEHAM, P. AND O'NEILL, E. (1998) 'The Role and Influence of Non-Executive Directors in Small Growing Companies', interim working paper, PERC, University of Paisley.
12. HUSE, M. (1990) 'Board Composition in Small Enterprises', *Entrepreneurship and Regional Development*, vol. 2, pp. 363–73.
13. TRUELL, E. (1998) 'Hunt for Innovation: where to get the best returns in the European buyout market over the next five years', paper presented to the ESRC Finance of Small Firms Seminar Group, Cambridge, June.
14. MacMILLAN, I.C., SIEGEL, R. AND SUBBA NARASHIMA, P.N. (1985) 'Criteria Used by Venture Capitalists to Evaluate New Venture Proposals', *Journal of Business Venturing*, vol. 1, pp. 119–28.
15. DIXON, R. (1991) 'Venture Capitalists and the Appraisal of Investments', *Omega*, vol. 19, no. 5, pp. 333–44.
16. BOOCOCK, G. AND WOODS, M. (1997) 'The Evaluation Criteria Used by Venture Capitalists: Evidence from a UK Venture Fund', *International Small Business Journal*, vol. 16, no. 1, pp. 36–57.
17. MASON, C.M. AND HARRISON, R.T. (1991) 'Informal Investment Networks: a case study from the UK', *Entrepreneurship and Regional Development*, vol. 3, no. 2, pp. 269–79.
19. MASON, C.M. AND HARRISON, R.T. (1994) 'The Informal Venture Capital Market in the UK', in Hughes, A. and Storey, D. (eds) *Financing Small Firms*, Routledge, London, pp. 64–111.
19. MASON, C.M. AND HARRISON, R.T. (1998) 'Stimulating Investments by Business Angels in Technology-based Ventures: the potential of an independent technology appraisal service', in Oakey, R. and During, W. (eds) *New Technology-Based Firms in the 1990s*, Paul Chapman, London, pp. 81–96.
20. HARRISON, R.T. AND MASON, C.M. (eds) (1996) *Informal Venture Capital: Evaluating the Impact of Business Introduction Services*, Woodhead-Faulkner, Hemel Hempstead.

21. GRAHAME, D. (1997) 'LINC Scotland', presentation to the ESRC Finance of Small Firms Seminar Group, Paisley, January.

22. LENGEL, Z. AND GULLIFORD, J. (1997) *The Informal Venture Capital Experience: A follow up study of the investment process, the post-investment experience and investment performance of LINC investors and investee companies in the period 1994–96*, LINC.

23. HARRISON, R.T. AND MASON, C.M. (1996) 'Developing the Informal Venture Capital Market: A Review of the Department of Trade and Industry's Informal Investment Demonstration Projects', *Regional Studies*, vol. 30, no. 8, pp. 765–71.

24. HARRISON, R.T. AND MASON, C.M. (1998) 'Backing the Horse or the Jockey: information and the evaluation of risk by informal venture capitalists', paper presented to the ESRC Finance of Small Firms Seminar Group, Cambridge, June.

25. McNALLY, K. (1997) *Corporate Venturing*, Routledge, London.

26. ALTERNATIVE INVESTMENT MARKET (1997) *Annual Report*, AiM, London.

27. STODDART, R. (1997) 'Taking AiM to Hit a Fast Moving Target', *Guardian*, January, September.

28. MANPOWER SERVICES COMMISSION (1988) *Enterprise Allowance Scheme Evaluation, Final Report*, MSC, Sheffield.

29. DEAKINS, D., GRAHAM, L., SULLIVAN, R. AND WHITTAM, G. (1997) *New Venture Support: an analysis of mentoring provision for new entrepreneurs*, PERC, University of Paisley.

30. BANK OF ENGLAND (1998) *Finance for Small Firms*, Bank of England, London.

31. SCOTTISH ENTERPRISE AND ROYAL SOCIETY OF EDINBURGH (1996) *Commercialisation Enquiry: Final Report*, Scottish Enterprise, Glasgow.

32. BANK OF ENGLAND (1996) *The Financing of Technology-Based Small Firms*, Bank of England, London.

33. NAMGS (1997) 'Mutual Guarantee Schemes: An Overview', NAMGS paper, Altrincham.

34. AECM (1995) *European Mutual Guarantee Association Annual Report*, AECM.

35. AECM (1994) *European Mutual Guarantee Association Annual Report*, AECM.

36. HUGHES, A. AND LEUBE, B. (1997) 'The Extent and Nature of Mutual Guarantee Schemes in Europe', paper presented to ESRC Seminar on Finance of Small Firms, Durham.

37. IPPR (1997) *Promoting Prosperity: A Business Agenda for Britain*, Commission on Public Policy and British Business, IPPR, London.

38. NAMGS (1998a) 'Procedure Manual', NAMGS, Altrincham.

39. EUROPEAN COMMISSION (1994) *Growth, Competitiveness, Employment*, White Paper, European Commission, Brussels.

40. OUGHTON, C. AND WHITTAM, G. (1997) 'Competition and Co-operation in the Small Firm Sector', *Scottish Journal of Political Economy*, vol. 44, no. 1.

41. NAMGS (1998b) 'Mutual Businesses', NAMGS Newsletter, issue 3, Spring, Altrincham.

42. SCOTTISH ENTERPRISE (1993) *Scotland's Business Birth Rate: A National Enquiry*, Scottish Enterprise, Glasgow.

43. LEVY, J. AND WARHUUS, J.P. (1998) 'A Four Nation Study of Entrepreneur–Banker

Interaction in Young Growing Firms', paper presented to the Babson Entrepreneurship Research Conference, Ghent, Belgium, May.

RECOMMENDED READING

BANK OF ENGLAND (1996) *The Financing of Technology-Based Small Firms*, Bank of England, London.

BANK OF ENGLAND (1997) *Finance for Small Firms, Fourth Report*, Bank of England, London.

BANK OF ENGLAND (1998) *Finance for Small Firms, Fifth Report*, Bank of England, London.

BOOCOCK, G. AND WOODS, M. (1997) 'The Evaluation Criteria Used by Venture Capitalists: Evidence from a UK Venture Fund', *International Small Business Journal*, vol. 16, no. 1, pp. 36–57.

HUGHES, A. AND STOREY, D. (eds) (1994) *Financing Small Firms*, Routledge, London.

MASON, C.M. AND HARRISON, R.T. (1991) 'Informal Investment Networks: a case study from the UK', *Entrepreneurship and Regional Development*, vol. 3, no. 2, pp. 269–79.

7. Innovation and Entrepreneurship

INTRODUCTION

Innovation and entrepreneurship is potentially a vast topic and for the purposes of this chapter we concentrate on issues that face the small firm entrepreneur who is engaged in some form of innovation. Innovation, itself, is a tricky concept to pin down—writers often consider the high technology-based small firm when discussing entrepreneurs concerned with innovation. Yet it can occur with low technology as well as high technology-based firms. It may simply involve 'managing change'; the entrepreneur may find a novel method of changing the process of production as well as the product. The product is loosely defined here to include services; innovation can occur through new variations in the service provided which are often called new 'products'. Drucker (1) cites the example of MacDonalds transforming the humble hamburger stall into a mega-multinational enterprise as 'innovation'. In his seminal work, Schmookler (2) defines innovation in the following way:

> When an enterprise produces a good or service or uses a method or input that is new to it, it makes a technical change. The first enterprise to make a given technical change is an innovator. Its action is innovation.

In order to illustrate the elusive nature of the concept of innovation and entrepreneurship, consider a small craft manufacturer making earrings. Let us assume he/she is skilled and finds that he/she is able to use new material that has been developed elsewhere, say in the aircraft industry by a major manufacturer. The manufacturer is taking technology that has been developed elsewhere and applying it to an everyday use. The question is whether he/she is an innovative entrepreneur? There is no R&D—it can be merely an application or incremental change to existing technology. For the purposes of this chapter, this manufacturer is an innovative entrepreneur, having found a way of applying technological change in a new way, perhaps from the commercialization of technology developed elsewhere.

Thus the innovative entrepreneur is more than just the pure scientist. He/she has to have the additional skills and abilities that we met with Schumpeter in Chapter 1, i.e. they need to have the ability to recognize the commercial application of technological advance. This chapter will provide a case study of that process. Of course to get to the commercialization stage, a marketable product, further R&D may be necessary.

Having defined our terms of reference, we can identify particular issues: for example, whether small, innovatory firms can successfully raise finance; whether entrepreneurs can successfully manage technological change; whether entrepreneurs can protect their investment and ideas through the patent system; whether a specific support infrastructure (such as a science park or incubator) can successfully nurture and develop innovatory small firms. All these questions have attracted some interest. It is assumed that we can identify innovatory entrepreneurs as a distinct group and that their characteristics are sufficiently different from other (non-innovatory) entrepreneurs. In reality, there are differences within innovatory small firms, for example, we might want to distinguish between *high technology* small firms and *new technology* small firms. New technology may be novel but not necessarily high technology and in many developing countries new technology solutions to areas such as irrigation may involve alternative technology as well as new technology.

What is different about the entrepreneur engaged in the innovation process? It can be argued that such entrepreneurs and small firms are worthy of special study and interest because of a number of characteristics as follows.

1. They have different and special financing requirements. The financing requirements are illustrated in Fig. 7.1. These arise because of the need for *seed capital*. The R&D process can take some time before the firm has a marketable product. During this period there is no return for the investor. It is sometimes argued that innovatory entrepreneurs will have greater needs for venture finance and long-term capital. In the development of the technology there will be a further need for *development capital*. When we discussed Schumpeter's definitions of innovation we saw that there were three distinct phases,

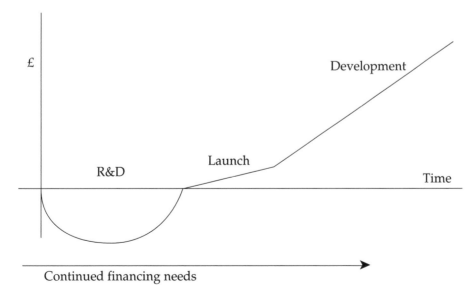

Figure 7.1   The Financing Requirements of High Technology Small Firms

invention, innovation and diffusion. The diffusion stage requires the development of the technology so that it can be applied in different uses and adopted throughout the economy.

2. The entrepreneur will require distinct and different managerial skills. The management of innovation requires a combination of technical and managerial ability that is different from other small firms. For example, the R&D process can be modelled as a time decision-making problem. Timing of decisions such as the taking out of patents can be crucial. Scherer and Ross (3) have modelled technological development within firms as a trade-off between development costs and market revenues and demonstrate that there are considerable *first mover* advantages in the innovation process. It can often be more advantageous to be first on the market with a new product rather than be first with a patent. This is particularly true for leading edge technology where suppliers may be sufficiently influenced to follow the market leader rather than necessarily the best technology. This has happened, for example, with the suppliers of software for IBM-type PCs. IBM has become the market leader even though it could be claimed that Apple MacIntosh had superior technology.

3. Further problems arise with *technology transfer*, which involves the commercial application of research carried out in a different environment such as a science laboratory in a university. It is argued that innovatory entrepreneurs have different support needs. Special environments may need to be created to facilitate successful technology transfer, e.g., from pure scientific research in universities to production techniques in firms. Hence the establishment of some science parks attached to universities in the UK and the network of Business Innovation Centres (incubators) that have now spread across the EU countries. Business Innovation Centres, however, tend to be more generally based than science parks.

4. It has been claimed that high technology small firms (HTSFs) require a network or *cluster* of like firms to be successful, the most famous example being Silicon Valley in the USA. In addition, the Massachusetts model of successful high technology development of small firms as spin-outs from the university has led to attempts to re-create that success here in the UK through the establishment of science parks attached to universities. The most successful of these has been the Cambridge Science Park. Sometimes identified as the *Cambridge Phenomenon* (4)—the spin-off from technical developments in scientific research carried out at Cambridge University. To begin with firms were closely dependent on research carried out at the university.

5. Finally, it can be argued that such firms are worthy of study because they are crucial to the development of the regional and national economy. Solow (5) first identified the importance of innovation for economic development. Over 60 per cent of all economic growth is due to technological advance rather than through improvements in labour productivity. A number of official reports, such as the 1993 White Paper on Science and Technology (6), have identified the potential from the encouragement of entrepreneurs that are engaged in

innovation or technical change and the need to transfer technology successfully. Unfortunately, the author concludes at the end of this chapter that the UK does not contain an environment that fosters entrepreneurs who are engaged in the innovation process. The classic scenario for the UK still exists that we are good at ideas (invention) but poor at the commercialization of ideas (innovation and diffusion).

The Nature of Technology-based Entrepreneurship

Research into the nature of technology-based entrepreneurship has suggested that technology entrepreneurs can be classified into either scientist or technician-based entrepreneurs, and commercially-based (or opportunist) entrepreneurs (7). This classification has been extended by Jones-Evans (8) who has suggested a similar typology of entrepreneurs in HTSFs. The implication, of an acceptance of such a typology, for intervention and policy making is that it should be worth while providing commercial expertise, where this is lacking, for the technically-based scientist who is seeking to commercialize new technology. Alternatively, the commercially-oriented entrepreneur may require technical assistance through specialized expertise. However, most technology-based firms are considered to be technician/scientist entrepreneurs. For example, Oakey (9) considers that:

> While it is theoretically possible for a businessman with substantial surplus capital and no technical experience, to begin a new high technology business, most new high technology small firm founders are technical entrepreneurs. (pp. 12–13)

The nature of R&D and the innovation process will obviously impact on the entrepreneurship process. In particular, the difficulty attached to risk assessment with technology-based products means that the technology-based entrepreneur will exhaust personal sources of capital, even if commercialization is possible, and be under-funded at the critical launch stage. Oakey (10) has modelled the problems inherent in this fundamental process and argued that such entrepreneurs, as a result, will pay insufficient attention to marketing. However, Jones-Evans (11) found from 38 technology-based entrepreneurs, in his interview survey, that:

> . . . an interesting discovery of this research is that 21 of the technical entrepreneurs sampled had assumed responsibility for marketing within their businesses, although less than half had any formal marketing experience in their previous occupations. (p. 85)

As the firm develops, the entrepreneurial function may get diluted away from the individual to a team of entrepreneurs or a management team. Roberts (7) has suggested that the potentially autocratic style of single founder will become difficult to maintain as the firm develops and delegation of key functions becomes necessary to a management team.

IDENTIFYING ENTREPRENEURS CONCERNED WITH INNOVATION

To identify entrepreneurs that are concerned with innovation is a problem that is not easily overcome for researchers or for our purposes in this chapter. One way that has been adopted is to identify high technology small firms by industrial sector and hence assume that they will include the entrepreneur that is concerned with R&D. This approach assumes that the key entrepreneur can be identified.

It has been suggested by Butchart (12) that high technology small firms can be classified according to industrial sector. Butchart defines high technology according to the intensity of R&D to turnover and science-based industries. The suggestion is that there are only certain industrial sectors that will meet Butchart's criteria. These will tend to be science-based manufacturing or engineering industries and services connected to those industries.

There are a number of problems with this approach:

1. It will exclude industrial sectors where the management of technological change and adoption of such change will still be important.
2. It is difficult to measure the intensity of R&D, e.g., it could be on the basis of expenditure or number of employees in R&D.
3. R&D is a less than perfect measure of innovatory activity, e.g., spend does not necessarily correlate with how innovative a firm is, nor does it correlate with the number of patent applications lodged by firms.

Any approach to define high technology or new technology small firms is fraught with difficulty. Further, because technology itself is rapidly changing, using industrial sector definitions can become outdated quite rapidly. Researchers have tried to get around these problems by concentrating on specific industries such as biotechnology or on specific locations such as science parks.

ISSUES IN INNOVATION AND ENTREPRENEURSHIP

Are entrepreneurs at a disadvantage in the innovation process?

The contributions of Schumpeter and Galbraith would suggest that entrepreneurs and small firms are at a disadvantage, compared to the larger firm, in the innovation process. Schumpeter (13) was more concerned with the effect of market structure. However, we have already seen in an earlier chapter that he considered the entrepreneur to be an innovator. The role of the entrepreneur was crucial in economic development. For Schumpeter the entrepreneur was a person who created new ways of fulfilling currently unsatisfied needs or created more efficient ways of satisfying those needs. The act of entrepreneurship sets the innovation process in motion. The reward is extraordinary profit, but this is eroded by imitation. More competition increases the likelihood of imitation and hence the reward for innovation is reduced. From this Schumpeter argued that oligopolistic or monopolistic market structures were necessary to provide the rewards for entrepreneurial innovation. Perfect competition would stifle innovation because there is no motive from profits to innovate.

As developed by Galbraith (14), large firms were seen to have distinct advantages in the innovation process. They were essential to the process of technological advance, but we can see that there was an inherent conflict in the Schumpeter view. This is because entrepreneurs were the movers of technological change, but monopolistic structures were necessary to provide the motives (of profit) to innovate. Galbraith argued that the costs of invention could only be undertaken with the resources at the disposal of the large firm. In addition, economies of scale existed in R&D which meant that large firms could develop new products more cheaply than small firms.

Phillips (15) has also developed the Galbraithian view into a technology 'push' hypothesis. This states that the research staff of a firm are the main instigators of innovation. Basic scientific advances are brought forward to the main organization for commercial development. The larger a firm's research staff the more it can benefit from this technological push.

An alternative hypothesis is associated with 'demand pull'. The main driving force behind technological innovation comes from the marketing staff of the firm who, in dealing with customers, identify problems and engage the research staff to solve the problems.

The evidence from market structure suggests that there are advantages with oligopolistic firms, but the rate of successful R&D falls with monopoly. Despite the disadvantages faced by small firms there is evidence that they are more efficient in the technological and innovatory process. Robson and Townsend (16), for example, have produced evidence to suggest that SMEs have increasingly provided a greater share of the number of innovations in the UK over the period 1945–83. They also show that SMEs have increased their innovative efficiency over this period (the ratio of innovation share and employment share).

Innovative entrepreneurs face disadvantages in raising finance and obtaining other resources

In theory, entrepreneurs and small firms concerned with the innovation process face disadvantages with bank finance. This is due to a number of factors:

1. Banks are primarily concerned with short-term finance. They will not be prepared to lend seed capital.
2. Banks face increased problems in risk assessment due to increased uncertainty associated with new or high technology (17). In the UK the NatWest Bank has introduced 'technology managers' whose role is to specialize in the assessment of new technology applications. If a technology manager receives an application it can be referred to consultants for assessment. However, we have found that the extent of training of such technology managers is only 'two to three days' (18).

3. Entrepreneurs and small firms may not be able to protect their investment through patents or other means. Hence this can increase the difficulties that they face in obtaining funding.
4. The tradition in banks that managers are generalists means that they will not have the skills to assess high technology applications.
5. Banks do not place any value on R&D in the balance sheet, because it is an intangible asset.
6. Entrepreneurs with a small high technology firm may be reliant instead on venture capital. However, recent research suggests that there has been a retreat of the venture capital sector in the UK from funding the high technology small firm (19).
7. Government schemes designed to relieve some of these funding problems are relatively short scale and are not easily available or promoted. For example, SMART and SPUR (see Chapter 6) have relatively small budgets and the size of their awards will not cover the financing needs of entrepreneurs that do qualify.

Entrepreneurs face difficulties in protecting intellectual property rights (IPR)

The IPR system in the UK and worldwide can operate against the successful protection of IPR by entrepreneurs and small firms, due to the time involved and the legal complexities of the system. Although the legal system offers the entrepreneur concerned with the innovation process a method of enforcement of patent (or other IPR) rights, it is a veritable minefield of regulation. Registration of IPR can be a lengthy and expensive process since the entrepreneur will often have to engage special legal experts.

Main Methods of Protection of IPR

- Patents system
- Copyright
- Trademarks
- Others (see below).

(a) Patents
A patent is a monopoly right to the exclusive use of an idea or invention within the geographical boundaries specified. In the UK it can last for 20 years. Note that this is the normal period in most countries, since it follows the guidelines of the Paris Convention of 1898 where all the leading industrial countries signed the convention and the time period for patents to apply. Given that technological advance is now much more rapid (in every five-year period we have doubled our knowledge), there is a strong case for the time period of patents to be reduced. However, agreement on the optimum time period for a patent is much more difficult to achieve since the reward for the entrepreneur needs to be balanced against the need for society to diffuse the technology.

Machines, products or processes are patentable if they are:

- New
- Inventive
- Capable of industrial application.

Sometimes individuals choose not to patent an invention but just to work to protect the idea with a 'know how' or confidentiality agreement.

(b) Copyright

The author of a work is the person who creates it and he/she or his/her employer owns the copyright which will last either 50 years after the author's death or 50 years after it was created.

(c) Trademarks

Trademarks give goodwill or reputation belonging to a firm which attaches to its products or services. The trademark needs to be registered to secure legal protection.

(d) Others

These include 'know-how' which can be protected with a special agreement, design right, and registered designs.

All of these forms of IPR are like any other form of property in that they can be traded, bought or sold. Often firms will come to an agreement to license the production of their new product or service by another firm, perhaps in another country. Royalties are then paid to the entrepreneur or firm that holds the patent or copyright.

One of the problems with the patent system for entrepreneurs and small firms is that the geographical areas that are covered by the patent can be quite limited. For example, until recently a firm would have to take out patents in separate European countries to protect an invention in these countries. This has become easier with the European Patent Office of the EU, but the extent of legal protection is still limited.

Patents can be difficult to enforce. Copying and imitating products is quite common. Often products do not infringe the patent right if made abroad and imported into the UK. In addition, they may just imitate the product and be marketed as a different product.

The high technology entrepreneur or small firm has the problem that registering for patents is expensive, complicated, takes time and still does not guarantee protection. It is not surprising, therefore, that the evidence suggests that the take-up of the patent system is low among such entrepreneurs and small firms (20). In Chapter 1 we discussed recent research by the author which indicated that there was a very low take-up of IPR protection cover through insurance from a sample of high technology-based entrepreneurs (21). This would seem to indicate that entrepreneurs do not take out patents or other forms of IPR protection because they find such protection too difficult or expensive to obtain.

We have met the concept of moral hazard in Chapter 5. The operation of the patent system also contains a moral hazard problem. In theory, the patent system may be viewed as a race with the winner taking all (22). Moral hazard arises because other entrepreneurs or small firms that have engaged in R&D lose out and potentially gain nothing, since under the patent system there is only one winner, however imperfect that patent protection may be. As we have stated before, it pays an entrepreneur to be first on the market, rather than first to patent. Thus the entrepreneur and small firm may be more concerned with being first and first mover advantages than with acquiring legal protection of their invention or new product.

Entrepreneurs and special supportive environments such as science parks and incubators

Segal *et al.* (4) highlighted the supportive network of a cluster of high technology small firms with the study of firms that had developed technological spin-offs from Cambridge University. The extraordinary growth in the number of new high technology small firms that developed around Cambridge, using the infrastructure and network of contacts, was termed the 'Cambridge Phenomenon'. It is possible to point to other clusters of high technology new firms that have developed spontaneously, the most famous at Silicon Valley in California.

Science parks have been established, in some cases linked to universities, to create a favourable environment for the development of high technology-based entrepreneurs. It is assumed that new technology small firms need the contacts and network of support that may be provided, perhaps relating to the more favourable treatment by financial institutions, use of skilled labour and support services attracted to the park. There is little direct evidence so far, however, that science parks provide any more benefits than could occur through the natural networking of such firms as occurs, for example, in the Thames Valley. A study by Warwick SME Centre for the DTI (23) comparing firms on and off science parks found little difference in performance.

In Germany we have found from our own research that some success has been achieved by targeting assistance at special centres. The Länder are powerful regional bodies that have considerable independence to invest money in their own schemes. Thus in Baden-Württemberg we found that special assistance had been provided for new technology firms through grants and soft loans. The difference in Germany to success of such firms was the extent of promotion of such schemes by the Chambers of Commerce.

To improve the survival and development rates of start-up firms with high potential and commitment to growth, incubators are believed to help 'by addressing the common reasons for failure such as lack of business skills or difficulties accessing know-how or finance' (24). The DTI further recognizes that business incubators can assist in promoting 'technological interweavements' (24) which can be critical in their success. The Enterprise Panel report (25) concluded that:

- Incubators can help business start-ups and businesses with high growth potential to succeed

- Incubators are an effective way of promoting technology transfer, of developing innovation and of generating local jobs and economic development
- While there is much activity in the UK, there is a lack of co-ordination.

However, most of the innovation centres and incubators have only enhanced new firm performances where certain conditions are present. Either they have established strong linkages with academic institutions, symbiotically existing of academic spin-outs and resources where an enterprise culture can be discerned; or they have specialized in particular sectors, creating effective innovative elements of pre-existing industrial clusters. The experience in many other cases, especially where the incubator has not been sufficiently integrated into the local innovation strategy of the public and private sectors, has been to 'become no more than managed workspaces' (26).

An incubator is designed to be a dedicated building to nurture small emerging firms. Typically, 'The incubator firms share business support services such as typing, copying, computer, telephone, and occupy space at reduced rates' (27, p. 43). Incubators seek to try and support companies over their most difficult years, the first three years in operation. This supportive environment is developed by the provision of facilities which are often beyond the reach of small companies. The sharing of facilities such as typing, copying, phone answering and telecommunication services allows individual firms to overcome this disadvantage. Additionally, the management of the physical environment is undertaken by a dedicated staff which frees the entrepreneur from matters such as building maintenance, the provision of conference rooms, reception facilities, furnishings etc. A further feature of incubator facilities is that they can provide 'networking' opportunities both within the incubator itself and, given the experience and contacts of the management team, in the wider economy. Incubator facilities are usually flexible in terms of availability of floor space. Incubators can have further advantages to the community at large. They can lead to the transformation of 'brown field' sites thus enhancing the locality and leading to a revitalization of the immediate surrounding area. The impact of attracting new high tech firms can lead to the diversification of the local economic base with consequent new job opportunities.

According to one case study of an incubator in Cambridge (28), such a facility can be remarkably successful. The case study incubator had 64 companies, employing over 1000 staff. Tenants for the incubator came from three sources: start-ups, young one to five years old technology-based companies who have the potential for spin-outs, and support companies with a technology bias who can provide services for other companies. This third section comprised around 10 per cent of the total. The authors concluded that the incubator performs two key functions as a resource provider:

1. It offers specific input to support the growing firm which is resource-constrained—help with cashflow/property costs, suitable prestige premises and advice.

2. It, in effect, brokers partnerships and alliances which are essential to firms by encouraging inter-tenant contact; acting as a gateway to other services.

However, other studies based on incubator facilities, contain much more equivocal findings. For example, one study of such facilities in Scotland found that 62 per cent of firms in such facilities were consultants and 88 per cent stated they had not received any professional advice or assistance while in the incubator (29). If there is no strategy concerning how long companies expect to remain in the premises, this can lead to incubators merely becoming real estate managers with the management spending most of their time collecting rent and firms which can pay the rents being offered premises (29).

PERFORMANCE OF ENTREPRENEURS CONCERNED WITH INNOVATION

While it is accepted that innovative small firms and entrepreneurs provide high value added to the local economy, they appear to perform little differently from other small firms, at least in the UK. For example, Oakey (30) comments: 'analysis of the growth performance of high technology small firms in the UK during the 1980s . . . has been unimpressive' (p. 2).

As well as overall performance, if we examine at the UK micro-level individual firm performance, there is little evidence of fast growth; despite the evidence from the US in areas such as Silicon Valley, where impressive growth has been recorded (31). In some cases this spectacular growth has led to the view that the high technology small firm or the innovative entrepreneur could be a panacea for some of the UK's problems of industrial restructuring. The 'Cambridge Phenomenon' also seemed to hold out hope that the growth of the small innovative firm in clusters of networking, exploiting technology transfer would be successful in specially created environments such as science parks. Yet, as Oakey (10) points out, by the time that European governments were attempting to foster the growth of such firms, the narrow window of opportunity had been closed. The result in the UK is that the high technology small firm entrepreneur has never been able to deliver the hoped for growth in special environments.

The result is that the entrepreneur still faces the same, if not higher, constraints as 10 years ago, resulting for the UK, according to Oakey, in 'a lost decade' (30). This loss of potential for entrepreneurship and innovation has been reflected in the performance of the venture capital industry. In the early 1980s venture capital supported small innovatory firms. By the end of the 1980s most of the funds from venture capitalists went into well established firms as management buy-outs or management buy-ins. As Oakey also comments:

> Now, at the beginning of the 1990s, the UK venture capital industry . . . has virtually abandoned new technology-based firm (NTBF) start ups as too risky and unrewarding . . . (and) . . . the conditions for innovation and growth in NTBFs is probably bleaker now than was the case in 1980. (p. 5)

This lost opportunity for the UK may have many causes—an over-optimistic assessment of the potential of small innovatory firms; short-termism on the part of investors; lack of the right support from Government and other bodies; and insufficient infrastructure of risk-taking venture capitalists to support high technology small firms or entrepreneurs and innovation, an infrastructure that does seem to exist, for example, in Massachusetts in the USA.

Whatever the reason, innovative entrepreneurs face tremendous barriers to development. If we consider that R&D periods are often long, resources are scarce, equity will be exhausted, and patents are expensive, then we can appreciate that the innovative entrepreneur faces special and acute barriers and problems. An entrepreneur may face ten years developing a product and even after development there are marketing and promotion problems; there are continued development problems after prototypes have been produced. Despite the occasional special assistance, these problems are often insurmountable.

To consider these special problems in more detail, it is useful to consider how they operate in a case study. An example is provided at the end of this chapter, which illustrates some of the problems faced by innovative entrepreneurs in the UK. Given the difficulties that have been outlined above we argue that there must be 'innovative' support mechanisms. For the remainder of this chapter we focus on some of the support measures that could be taken to realize and develop the (lost) potential from entrepreneurs concerned with the innovation process.

SUPPORTING THE INNOVATIVE ENTREPRENEUR

Innovative funding mechanisms

We have identified some of the problems that high technology-based entrepreneurs face. It is possible to argue that the funding problems are also faced by low technology applications—any innovatory process requires some R&D and it is this stage of the process that requires support. However, funding is only one aspect of this support; a holistic approach needs to be taken. Philpott (32) has shown from his research that there are information and funding gaps with innovatory entrepreneurs. Clearly, despite the improvements that have been made by some of the clearing banks such as the NatWest Bank (33), which does have a coherent policy for supporting technology, we cannot expect existing funding to close the gap for innovatory entrepreneurs. It requires state support, perhaps a state investment bank that has frequently been called for along the lines of the German state investment bank, the KfW.

It is clear that normal commercial banking principles preclude the banks from any heavy investment in high tech at the R&D stage. The lack of such a state policy, until recently, towards high technology means that an investment bank of this sort is unlikely in the near future. Also, given the Government's desire to promote self-help schemes, it would seem that Mutual Guarantee Schemes (MGSs) have far more potential in the UK, especially when one considers that technical advance is often incremental, that is, a firm will make a small advance on existing technology, perhaps by applying it to a different application. In these circumstances, particularly in the UK, MGSs possess potential not just for high technology-based small firms but for all SMEs engaged in innovatory product and process development.

The Role of the DTI

Broadwith (34) has shown that the DTI recognizes that: 'Innovation is critical for sustainable wealth creation' (p. 2). A CBI study has shown that there are critical success factors that determine whether entrepreneurs are able to exploit technology (35). The emphasis of the DTI, however, seems to be on regional delivery through the spread of best practice. The Austrian School principle of force of competition is quoted as providing the spur to innovate and develop. Unfortunately, market competition can be haphazard in the selection of best practice. In the face of severe competition, the innovative entrepreneur faces particular competitive disadvantages and we have argued that these are serious enough to warrant special support through a coherent technology policy. Identification of best practice and successful role models can be encouraged as through the SMART awards.

CONCLUSIONS

This chapter has attempted to synthesize and present some of the issues that surround entrepreneurship and innovation. We have concentrated on those that are important for small firm entrepreneurs, and we have attempted to suggest some policy measures that could be taken to encourage the important function of the entrepreneur in terms of innovation. However, it is a salutary fact that documented cases exist of entrepreneurs who have 'given up' the uneven struggle with innovation and R&D in the UK (36). The Government's own White Paper on Science and Technology (6) recognized the untapped potential that still exists from our failure to commercialize inventions and capitalize on British technology. One of the reasons for this failure must be the inhospitable environment faced by the innovative entrepreneur.

To tackle this failure we need a radical change of policy and thinking. No amount of tinkering with the support system will make much difference. Business Links will not make more than a superficial change in the networking abilities; the evidence already is that they add yet another layer to the confusing range of support faced by small firm entrepreneurs (37). There are some signs of the beginnings of specialized targeted support (38), yet to make any significant impact, changes are required in all the institutions concerned with the support infrastructure. This infrastructure includes banks, chambers of commerce and local authorities. Even universities need to be more entrepreneurial in their outlook. Comparing the UK to an area that is successful, such as Massachusetts in the USA or Baden-Württemberg in Germany, we can see that a radical change in the infrastructure is required, if UK innovative entrepreneurs are ever to compete on equal terms with their North American and German counterparts. This situation will only change if the Government improves support to innovative SMEs.

CASE STUDY

We conclude with a case study of a small innovatory firm—Aquamotive Control Systems Ltd. This case illustrates a number of issues concerned with entrepreneurs and the innovation process as discussed in the chapter. It also serves as the basis for suggested assignments which are set at the end of the chapter. Further developments in the Aquamotive case and discussion of some of the issues are available in the tutor's manual.

AQUAMOTIVE CONTROL SYSTEMS LTD

Introduction: Mauchline Business Services

Mauchline Business Services (MBS) was a precursor business start-up by two partners: Marion Welsh and Alex Howie. This service-based business was started by Marion and Alex in light of their successful experience in the effective daily operation and control of their previous employment. MBS offered a consultancy service to other SMEs. It was the partners' intention to offer a holistic, global solution to the administrative needs of small firms and to provide a 'one-stop-shop'.

During the initial start-up phase, the partners were able to take customers from their previous employer with them, but Marion and Alex faced difficulties in sourcing initial custom to create a broader, more secure customer base. MBS faced a further obstacle in the longer term. The nature of the service they were offering and the market they were targeting was such that their customer base was necessarily 'churning'. The essence of the service offered by MBS was the provision of administrative and commercial support to new-start and micro-firms until such times as these firms had enjoyed sufficient growth to enable them to bring these functions in-house. Although custom from individual client organizations was often on a repeat basis, it had a finite lifetime, averaging in the region of two years. As a result MBS was required to find new clients to replace those they had helped to grow. In effect they were assisting organizations to reach a situation whereby they no longer needed the services of MBS.

After two years trading MBS had achieved a turnover marginally in excess of £50 000 and was employing one additional member of staff in a clerical/administrative role. Although this situation was considerably short of the original targets the partners had set themselves, the company pre-tax profit (excluding partner remuneration) was £40 925. At this stage the temptation would have been to seek the consolidation and limited growth which marks the 'lifestyle firm', content with generating an acceptable level of personal income and enjoying continued autonomy. However, the partners remained intent on growing the business. A possible opportunity was soon to present itself.

Alex had received several phone calls from his brother, who was a maintenance foreman at a fish farm, asking advice on a feeding system that didn't work very well. There had been several lengthy sessions on the phone and eventually his brother invited Alex and Marion to the site of the fish farm. The feeding system was manufactured in Norway, with the result that obtaining service and an engineer from Norway was both time consuming and very expensive. Alex and Marion visited the site and on opening the control panel box, they found a programme logic controller (PLC). This was exactly the type of technology they had been working with in their former employment. They found that the system in place at the fish farm was adapted from other land-based systems. They were able to repair the system, but as they were leaving they both thought: 'There has got to be a better way of engineering a fish feeding system'. In addition, they were of the opinion that the existing technology was being utilized in an incomplete and piecemeal manner which, they felt, created as many difficulties as it was able to solve.

Aquamotive Control Systems Ltd

From the outset it had been the intention of Marion Welsh and Alex Howie to become involved in electronic control systems design. However, they realized that if this course was to be followed exclusively, the finances and time involved in creating a product/service range and establishing a reputation and customer base would render the venture unfeasible. Although the partners had no direct prior experience with regards to control systems within the fish farming industry it is true that many of the concepts involved were generic across industries. It was as a result of this truism that the partners felt problems were arising.

Product Development

These problems revolved around issues relating to:

- The harshness of environment and the inherent difficulties arising from exposure of electrical devices and other equipment
- The high maintenance requirements/costs of existing equipment in the event of blockages and disruption
- Wastage, destruction and uneven dispersal of foodstuff
- Algal growth and pollution.

These problems, in turn, resulted in existing technology being utilized in an incomplete and piecemeal manner which, they felt, created as many difficulties as it was able to solve.

After some initial market survey work designed to establish whether the problems they had identified were indeed prevalent throughout the fish farming industry, the partners determined to develop a system which would provide a global solution for the sector and prototype development begun. The original intention in developing a system and its companion software had been to utilize existing technology in a more efficient and comprehensive manner. However, during the design process they discovered that the necessary technology was unable adequately to meet the requirements which they had set the system.

Fish farming involves a significant amount of water. The risks and potential costs involved when electricity comes into close proximity with water led the partners to the conviction that traditional control systems, involving on-site electrical currents, could not be the cheapest and most effective method of meeting control requirements. The task with which they were faced was to design a system which would withdraw the necessary electrical components from the site and the water tanks. To facilitate the development project that was to be at the centre of their activities the company was able to secure a public sector innovation grant which represented 50 per cent of estimated costs involved (including wages, travelling expenses, etc.—amounting to £25 000).

The key innovative elements of this finished system were the Aquamatic control valves. These valves effectively take hydraulics into the realms of digital computing. Current systems use 1 valve: 1 hydraulic line. By digitizing the system, the addition of one hydraulic line doubles the number of valves which can be controlled, so that 16 valves can be controlled by 4 hydraulic lines. Control was therefore by means of a digital address. This address, however, was created by means of water pressure, not by electrical signals. In addition to the obvious electrical safety considerations the system offered another principal benefit, in the event of leakage, in its use of salt water as the hydraulic fluid as opposed to the more conventional oil. Hence, the hydraulic fluid used is free, in plentiful supply, non-toxic and safe.

Market Positioning

The technology had originally been developed to create a more efficient automated fish feeding system. However, it became obvious to the partners during, and immediately after, the design stage of their project that the breadth of applicability of their 'invention' was far greater than they had originally appreciated.

For example, it could be adapted for application in the:

- Horticulture industry (primarily large-scale greenhouse facilities)
- Oil and gas industry (including extraction, transport and storage activities)
- Chemical industry (principally transport and storage activities).

Despite this diverse technological applicability it was decided that the company should concentrate its initial activities on tailoring, and subsequently marketing, the technology for one distinct industry. The rationale for this decision lay in part in the desire to maintain effective control of the company's growth and in part in the limiting nature of finance—fearing that potential financiers would perceive the company to be spreading itself too thinly. Superficially it could be assumed that concentration on one or more of these alternative market opportunities would offer greater scope for remuneration than that offered by the low profile, 'unfashionable' fish farming industry. However, in deciding on their initial market positioning and developing a market strategy the partners highlighted several drawbacks associated with entry into these alternative markets:

- Development for the oil and gas or chemical industries would prove to be too costly at this stage of the company's development (e.g., due to material and time costs, valves for petrochemical industries would cost in the region of £300 as opposed to £30 for the fish farming industry).
- There are no technological barriers to development specifically for the horticulture market. Specification limits and tolerances are of a similarly low nature to those required for the fish farming market and the valves themselves would require little further research and development time. However, the profit margins and attitudes to investment within these markets are such that investment in automation would only be undertaken at prices incompatible with development costs to date.

By contrast the fish farming industry offered some distinct benefits, such as:

- Comparatively low levels of competition. There existed no direct competition for the valve component of the system and automation in general is relatively low, though a growth area within the industry.
- Low materials costs, and subsequent relative selling price (due to looseness of technical specification requirements).
- Direct and obvious applicability of technology.
- Immediate potential customer base.
- Proximity of potential test facility offering mutual benefit (i.e., opportunity for 'real life' testing allowing problem identification and resolution—in addition, potential subsequent saleability at reduced cost).

Marketing Strategy

Given that feed costs for the average medium-sized fish farm were circa £30 000 per month and that the technology for such an enterprise, costing £10 000–£30 000 (depending on complexity of system), promised savings in the region of 30 per cent, farmers investing in the system could expect it to pay for itself within a year of purchase.

Appreciating the fact that technological value and associated benefits were not in themselves guarantors of success, the partners sought to develop a profile of potential customers who would be targeted in the first instance—dividing the overall market into groupings by type and size. To this end it was decided that the immediate focus of attention would be directed at salmon farms with a least 8 cages and having 2–3 sites, where profit margins and potential returns to investment were greatest. Having established a customer base within this market and developed a degree of visibility within the industry, it would then be possible to consider diversification into fresh water and other specialist fish farming fields.

Previous promotion and marketing activities for the administrative and system-related services of MBS comprised advertising in the local press, local exhibitions and direct personal selling. The company recognized that, due to the nature of the product and services that were offered by Aquamotive Control Systems Ltd and the relative dimensions of the proposed market place, a different approach should be taken.

The activities identified for involvement in the process of gearing up for the launch of the Aquamatic control valves and the Aquamotive control systems for the fish farming industry included:

- Development of a new company image. To protect its identity Aquamotive Control Systems Ltd was registered as a company name in March 1995, professional brochures and marketing material were commissioned under this name, and the company began trading under the trade-name/trademark Aquamotive Control Systems (though still through the 'books' of the original company, MBS).
- Construction of a Beta-Test Facility. Construction of this facility was nearing completion and provided the company with exact information regarding the capabilities of the system and allowed it to detail more accurately the expected benefits and savings associated with farm investment in this area. Once the facility had been established, the intention was to produce a video to act as a complementary promotional tool.
- Establishment of a network of contacts within the industry. In addition to farm contacts established during the prototype development stage, and with the assistance of the agency funding, the company was able to make visits to Sweden, in the first instance, and other European/Scandinavian countries. These trips were made with a view to making direct contacts with firms operating in a similar sphere to determine the possibility of some form of co-operative venture, whereby Aquamotive would be willing to act as

an agent for other organizations' products if a reciprocal agreement could be reached. On a more direct sales front the company attended the industry's annual trade fair to gauge market reactions to its technology.

Perhaps of greatest importance in establishing a reputation from which to build a client base is the role played by 'word of mouth' and referral business within the industry. Market research undertaken by the company had shown that '. . . the majority of technological advancements within the industry are as a result of recommendations made between the fish farms themselves'. In light of this, the Beta-Test Facility on the new site of an established and prominent fish farm was important to achieve demonstration and hence recommendation. 'Word of mouth' had already led to two requests from fish farms for the design and implementation of comprehensive feed control systems (values circa £30 000 each).

In a supplementary move to further increase the company's profile within the industry Aquamotive had been involved in the design and implementation of a crustacean feeding control system which, although not incorporating the innovative valves, had allowed them a smooth introduction to the market. An order was placed for this system by the North Atlantic Fisheries College in Shetland (circa £25 000), after having seen a ¼-scale prototype demonstration. The college intended to expand to five such systems, whilst several other establishments were keeping a close eye on the system's progress (including an institution in Wales which invited the company to tender for a system valued in the region of £120 000—arising through industry 'word of mouth').

Licensing

The company was approached by five separate organizations from Chile and Norway with a view to these organizations manufacturing under licence the technology currently being developed at Aquamotive Control Systems Ltd. These proposals were declined, not as a result of an aversion in principle to the concepts involved but rather to a general 'unreadiness' on the company's part to become involved in such a venture. The company felt that it would prove to be the ideal way in which to surmount the barriers to entry associated with international markets where competition and technological sophistication is far greater than those that would be encountered in the domestic market. The primary reasons for rejecting interest at the time were three-fold:

- Financial. The partners felt that they would like to '. . . learn to walk before we run' and were in danger of driving the company too fast.
- Uncertainty and lack of knowledge with respect to individual organizations and foreign markets. Though lack of knowledge of foreign markets was seen as a barrier to

direct entry, relative naiveté and asymmetric information were also seen as barriers to licensing. Consequently the company was determined to become more familiar with the environment in which it would be dealing and the actors within that arena before making a decision on this issue.

- Inability to adequately police use of technology once it was made available to external interests.

Patenting

Although patents have been applied for, and the company is confident of having its application accepted, completion of the patent application process is expected to take in the region of 3–4 years. As a result, the company was reluctant to license its technology for manufacture without advice from the appropriate quarters and a fuller understanding of the risks involved. The patenting process itself will prove to be a considerable financial burden on a company of this size. The original patent application cost circa £2500, while costs for further patents covering individual countries will be in the region of £2000. Thus with 20 countries immediately within the intended scope of coverage, final costs will be in excess of £40 000.

Short-Term Developments

In the short term the company's aims revolved around initial market penetration and active direct product sales (discussed above), the establishment of a manufacturing facility and the corresponding internal organizational development.

The need to establish a manufacturing facility in the immediate future was of paramount importance. One requirement, associated with the development work being carried out to date, which in turn has created an ongoing dilemma for the partners, revolves around the issue of premises. The company occupies reasonably sized premises on a small industrial complex, which ideally suited the function of MBS in the provision of administrative and rudimentary systems support. For the research and development and subsequent manufacturing activities in which Aquamotive was involved these facilities were inadequate. The specific systems being developed for the fish-farming market naturally, if testing is to be rigorous, require large quantities of water. This should be part of a recycling process, incorporating water storage facilities, to ensure maximum efficiency and minimum waste.

As a temporary measure the company took a short-term lease on an additional unit within its current industrial estate. This step, though providing sufficient accommodation, has insufficient facilities for further development work and was only suitable for small-scale production runs. Thus the company is exploring the possibility of purchasing or custom building premises with adequate scope for future growth in line with manufacturing output.

At the time only one individual (in a clerical and administrative capacity) was employed by the company. With the move to manufacturing, staffing levels would have to increase to fully service both the new custom generated by Aquamotive and existing/future business undertaken by MBS (dependent on any decision regarding the operating future of MBS). With this in mind Marion Welsh devised a proposed medium-term staffing structure which it was hoped would be achieved in a progressive manner (Fig. 7.2).

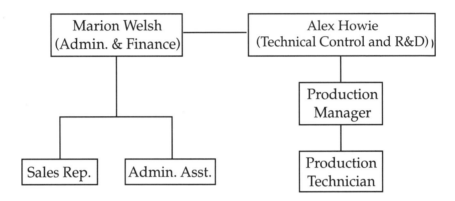

Figure 7.2   Organizational Structure of Aquamotive

The short-term/immediate plans with regards to this recruitment and organizational development process will involve the employment of a graduate electronic engineer to fill the position of Production Technician ('Though he will wear 40 hats like the rest of us'), with a view to promotion to the role of Production Manager when sales and output warrant the recruitment of further technical members of staff. A member of staff dedicated to sales will be employed once initial industry contacts have been established, production is underway and it is felt that the partners are unable to devote sufficient time to this function. Any moves in this direction were dependent on finance being made available.

Funding

Although the partners had identified aims, objectives and strategies for growth and development, these in turn were reliant upon the injection of considerable capital to allow their initial implementation and achievement regardless of the probability of ultimate success. The estimated financial package required to launch the first-stage plans for Aquamotive (namely the initial small-scale manufacturing and sales) was between £50 000–£60 000, depending on whether premises were bought, custom built or leased. In raising all, or part, of the necessary finance the company had several avenues which could be explored:

1. Further government/quasi-government grants and/or loans. This naturally represented the preferred option for the company whereby it is able to secure grants or low interest loans via Central Government (as was the case for the previous innovation grant), agencies or local authority. With this in mind the company had targeted a regional assistance manufacturing grant available through the Government (though the application process for this had not formally begun).

2. Bank/Financial institution funding. Since it was unlikely that government funding would fully satisfy the financial needs of initial development, overdraft extensions or bank loans would be sought to make up the shortfall. At the time the company had received an overdraft extension from £14 000 to £35 000 to allow the leasing of temporary premises (discussed above). This figure was expected to fall to £23 000 once the second instalment of the innovation grant had been received and was further expected to fall to zero on sale of the first feeding system. The company enjoyed an excellent relationship with its bank and required no guarantee for this facility.

3. Venture capital/external stakeholding. The entrepreneurs were not averse, in principle, to the notion of an external shareholding in their company, and the external influences that may come with this, believing in Marion's words: 'It is better to own part of something than all of nothing'. The company had no formal approaches from venture capitalists, however, the feeling within the networks it had established was that this would not prove to be a problem (particularly once small-scale manufacturing had begun and the first sales had been achieved).

4. Business angel venture financing. An individual angel may be more interested in providing the required funding level of £50 000–£60 000.

5. Manufacturing under licence. Despite the fact that approaches to this effect had been dismissed for reasons discussed previously, this course of action would offer an initial lump sum and a guaranteed income thereafter. If the concerns highlighted above could be adequately addressed, this would offer a partial solution to the financial needs of the company corresponding with organizational development.

The Future

Marion and Alex began to look forward to the future with some confidence and excitement. They felt that they had a sound trading record that counted highly with the bank, a solution to the fish farming industry's problem, a patentable product with a global market, good knowledge from market research on the fish farming industry and good contacts and high levels on interest from overseas at their exhibitions. To realize the potential, however, of Aquamotive Control Systems they needed to raise additional finance.

Financial Forecasts for Aquamotive Control Systems Ltd.

Profit & Loss Account Forecast	Year 1		Year 2		Year 3	
SALES FORECAST	£		£		£	
Administration	24 000		12 000		12 000	
Technical services	7 500		10 000		15 000	
Aquamatic systems	40 000		120 000		180 000	
Other fish farm equipment	10 000		24 000		24 000	
	81 500	81 500	166 000	166 000	231 000	231 000
COST OF SALES						
Administration	420		420		420	
Technical services	1 000		2 000		3 000	
Aquamatic systems	20 000		60 000		90 000	
Other fish farm equipment	5 000		12 000		12 000	
	26 420		74 420		105 420	
GROSS PROFIT		55 080		91 580		125 580
Grants		25 000		–		–
OVERHEADS						
Wages & salaries	–		9 300		28 400	
PAYE & NI	–		4 700		14 700	
Prototype materials	5 000		–		–	
Heat & light	1 200		1 200		1 800	
Rent & rates	2 650		2 650		2 650	
Motor & travel	5 000		5 500		6 050	
Post, stationery & adv.	4 400		2 500		4 400	
Telephones	2 000		2 200		2 420	
Office costs	500		550		605	
Insurance	2 200		2 420		2 662	
Repair & renewals	500		550		605	
Sundry expenses	500		550		605	
Accountancy fees	1 000		1 000		1 000	
Patent fees	2 000		20 000		2 000	
Bank charges	280		550		605	
Bank interest	–		–		–	
HP interest	1 122		1 224		1 224	
Loan interest	–		–		–	
Depreciation	7 050		7 050		7 050	
Bad debt provision	4 075		8 300		11 550	
	39 477	39 477	70 244	70 244	88 326	88 326
NET PROFIT		40 603		21 336		37 254

Balance Sheet Forecast	Year 1		Year 2		Year 3	
FIXED ASSETS	£		£		£	
Motor vehicle opening	–		6 375		4 250	
Motor vehicle additions	8 500		–		–	
Motor vehicle disposals	–		–		–	
Motor vehicle depreciation	2 125		2 125		2 125	
		6 375		4 250		2 125
Plant & equipment opening	–		9 750		6 500	
Plant & equipment additions	13 000		–		–	
Plant & equipment disposals	–		–		–	
Plant & equipment depreciation	3 250		3 250		3 250	
		9 750		6 500		3 250
Computer equip. opening	1 603		2 553		1 403	
Computer equip. additions	2 100		–		–	
Computer equip. disposals	–		–		–	
Computer equip. depreciation	1 150		1 150		1 150	
		2 553		1 403		253
Fixtures opening	88		1 563		1 038	
Fixtures additions	2 000		–		–	
Fixtures disposals	–		–		–	
Fixtures depreciation	525		525		525	
		1 563		1 038		513
TOTAL FIXED ASSETS		20 241		13 191		6 141
CURRENT ASSESTS						
Debtors	17 184		16 255		22 618	
Cash in bank	15 305		19 470		40 829	
Cash in hand	68		68		68	
	32 557		35 793		63 515	
CURRENT LIABILITIES						
Creditors	7 777		7 287		10 322	
HP creditor	9 510		4 755		–	
PAYE	–		392		1 225	
VAT	2 498		3 397		5 648	
Bad debt provision	4 075		12 375		23 925	
	23 860		28 206		41 120	
NET CURRENT ASSETS		8 697		7 587		22 395
SURPLUS		28 938		20 778		28 536
FINANCED BY						
Loans	–		–		–	
Capital account	17 831		28 938		20 778	
Less drawings	(29 496)		(29 496)		(29 496)	
Period profit/loss	40 603		21 336		37 254	
		28 938		20 778		28 536

Cash Flow Projection Year 1	Month 1	Month 2	Month 3	Month 4	Month 5	Month 6	Month 7	Month 8	Month 9	Month 10	Month 11	Month 12	Year 1 End
	£	£	£	£	£	£	£	£	£	£	£	£	£
INFLOW													
Administration	—	2 350	2 350	2 350	2 350	2 350	2 350	2 350	2 350	2 350	2 350	2 350	25 850
Technical services	—	734	734	734	734	734	734	734	734	734	734	734	8 074
Aquamatic systems	—	—	—	—	—	—	—	—	—	11 750	11 750	11 750	35 250
Other fish farm equipment	—	—	—	1 175	1 175	1 175	1 175	1 175	1 175	1 175	1 175	1 175	10 575
Debtors	19 727	—	—	—	—	—	—	—	—	—	—	—	19 727
Grants	—	—	12 500	—	—	—	—	12 500	—	—	—	—	25 000
TOTAL CASH INFLOW	19 727	3 084	15 584	4 259	4 259	4 259	4 259	16 759	4 259	16 009	16 009	16 009	124 476
OUTFLOW													
Administration	—	41	41	41	41	41	41	41	41	41	41	41	451
Technical services	—	98	98	98	98	98	98	98	98	98	98	98	1 078
Aquamatic systems	—	—	—	—	—	—	—	—	—	5 875	5 875	5 875	17 625
Other fish farm equipment	—	—	—	587	588	587	588	587	588	587	588	587	5 287
Creditors	3 878	—	—	—	—	—	—	—	—	—	—	—	3 878
OVERHEADS													
Wages & salaries	—	—	—	—	—	—	—	—	—	—	—	—	—
PAYE & NI	—	—	—	—	—	—	—	—	—	—	—	—	—
Prototype materials	2 350	—	—	2 350	—	1 175	—	—	—	—	—	—	5 875
Heat & light	353	—	—	352	—	—	353	—	—	352	—	—	1 410
Rent & rates	221	221	220	221	221	220	221	221	221	221	221	221	2 650
Motor & travel	489	490	489	490	489	490	490	489	490	490	489	490	5 875
Postage, stationery & adv.	1 175	150	150	150	150	150	150	2 350	150	150	100	100	4 925
Telephones	—	587	—	—	587	—	—	587	—	—	587	—	2 348
Office equipment costs	543	—	—	—	—	—	—	—	—	—	—	—	543
Insurance	184	183	183	184	183	184	183	183	183	184	183	183	2 200
Repair & renewals	543	—	—	—	—	—	—	—	—	—	—	—	543
Sundry expenses	543	—	—	—	—	—	—	—	—	—	—	—	543
Accountancy fees	—	—	293	—	—	—	—	294	—	—	—	588	1 175
Patent fees	—	—	—	—	—	—	—	2 350	—	—	—	—	2 350
Bank charges	15	15	15	15	15	15	15	15	40	40	40	40	280
Bank interest	—	—	—	—	—	—	—	—	—	—	—	—	—
HP interest	—	102	102	102	102	102	102	102	102	102	102	102	1 122
Loan interest	—	—	—	—	—	—	—	—	—	—	—	—	—
VAT	1 384	—	—	(£2 316)	—	—	1 159	—	—	1 815	—	—	2 042
HP repayments—cars	850	219	218	219	218	219	218	219	218	219	218	219	3 254
HP repayments—equipment	1 510	177	7 550	178	177	178	177	178	177	178	178	178	10 836
Capital equipment	2 642	2 350	—	—	—	—	—	—	—	—	—	—	4 992
Income tax payments	—	—	—	—	—	—	—	3 000	—	—	—	3 000	6 000
Drawings	1 958	1 958	1 958	1 958	1 958	1 958	1 958	1 958	1 958	1 958	1 958	1 958	23 496
TOTAL OUTFLOW	18 638	6 591	11 317	4 629	4 827	5 417	5 753	12 672	4 266	12 310	10 678	13 680	110 778
NET CASHFLOW	1 089	(£3 507)	4 267	(£370)	(£568)	(£1 158)	(£1 494)	4 087	(£7)	3 699	5 331	2 329	13 698
Opening bank balance	1 607	2 696	(£811)	3 456	3 086	2 518	1 360	(£134)	3 953	3 946	7 645	12 976	1 607
CLOSING BANK BALANCE	2 696	(£811)	3 456	3 086	2 518	1 360	(£134)	3 953	3 946	7 645	12 976	15 305	15 305

Cash Flow Projection Year 2	Qrt 1	Qrt 2	Qrt 3	Qrt 4
INFLOW	£	£	£	£
Administration	2 350	3 525	3 525	3 525
Technical services	2 206	2 940	2 940	2 940
Aquamatic systems	23 500	35 250	35 250	35 250
Other fish farm equipment	4 700	7 050	7 050	7 050
Debtors	17 184	–	–	–
Loans	–	–	–	–
TOTAL CASH INFLOW	49 940	48 765	48 765	48 765
OUTFLOW				
Administration	82	123	123	123
Technical services	490	588	588	588
Aquamatic systems	11 750	17 625	17 625	17 625
Other fish farm equipment	2 350	3 525	3 525	3 525
Creditors	7 777	–	–	–
OVERHEADS				
Wages & salaries	2 325	2 325	2 325	2 325
PAYE & NI	783	1 175	1 175	1 175
Prototype materials	–	–	–	–
Heat & light	352	353	352	353
Rent & rates	663	662	663	662
Motor & travel	1 615	1 615	1 615	1 615
Postage, stationery & adv.	1 175	255	1 175	250
Telephones	646	646	646	646
Office equipment costs	161	162	161	162
Insurance	605	605	605	605
Repair & renewals	161	162	161	162
Sundry expenses	161	162	161	162
Accountancy fees	–	–	–	1 175
Patent fees	–	23 500	–	–
Bank charges	137	138	137	138
Bank interest	–	–	–	–
HP interest	306	306	306	306
VAT	2 498	3 396	123	3 396
HP repayments	656	656	656	655
HP repayments—equip.	533	533	533	533
Drawings	5 874	8 874	5 874	8 874
TOTAL OUTFLOW	41 100	67 386	38 529	45 055
NET CASHFLOW	8 840	(£18 621)	10 236	3 710
Opening bank balance	15 305	24 145	5 524	15 760
CLOSING BANK BALANCE	24 145	5 524	15 760	19 470

Cash Flow Projection Year 3	Qrt 1	Qrt 2	Qrt 3	Qrt 4
INFLOW	£	£	£	£
Administration	2 350	3 525	3 525	3 525
Technical services	3 426	4 406	4 406	4 406
Aquamatic systems	41 125	52 875	52 875	52 875
Other fish farm equipment	4 700	7 050	7 050	7 050
Debtors	16 255	–	–	–
Loans	–	–	–	–
TOTAL CASH INFLOW	67 856	67 856	67 856	67 856
OUTFLOW				
Administration	82	123	123	123
Technical services	686	882	882	882
Aquamatic systems	20 562	26 437	26 437	26 437
Other fish farm equipment	2 350	3 525	3 525	3 525
Creditors	7 287	–	–	–
OVERHEADS				
Wages & salaries	7 100	7 100	7 100	7 100
PAYE & NI	2 842	3 675	3 675	3 675
Prototype materials	–	–	–	–
Heat & light	528	528	528	528
Rent & rates	663	662	663	662
Motor & travel	1 777	1 777	1 777	1 777
Postage, stationery & adv.	1 475	450	2 650	350
Telephones	711	711	711	711
Office equipment costs	177	177	177	177
Insurance	665	666	665	666
Repair & renewals	177	177	177	177
Sundry expenses	177	177	177	177
Accountancy fees	–	–	–	1 175
Patent fees	2 350	–	–	–
Bank charges	151	151	151	152
Bank interest	–	–	–	–
HP interest	306	306	306	306
VAT	3 397	5 253	5 822	5 428
HP repayments	656	656	656	655
HP repayments—equip.	533	533	533	533
Drawings	5 874	8 874	5 874	8 874
TOTAL OUTFLOW	60 526	62 840	62 609	64 090
NET CASHFLOW	7 330	5 016	5 247	3 766
Opening bank balance	19 470	26 800	31 816	37 063
CLOSING BANK BALANCE	26 800	31 816	37 063	40 829

Learning outcomes

At the end of this chapter students should be able to:

1. Appreciate and discuss the problems faced by small firm entrepreneurs in the innovation process.
2. Understand the concept of innovation as a process.
3. Recognize that innovation can take many forms and may involve low technology as well as high technology.
4. Discuss the value of creating special environments such as incubators and science parks.
5. Appreciate the value of full external networking by the support infrastructure for entrepreneurship and innovation.

Suggested assignments

The following questions are based on the Aquamotive case.

As a basis for discussion

Students are directed to some of the recommended reading and divided into groups as a basis for class discussion. Some questions for discussion include:

1. With hindsight, was the strategy to use MBS to gain time and finance as well as business experience correct?
2. What are the difficulties faced by entrepreneurs in the innovation process as demonstrated by Aquamotive?
3. How can these be overcome?
4. What are the risks for a potential investor in Aquamotive?

As a role play

Students are given a briefing sheet and asked to adopt one of the following roles:

- 2 students play the role of Alex and Marion
- 1 student plays the role of a 'business angel' who has £100 000 to invest and is searching for an engineering opportunity.

Students that take on the role of Marion and Alex must sell their idea to the business angel who then has to justify his/her decision of whether or not to invest in Aquamotive.

Assessment criteria

- Knowledge and understanding of the case study
- Participation in the role play
- Research undertaken.

REFERENCES

1. DRUCKER, P. (1985) *Innovation and Entrepreneurship*, Butterworth-Heinmann, Oxford.
2. SCHMOOKLER, J. (1996) *Invention and Economic Growth*, Harvard University Press, MA, USA.
3. SCHERER, F.M. AND ROSS, D. (1990) *Industrial Market Structure and Economic Performance*, 3rd edn, Houghton Mifflin, Boston.
4. SEGAL, QUINCE, WICKSTEED (1985) *The Cambridge Phenomenon*, Segal, Quince, Wicksteed, London.
5. SOLOW, R.M. (1957) 'Technical Change and the Aggregate Production Function', *Review of Economics and Statistics*, vol. 39, pp. 312–90.
6. WHITE PAPER ON SCIENCE AND TECHNOLOGY (1993) *Realising Our Potential: A Strategy for Science, Engineering and Technology*, HMSO, Cmnd 2250, London.
7. ROBERTS, E. (1991) *Entrepreneurs in High Technology—Lessons from MIT and beyond*, OUP, Oxford.
8. JONES-EVANS, D. (1995) 'A Typology of Technology-based Entrepreneurs: a model based on previous occupational background', *International Journal of Entrepreneurial Behaviour and Research*, vol. 1, no. 1, pp. 26–47.
9. OAKEY, R.P. (1984) *High Technology Small Firms*, Francis Pinter, London.
10. OAKEY, R.P. (1995) *High Technology Small Firms: Variable Barriers to Growth*, Paul Chapman, London.
11. JONES-EVANS, D. (1997) 'Technology Entrepreneurship, experience and the management of small technology-based firms—exploratory evidence from the UK', *Entrepreneurship and Regional Development*, vol. 9, no. 1, pp. 65–90.
12. BUTCHART, R.L. (1987) 'A New Definition of High Technology Industries', *Economic Trends*, vol. 400, pp. 82–9.
13. SCHUMPETER, J.A. (1942) *Capitalism, Socialism and Democracy*, Harper, New York.
14. GALBRAITH, J.K. (1967) *The New Industrial State*, Hamilton, London.
15. PHILLIPS, A. (1966) 'Patents, Potential Competition and Technical Progress', *American Economic Review*, vol. 56, pp. 301–10.
16. ROBSON, M. AND TOWNSEND, J. (1984) *Trends and Characteristics of Significant Innovations and Their Innovators in the UK since 1945*, Science Policy Research Unit, University of Sussex.
17. VYAKARNAM, S. AND JACOBS, R. (1991) 'How Do Bank Managers Construe High Technology Entrepreneurs?', paper presented to the 14th National Small Firms Policy and Research Conference, Blackpool, November.
18. DEAKINS, D. AND PHILPOTT, T. (1994) 'Comparative European Practices in the Finance of New Technology Entrepreneurs: UK, Germany and Holland', in Oakey R. (ed.) *New Technology-Based Firms in the 1990s*, Paul Chapman, London.
19. PRATT, G. (1990) 'Venture Capital in the UK', *Bank of England Quarterly Review*, vol. 30, pp. 78–83.
20. BAIN AND CO. REPORT (1990) *Innovation in Britain Today*, Bain and Co., London.
21. DEAKINS, D. AND BENTLEY, P. (1993) *The Small High Technology Firm, Risk Management and Broker Provision of Insurance*, Enterprise Research Centre, University of Central England, Birmingham.

22. KAUFER, E. (1988) *The Economics of the Patent System*, Churchill, Harvard.

23. WESTHEAD P. AND STOREY, D.J. (1994) *An Assessment of Firms Located On and Off Science Parks: Main Report*, DTI, HMSO, London.

24. DTI (1998) press release, February.

25. ENTERPRISE PANEL (1996) *Growing Success: helping companies to generate wealth and create jobs through business incubation*, Midland Bank, London.

26. BENNETT, R. AND McCOSHAN, A. (1993) *Enterprise and Human Resource Development*, Paul Chapman Publishing, London.

27. KURATKO, D.F. AND SABATINE, F.J. (1989) 'From Incubator to Incubation: A Conceptual Focus In The Development Of Innovation', *Economic Development Review*, Fall.

28. GARNSEY, E. AND REID, S. (1997) 'Incubation Policy and Resource Provision: meeting the needs of young innovative firms', paper presented at High Technology Small Firm Conference, Manchester, May.

29. MARTIN, F. (1997) 'Business Incubators And Enterprise Development: neither tried or tested', *Small Business and Enterprise Development*, vol. 4, no. 1, pp. 3–11.

30. OAKEY, R.P. (1994) 'New Technology-Based Firms: A Review of Progress', paper presented to the UCE/ISBA seminar, Innovation and Entrepreneurship, Birmingham Centre for Manufacturing, Birmingham, May.

31. OAKEY, R.P. (1991a) 'Government Policy Towards High Technology: Small Firms Beyond the Year 2000', in Curran, J. and Blackburn, R. (eds) *Paths of Enterprise*, Routledge, London.

32. PHILPOTT, T. (1994) 'Information Exchange Between the Banker and the High Technology Small Firm', paper presented to the UCE/ISBA seminar, Innovation and Entrepreneurship, Birmingham Centre for Manufacturing, Birmingham, May.

33. IVES, P. (1994) 'The NatWest Bank and Technology Policy', paper presented to the UCE/ISBA seminar, Innovation and Entrepreneurship, Birmingham Centre for Manufacturing, Birmingham, May.

34. BROADWITH, B. (1994) 'Supporting Innovation: DTI Policy', paper presented to the UCE/ISBA seminar, Innovation and Entrepreneurship, Birmingham Centre for Manufacturing, Birmingham, May.

35. CONFEDERATION OF BRITISH INDUSTRY (1997) *Tech Stars; breaking the growth barriers for technology-based SMEs*, CBI, London.

36. DAVIES, R. (1994) 'Innovation and Entrepreneurship: Developing Support', paper presented to the UCE/ISBA seminar, Innovation and Entrepreneurship, Birmingham Centre for Manufacturing, Birmingham, May, discussed in *Entrepreneurship and Small Firms*, 1st edn.

37. BENNETT, R.J. (1996) 'SMEs and Public Policy: present dilemmas, future priorities and the case of Business Links', paper presented to the 19th ISBA National Small Firms Conference, Birmingham, November.

38. SHUTT, J.D. AND BRADSHAW, N. (1994) 'The Design and Delivery of a Range of Management Support Services to Support SME Growth through Innovative Product Development and Technology Transfer', paper presented to the 2nd High Technology Small Firms Conference, Manchester, September.

RECOMMENDED READING

OAKEY, R.P. (1991a) 'Government Policy Towards High Technology: Small Firms Beyond the Year 2000', in Curran, J. and Blackburn, R. (eds) *Paths of Enterprise*, Routledge, London.

OAKEY, R.P. (1991b) 'High Technology Small Firms: Their Potential for Rapid Industrial Growth', *International Small Business Journal*, vol. 9, no. 4, pp. 30–42.

OAKEY, R.P. (1995) *High Technology Small Firms: Variable Barriers to Growth*, Paul Chapman, London.

ROBERTS, E. (1991) *Entrepreneurs in High Technology—Lessons from MIT and beyond*, OUP, Oxford.

8. Enterprise Support and Government Policy

INTRODUCTION

The election of the Conservative administration in 1979, under Margaret Thatcher, coincided with recent growth in, and attention given to, the SME sector of the economy (see Chapter 2 on the importance of small firms in the UK economy). The free market philosophy of this administration fitted the more important role given to entrepreneurship and enterprise. The early years of the Government also took place against the background of the severest recession in the UK since the 1930s. Many large firms were making workers redundant. The small firm and 'enterprise' were seen as the key to reducing unemployment and job creation. At the time evidence was also beginning to emerge that small firms could be important for future job creation. For example, the Birch Study claimed that it was small firms (rather than large firms) that accounted for the majority of jobs created (1).

The advantage of placing a greater role on the small firm and the individual in job and wealth creation was that it avoided large-scale state intervention in the economy, through, say, state subsidies to large manufacturing concerns. The very tight monetary régime that had been adopted did not permit such public expenditure programmes. Indeed, part of the policy was to cut state expenditure during a period of very severe recession, a decision that caused extreme controversy with over 400 leading economists stating their written objection and opposition to such cuts and state economic policies. The Government turned to supply side measures that were inexpensive and fitted the philosophy that individuals would create their own wealth and hence jobs, if they were given the opportunity and freedom to start their own businesses.

The introduction of the term 'enterprise culture' has been attributed to Lord Young; the belief was that a new enterprise spirit had been regained is encapsulated in his following comment (2): 'The restoration of enterprise in Britain has played a major role in the revival of growth, employment and prosperity' (p. 34).

The Government fostered the idea that before 1979 the UK economy suffered because the culture of society did not encourage enterprise. The standard career was to work for a large firm rather than start your own business. Role models of successful businessmen had not been promoted by the state before. Although they certainly existed they were not promoted. Now the Government did more to encourage the publicity of successful entrepreneurs who had created their own businesses, such as Alan Sugar and Richard Branson. The belief was that the environment, both economically and socially, had been inappropriate before 1979. Now the state would take a range of measures designed to create the right environment for successful enterprise and entrepreneurship.

At the heart of these developments were support agencies and, in particular, the development of the enterprise agencies (or in Scotland, enterprise trusts), Training and Enterprise Councils (TECs) and in Scotland the Local Enterprise Companies (LECs). More recently a network of Business Links (with over 200 outlets) has been created in an attempt to co-ordinate support provision in England and Wales. (Scotland has Business Shops, but their role is more concerned with signposting than with a co-ordinating role.) In the 1990s the provision of enterprise support as part of government policy has lost much of its political dimension. The election of a Labour Government in 1997 (with a landslide majority) has, if anything, reinforced enterprise support policy. For example, Barbara Roche, the Small Firms' Minister at the time (1997), indicated that Business Links were to be the prime vehicle of support for small firms (3). However, at the time of writing there is some speculation over the continued future for Business Links and TECs as separate agencies. There have already been some mergers of separate agencies and more seem to be likely in an attempt to further rationalize support provision. A recent White Paper proposes new Regional Development Agencies (RDAs), which may well take over the functions of TECs in some areas (4). The future for enterprise support provision, as ever, is somewhat uncertain.

Although Business Links and TECs/LECs are often seen as the primary vehicle for enterprise support there are, in practice, many organizations involved in the infrastructure in any one area, including local authorities, chambers of commerce, banks, training agencies and others. This chapter reviews methods of enterprise support and some of the associated issues; examines the role of support agencies and makes some comparisons with the alternative model of support through strong chambers of commerce in Germany and France. The conclusions compare these different models of support and we find that there are some advantages in having strong chambers of commerce.

TYPE AND METHOD OF SUPPORT

Leaving aside a discussion of whether enterprise support should be targeted at existing firms (the policy of Business Links), there are considerable differences in the way that support can be provided. For example, there may be provision of short-term (part-funded) consultancy to meet a specific short-term need for expert advice. Alternatively, other programmes may provide longer-term support to meet an ongoing need for general business advice. These different forms of advice/counselling may be supplemented by other support such as grant aid, access to finance and training.

Part-funded Consultancy

The use of business consultants has grown dramatically by both the private sector and the public sector in the last decade. As a result consultancy has become a virtual industry in its own right, with nearly 12 000 consultancy firms by the end of the 1980s (5). One of the reasons for this growth has been the use of (part) publicly funded use of consultants, in the belief that small and medium-sized enterprises (SMEs) do not have the resources or the time to undertake specialized market research or other functions that larger firms can carry out, but would benefit from having greater access to such expertise.

Much of the research on the impact of consultancy utilizes satisfaction measures (6, 7). Segal *et al.*'s study (8) into the Government's consultancy initiatives also utilized 'hard' impact measures. Two main measures, turnover and value added, were used to reflect different types of the potential impact of consultancy on businesses. The satisfaction measures were high (77 per cent of the firms rated the scheme as satisfactory or better in terms of their part of the consultancy cost) whereas the hard measures demonstrated a substantial shortfall between what consultants promised and subsequently delivered (on average, gross impact as measured at the follow-up interview was 40 per cent of the forecast of impact made at the initial interview). However, there was a striking variation on the impact of the initiative. For the smallest firms, those with less than 10 employees, actual gross impact was only 9 per cent of the forecast; for firms with 100–249 employees the corresponding figure was 10 per cent; however, for other size groups, actual/forecast gross impact on turnover ranged from 40 to 167 per cent.

Most references to models of the consulting process invariably serve to underline Schein's classic consulting typology (9) in which he advocates a collaborative, non-expert role for the consultant with the focus on the process and helping the client to define diagnostic interventions. Schein's vision of the consultant is in a non-expert, collaborative capacity. This difference between the process and task consultants is particularly important for the appropriate role of the consultant with small firms. For smaller firms it is suggested that Schein's process consultation role for the consultant is more appropriate than the expert role. Under the expert role, which frequently occurs when small firm owner-managers are referred for specialist help, successful outcomes are crucially dependent on self-diagnosis by the small firm owner-manager/entrepreneur. Under the process consultation role, the consultant is involved through helping clients help themselves, and assumes that the client is unable to diagnose the problem. As a result, the key to successful consultation is diagnosis. Since it can be questioned whether small firms can successfully self-diagnose, it is arguable that the process consultation model or role is more appropriate for small firms. There is then a role, in theory, for support agencies in the diagnosis process.

Research carried out by the author into one part-funded consultancy scheme (10) found that there was an inappropriate match between the use of expert consultancy and the needs of small firms on the scheme.

Longer-Term Relationships with Small Firms

There are a variety of ways in which longer-term relationships may be developed. For example, Business Links have introduced the principle of an in-depth diagnostic service available to growth-seeking companies. This investment of over £250 million (11) by the Government has swelled the ranks of small firm business consultants through the consultancy role of the Personal Business Advisers (PBAs). It can be disputed whether PBAs see themselves as consultants, but as a recent survey points out, 'a number of pressures are shifting the focus of the role of PBAs to that of consultant' (12). The creation of Business Links and hence PBAs, who have a pivotal role at the crux of the Business Link service, has already been the subject of heavy criticism, despite their relatively brief existence (13). The expense associated with providing an extensive up-front consultancy service, available on demand, is already showing signs of crisis (13). The creation of Business Links and the pivotal role of the PBA has been made at considerable public expense, but with very little knowledge of the potential value-added or 'mentoring' role of the PBA/consultant with small firms and little previous research into this relationship and the impact that it can have on small firm development.

Research by the author with a local scheme in Scotland (14), that provided mentors for selected start-up small firms, found that there was considerable value added by the mentoring support. The study confirmed that the programme of mentoring support was highly valued by the clients. Following the second-stage analysis it was possible to identify the main areas of value added by the mentoring support as:

- Clients had a clearer focus on achieving objectives
- Clients were more likely to use business planning
- Clients were focused on profitability rather than just turnover or cash
- New entrepreneurs were helped to learn, manage their businesses and to cope with change.

Value added of such impacts cannot be measured precisely, but mentoring support did have results in terms of better performance of new start businesses, better competitiveness and hence better survival rates. The impact on performance and achieving objectives was validated through the performance of the clients in the sample who, on average, met or exceeded their projected performance targets from the first stage. This was an important test of the value of the programme, and the success of mentors in keeping clients to their targets and objectives, identified in their original business plan.

Providing publicly-funded long-term support, however, may be prohibitively expensive for some agencies. They may overcome this through having free diagnostic service, followed by a fee-based advice/counselling service. As stated above, this can increase pressure on PBAs to become consultants. An appropriate alternative for some small firms, particularly strong growth performers, is to provide an initial mentoring service which may convert into the mentor taking a non-executive director (NED) role in the later development of the company. At the time of writing, research by the author into the role of NEDs in small companies (15) found largely positive results. One recommendation made by the research team (16) concerned the continuation of support after the mentor period was completed. For carefully selected firms, NEDs provided a close model of the mentor relationship for small, growing firms. Such selected firms could be encouraged to appoint a NED on a purely commercial basis. Agencies could promote and support the development of a list of appropriate people to be NEDs in such growing small firms.

THE ROLE OF SUPPORT AGENCIES

Enterprise Agencies (EAs) have mirrored the development of state concern with support for small firms. The first agency was established at St Helens in 1978 and since then they have grown in an *ad hoc* way, with, at one time, over 300 such agencies in the UK. Part of their role has been to nurture the growth of start-up business, to unlock the potential for entrepreneurial activity and to raise enterprise awareness. This diverse pattern of support agencies has been augmented with the establishment of TECs in England and Wales and the equivalent Local Enterprise Companies (LECs) in Scotland. Together with Business Links and the new RDAs they may be seen as adding to an already confusing range of alternative agencies.

The *ad hoc* development of the enterprise agency movement means that provision of support, spatially and vertically, is the result of chance and accidents of geography and the economic mix of the environment that happened to exist at the time that different EAs were formed. The agency movement has been criticized for the lack of strategic focus of interventions (17). There is some evidence that agencies have a low profile in the small business community (18), and they can be criticized for being reactive in provision rather than pro-active (19).

Despite the considerable framework of support that now exists (established in the 1990s), the delivery of small business advice varies from agency to agency. There are huge asymmetries in the size, staffing and operation of individual agencies. Some provide merely basic counselling advice for start-ups; others have a full range of training and consultancy services for the SME community. An earlier study by the author (20) revealed that a range of support services was common, such as business clubs, financial support, clerical services, databases and additional business services. There was an uneven geographical pattern of support with over-provision in some areas and under-provision in others. Diversity is illustrated by the agencies in Scotland, which are called enterprise trusts, and operate under a rather different environment from those in England and Wales. Also the LECs in Scotland are development agencies and thus have a wider remit than the TECs in England and Wales.

TECs and LECs also vary in size (and budget) even though they were supposed to be based on local labour markets with populations of 250 000. There have been a number of studies that have examined the concept and remit of TECs. Bennett *et al.* (21) have argued that the TECs have been given insufficient empowerment:

> The key impediments to business development in the UK is that not enough power has yet been given out to redress a century long imbalance that has frustrated Britain's economic growth. (p. vii)

Emmerich and Peck (22), however, argue that the TECs are likely to focus on low-level skills and that the composition of the board members is too dominated by representatives of large rather than small firms. A study by Topham *et al.* (23) compared the budgets of TECs to social and business needs of their areas. Ranking by budget did not match local needs, the implicit conclusion being that many TECs will not be able to meet local needs. Curran (24) has argued that there was a low-level of awareness of local TECs by the small business community and concluded that TECs were unlikely to reach small firms and provide appropriate enterprise support. More recent evidence indicates that TECs have raised their profile with the local enterprise community (25).

Discussion of the funding of agencies has been concerned with whether it should be from public funds or private sponsorship. For example, Smallbone (26) has suggested a classification for agencies in the London area based on the degree of public sector involvement and funding. This view of EAs as a 'partnership' between the public and private sectors is becoming less relevant as agencies are attempting to increase their degree of autonomy. TECs and LECs have become the fund holders for enterprise support and training. Agencies are now dependent on them for contracts and have to bid for enterprise funding. Agencies have attempted to make some progress towards financial independence but are still dependent on TEC and LEC funding and therefore indirectly on state funds. This dependency on the TECs for funding was confirmed in a survey by Durham University Business School in 1992 (27) which suggested that 50 per cent of EAs in England and Wales were dependent on TEC funding for the delivery of business counselling services.

Whether agency intervention makes an effective difference to small business development is a moot point. If agencies are to be effective then their role lies in unlocking latent entrepreneurial talent. This is obviously difficult to achieve, but is associated with their effectiveness in raising their profile in the small business community and the extent to which members of the community can be targeted. Since agencies have been criticized for blanket support and their low profile, it is possible to argue they have had little impact on small business development. For example, Casson (28) has argued that empirical evidence suggests that interventions to promote small firm start-ups are unlikely to stimulate entrepreneurship. Business In The Community (BITC) commissioned reports (29, 30) suggest support is effective in creating sustainable businesses but the actual difference that the agency makes is difficult to assess. Moore (31) has suggested that the impact of EAs can vary from 'marginal to significant' (pp. 24–5). Another study has suggested their impact has been quite low (32). A review of the evidence by Storey (33) suggests that the level of enterprise support is not a significant factor in the development of SMEs. However, an evaluation of TEC services for the DTI by PA Cambridge consultants (34) concluded that:

> (Overall) some jobs are created—but are largely offset—by displacement . . . the more significant benefits arise through increased efficiency and profitability in small firms. (p. 1)

The quality of support in the UK has, so far, been variable. The effectiveness of support is determined by the degree of selectivity, of co-ordination and collaboration of different agencies and the profile of the agency. Our research has suggested that the collaboration and co-ordination between agencies is, as yet, very limited when compared to other levels of networking that take place, for example in Germany (35). Other studies have supported the view that the links between agencies and other institutions in the infrastructure of support are undeveloped (36). Co-ordination of support between EAs and other institutions has been slow to develop.

THE ROLE OF BUSINESS LINKS

Business Links were charged with the role of bringing together the often confusing pattern of support that faces the entrepreneur or small firm owner. In a paper addressing specifically the role of Business Links, Bennett (37) claimed that such institutions have the potential to meet the needs of SMEs for assistance, but policy suffered from bureaucratic and financial constraints. We draw upon the example of Business Link Birmingham (BLB) to illustrate their role. BLB saw itself as a single gateway for existing firms seeking assistance with their business problems. In general, Business Links provide support in the following areas: marketing, business survival, staff and management training, quality management, corporate and business planning, European issues and information (38). In BLB's case eight areas had been identified: exporting, sales and marketing, quality, team development, management and finance, legal and regulation, property, and technology.

BLB offered help at three levels. The first level was information and advice in response to enquiries through an easy-to-remember phone number. The second level involved the business adviser service. If the client wished they could be allocated a Personal Business Adviser (PBA) whose role was to carry out a diagnostic check or 'health check' on the business. For example an officer commented: 'It is at that point that we bring the PBA in, which is a free service, which is working with the client anything up to 3 days to assess the real needs of the business'. The third level involves the referral of the client to an agency who will attempt to carry out the PBA's recommendations. It was regarded that this was simply more than a referral with a continual review by the PBA, who is charged with the responsibility of ensuring that the project is completed successfully.

Although, in theory, Business Links are meant to target existing SMEs that employ between 10 to 200 employees, we found in BLB's case that this target had already been revised downwards, after six months of operation, to include firms that employed five or more. In addition the idea that Business Links could target 'winners' (i.e. the small number of fast growth firms) was not backed by any criteria for targeting such firms beyond a belief that they would be self-selecting. In BLB's case it was believed that such firms would select themselves by coming forward for assistance.

TARGETING OF SUPPORT BY AGENCIES

Our earlier study (20) found little evidence of targeted support to different clients. It was found that the main bases of targeting support were age (26 per cent), gender (13 per cent), prior employment (11 per cent) and ethnicity (9 per cent). The size of the agency (FTEs) was significantly associated with any targeted support. Larger agencies were significantly more likely to develop some form of policy to different client groups. The second stage research confirmed that relatively little attempts are made at providing specialized assistance to specific groups of clients. Only a minority of agencies attempted special provision such as Women into Business seminars. Where directors had previously been sceptical of the benefits of such courses, they had changed their views after attending or running such courses.

The creation of Business Links has offered an opportunity both to rationalize support in the UK (by reducing duplication) and to develop some specialization by different EAs. In the case of Birmingham, however, there was little attempt to do either. Some provision for targeted support to ethnic minority clients was provided, as might be expected, but there was no attempt to encourage specialization beyond that which already existed. For example, the director of BLB was of the opinion that:

> I do not see it (rationalisation) personally as a saving, I see it as an opportunity to spot the gaps—and retrain the resource to the gaps which we may well define as a service that is needed.

In Germany, all manufacturing SMEs belong to the Industrie-und Handelskammern (IHK), the local chambers of commerce. These institutions are much stronger than UK chambers of commerce and play a much more pivotal role in promotion and dissemination of information. There is also a greater diversity of financial institutions. The regional states, the Länder, have considerable independence and power to implement their own investment and funding programmes. In the UK there are no such powerful organizations as the IHK and the regional Länder. In the West Midlands alone there were 10 TECs. We have argued that such agencies are too small to make an effective difference to the level of enterprise support and training.

In Baden-Württemberg the IHK was able to provide specialist support and training for high technology small firms by having a director who specialized in technology. His role was seen as that of promoting the interests of technology-based firms, co-ordinating resources and support. Specialized start-up support was available at the chamber even though its members were small and medium-sized manufacturing firms. The difference in support was the way in which the chamber could bring its influence to bear on other institutions such as the banks to provide support. The co-ordinating role was more effective than equivalent organizations in the UK. This included providing information and seminars for the local banks as well as venture capital providers. For example, a comment by a representative of one of the local banks was that: 'The IHK, once a year, hold special seminars on advice to small firms, which bank staff attend'.

In Baden-Württemberg there was also a range of special assistance to help different industrial sectors such as high technology small firms. This was in the form of grants, subsidies, guarantees and soft loans. But beyond industrial sectors there was little in the way of targeting assistance to other categories. Similar to both the UK and France, the chamber provided seminars on specialized help for areas such as exporting, marketing and development. The IHK saw the promotional role as being more important than direct support especially with start-up concerns. In this way it could co-ordinate support such as finance or other requirements of its members.

NETWORKING BETWEEN AGENCIES AND THE CO-ORDINATION OF SUPPORT

Our UK study revealed that different agencies employed counsellors and trainers as generalists or specialists. Although there were attempts by agencies not in formal networks to break away from a generalist approach, it was noticeable that those in a formal network had greater opportunities to break away from the traditional generalist start-up advice that has characterized EA support in the past. The more formal the network, the greater the possibility of developing niche roles for individual agencies with the employment of full-time professional staff who have recognized specialist skills and experience in providing support to different categories of clients. Implicit in this development is the cross-referral of clients that may need specialist help and advice. There are other advantages from the efficient use of staff resources. It can be possible to free resources and staff time so that other issues can be investigated. Examples of this included the delegation of responsibility for marketing and public relations for agencies in the network to one individual and responsibility for developing sources of funding to another. Networking places agencies in a stronger position to develop funds for clients. Some of the larger agencies were able to administer their own venture capital funds for clients, including both first-stage and second-stage funding. If these were administered centrally through networking, it might be possible to widen the benefits of such schemes to more clients, where accessing risk capital is often a problem, to increase the attractiveness of the schemes to potential investors, and to cross-refer clients in the network who may need specialist advice and assistance.

The diversity of the pattern of small business support provided by EAs gives them the flexibility to meet local needs. However, this very diversity can operate as an inhibitor to developing an effective and collaborative network.

Asymmetries between agencies in size, resources, sponsorship, personnel and attitudes can operate to prevent integration. Our study demonstrated a strong independence of agency directors and a desire to retain their own tradition of provision, even though they were prepared to admit that they could see advantages in a more co-ordinated network of support. This means that it can be difficult, even in the more developed networks, to resolve conflicting views and personalities. The harbouring of jealousy of other agencies' roles can inhibit progress and co-operation. The extent of competition for funding affected the ability and propensity of agencies to network, sometimes inhibiting closer co-operation between individual agencies. The impact of TECs and LECs on this extent of networking has been mixed. In some cases the TECs had forced agencies to form a consortium to bid for TEC funding; in other cases the formation of the TEC had cut across agency boundaries and co-operation.

One survey of British and German chambers of commerce (39) found that the resources of British chambers were on average only 7 per cent of those in Germany and they had only 17 per cent of the staff. For example, the Germans do not have to bid for contracts like an enterprise agency and their income from year to year can be calculated with relative certainty. This contrasts with the relative uncertainty of funding for local EAs in the UK. When we carried out the interviews with EA directors, some of them were not only unsure what their income would be for the following year, but in some cases were unsure whether they would still be in existence in a year's time.

The certainty of income allows the IHK to plan support, training programmes and counselling. By the nature of provision, the German system also avoids any duplication. Other institutions work with the IHK rather than try to set up their own support system. Local authorities and regional authorities provide schemes that complement the provision of the IHK rather than set up agencies that may be in competition or offer duplication of support from the IHK. The IHK is relatively independent and powerful and, as a result, is able to employ specialist staff. For example, we were able to interview a director of the IHK responsible for advice and support for technology based firms.

Where other agencies existed they met a specific and identified need and complemented the work of the IHK. For example, in Pforzheim, a specialized agency for the jewellery industry existed, the Creditoren-Verein (CV). Its role was to provide debt collecting for the jewellery industry where that was seen as a specific problem. Again the agency had the characteristics of independence, membership by subscription and power that was supported by law.

There are similarities between the German and the French chambers of commerce. The local chambre de commerce et d'industrie is independent, powerful and membership is again compulsory. The agencies concerned with support and regeneration in Clermont-Ferrand proved to be atypical for France, because there was special provision due to the need to reconstruct and diversify the local economy from its dependence on Michelin as a major employer. However, there was evidence of co-operation between these agencies concerned with enterprise support. For example, a director from the chambre commented: 'We work together (with the Development Commission) but . . . there is some competition'. This point was developed by an officer from the Comité d'Expansion Economique (of the Puy de Dôme department). He considered that the relationship with the chambre was:

> A sort of partnership, yes. The success depends on the relationship between the entrepreneur and the Chambre. If things are going well between the entrepreneur and the Chambre, then they will stay with the Chambre. If not, they will come here and vice versa.

In addition there was a number of smaller chambers for shopkeepers and smaller firms; the chambre de métié. There was one chambre de métié in the department (the Puy de Dôme). The services of this smaller chamber, however, were distinctly different from the main chambers of commerce. The main chambers have members whose employment varies from 10 to 100 employees, whereas the chambre de métié is more likely to serve the 'petite de commerce', the self-employed and skilled trades people. Thus there was some competition, but co-operation also seemed to be effective between different support institutions.

The level of collaboration that exists in Germany between support agencies and financial institutions means that better quality start-ups are ensured. It may be more difficult to establish a new business because informational requirements are higher, but the quality of those start-ups is also higher (35). One of the problems in the UK is that the extent of new small firm creation has been subject to much volatility (40, 41).

SUPPORTING GROWTH FIRMS

In the UK, Business Links have been established with the aim of targeting support at enterprise development. Comparisons with France and Germany are borne out with the emphasis on firms that employ 10 to 100 employees. The methods for reaching such firms are not clear beyond marketing a series of 'events' such as workshops and business development programmes. Business Link Birmingham (BLB) attempts to achieve this aim of targeting growth firms. In the original prospectus BLB was to target existing businesses that employ 20–200. In practice they have been operating with firms that employ 10 to 200 and we have mentioned before that this has now been adjusted downwards to include those employing five or more.

Although BLB has a clear policy of providing support through PBAs to existing firms the criteria for supporting growth firms were admitted to be unknown. As the director also commented: 'I can't offer a solution to that point. Clearly picking winners in my City Council's minds would be a different formula from my DTI requirements and arguably from the TEC'. (BLB is funded by three different bodies, DTI, Birmingham TEC and Birmingham City Council.)

At the same time, the Business Start-Up Scheme has been phased out, accompanied by a reduction in schemes of blanket support. Although there is a powerful argument for switching resources away from start-up support, the criteria for selecting growth firms have not been developed. 'Picking winners' has been advocated yet we are still no nearer developing criteria that will identify so-called 'fast-track' firms. As another officer has admitted: 'We don't know what the answer is (to picking winners)—at the end of the day it comes down to self-selection'. It is hoped that growth firms will phone into BLB for advice and support with their business development. There has been some evidence to show that start-ups can achieve more success where different skills are identified and developed through a 'team start' (42).

Despite the desirability of targeting public sector support to growth firms, in practice it has not been possible to 'pick winners'. This view (that it is impossible to pre-select growth firms) has been supported by an in-depth case study of growth firms in Scotland by Freel (43). He concluded that evidence from the early stage development of such firms did not support a predictive policy of selection, or support a 'picking winners' policy.

A further issue arose with the potential conflict in the provision of a quality service that is required to provide support for fast growth and developing firms, yet at the same time meet quantitative indicators of support provided to meet targets set (in BLB's case) of three different funders. As the director of BLB commented: 'I have to do both. All the grant schemes that I have, have quantitative indicators and output related activity to get the money'.

The interviews with EA directors also revealed that there was some complacency in developing quality indicators. Most directors were content to monitor counselling sessions through quantity indicators such as records of enquiries, but there was relatively little in the way of developing quality indicators such as whether value has been added to the firm. This dilemma exists in the UK because the current provision of support is targeted through Business Links or TECs and LECs. These are not independently funded and will have to meet quantitative criteria of supporting 'X' number of firms. This conflicts with any attempt to provide quality support to a small number of fast growth firms.

In Germany there is some selectivity of support. The IHK by its nature will tend to direct support more to existing firms and respond to their needs rather than start-ups. Seminars tend to be provided not for start-ups or to raise enterprise awareness but for retraining, technology or exporting. The programme tends to be a series of support seminars and training that is geared at existing firms and at Germany's famous Mittelstand, the medium-sized firm, of 50 to 250 employees.

In France, a similar emphasis on developing firms rather than directing aid at start-ups was more normal. Start-up clients were more likely to go to the department agency, the Comité d'Expansion Economique. For example the officer concerned considered that of his clients: 'One third are people who want to start a new business; one third are clients who want to develop an existing business and one third were people who were facing difficulties'. The director of the chambre considered that his typical client was a 'medium-sized firm' and considered that he wished to develop a long-term relationship with these medium-sized firms although they did provide advice and support for the creation of new firms.

There are distinct parallels with the development of one-stop shops in the UK and some of the work and emphasis of French and German chambers of commerce. In the UK there are the beginnings of the development of longer-term relationships with existing firms, providing support more in response to firm needs when it is required, rather than some policies which have been seen as top-down and 'off the shelf' by some commentators (24).

OTHER ENTERPRISE INITIATIVES

There are a number of state initiatives designed to encourage small firm start-up and growth. At the same time, set in the background to these initiatives has been a general withdrawal of the state from the production and provision of goods and services. The extensive programme of privatization and other major economic changes such as in income taxes and corporation taxes cannot be discussed here, but they form the background of general state measures designed to increase and promote the opportunities for private sector enterprise and development. Specific state measures designed to encourage small firm formation and growth are much more limited. They concentrate on relieving perceived constraints on small firm formation and growth. As such they tend to be concerned with funding and other resource constraints. The main schemes are identified below. We merely list and describe them briefly before turning to an examination of whether there has been any significant change, as a result, in our culture.

Enterprise zones

These were created in a limited number of areas designed to provide special conditions that would foster the growth of new businesses. They represented a special 'tax free' zone where the firm did not have to pay local authority rates. Each zone was created for ten years. The most famous enterprise zone has been the Isle of Dogs since it attracted the Canary Wharf investment and development. The Isle of Dogs illustrates the major problem with enterprise zones: they have attracted large-scale firms and funding which, it is arguable, would have been invested anyway but in other areas where firms would have more long-term viability. In addition the enterprise zones do not have the infrastructure to support long-term growth and viability. The Isle of Dogs, for example, has continued to suffer from poor transport links compared to the City of London and it has never attracted the amount of office space that it needed to establish itself as a major centre of regeneration. Amin and Tomaney (44) in a study of the North East were critical of the creation of enterprise zones, where investment has gone into property development rather than into manufacturing.

The Enterprise Allowance Scheme (EAS)

Designed to encourage unemployed people to start their own businesses, the EAS has now largely been withdrawn; although some TECs/LECs do have variations of this scheme funded with European assistance. The original requirement that an individual had to be unemployed for a period of up to six months has been dropped. Like other funding schemes this has been discussed in Chapter 6. As explained there, it provided a start-up grant during the first year of operation. Like the pattern of UK support discussed above, there was diversity in this support. There could, for example, be different levels of enterprise training and requirements under the scheme depending on the TEC/LEC which was responsible. In general, however, the EAS has been criticized for creating businesses that may not be viable, for subsidizing inefficient businesses, for creating unemployment since other businesses may be forced to stop trading through 'unfair competition', and for not tackling the problem of the long-term unemployed for which group it was designed to help (45). Official evaluation reports can often paint a rosy picture. For example, one MSC Report (46) claimed survival rates of 74 per cent after eighteen months for businesses on the scheme. However, such crude survival rates tell us little about the effective quality of such start-ups. The repeated criticism of the EAS is that jobs and businesses were being created at the expense of others. Official reports tend to ignore such opportunity costs.

The Small Firms' Loan Guarantee Scheme (SFLGS)

Finance was seen as a potential constraint on individual enterprise. The SFLGS was designed to relieve problems that might exist in raising finance for viable ventures that lacked security. As discussed in Chapter 6, the problem with this scheme has been that banks have to put forward a venture to qualify and they have not been enthusiastic supporters. Compared to similar schemes in Germany, take-up rates have been only at 10 per cent of such levels (47). Since the scheme was enhanced (in 1993) take-up rates have improved (48), but levels are still below other countries' equivalent schemes and default rates have remained high (49).

As discussed above, the extent and level of networking is one of the reasons for the higher take-up of an equivalent scheme in Germany. The role of institutions such as the IHK means that the promotion and subsequent take-up of such a scheme is on a far higher level. The low take-up in the UK reflects, in part, the lack of collaboration and effective networking between the banks and external support agencies.

The enterprise initiative

A Department of Trade and Industry (DTI) scheme which offered help to small businesses to get professional advice and consultancy. Launched in 1988, it was part of the Government's switch from specific help with funding to more emphasis on advice and consultancy. It was designed particularly to help existing small businesses to expand by providing financial assistance for them to employ consultants. It represented a scheme targeted at perceived management constraints that face small businesses. The main component of the initiative was the Consultancy Initiatives (CI) programme, which provided assistance for consultancy in defined areas such as marketing, design and business planning. The Enterprise Initiative and CI scheme seem to have some impact although it can be argued, as with other schemes, that take-up rates were low (50). The main problem seems to have been lack of adequate follow through on implementation by firms and the perception that the scheme was more suited to medium-sized rather than small firms. An evaluation of the scheme (8) claimed considerable value-added but, as with many such schemes, assessing additionality is difficult because of the subjective nature of advice as part of the consultancy provided under the scheme. For example, it is very difficult to place a value on 'expert' advice—it may take considerable time for the benefits of such advice to materialize. The evaluation (51) did attempt to track changes in firms before and after the consultancy; but, as with most such evaluation, such assessments are inevitably retrospective and rely (as a result) on subjective assessments.

The Business Expansion Scheme (BES)

The BES was intended to help existing businesses with expansion plans who were seeking additional equity. The relative failure of this scheme to attract additional sources of equity for small firms resulted in its withdrawal in 1993. The problem was not that it failed to provide equity finance. According to Mason *et al.* (52), between 1982 to 1988, £700 million of equity capital was invested under the scheme, but much of the equity raised went into property firms in the South East rather than manufacturing concerns. It has been replaced by the Enterprise Investment Scheme (EIS), designed to encourage potential investors to invest in small amounts of equity (see Chapter 6).

Semi-official schemes

A number of other semi-official schemes were established to encourage small firm start-ups. For example, in some areas funding is available under British Coal redundancy schemes. British Steel also has similar schemes; and there is the role of task force funding in inner-city areas. City Challenge, designed to revitalize inner-city areas also adds to the wide range of potential assistance.

When added together, the combination of these different enterprise initiatives and the background of the broadbrush government economic changes in taxation and privatization provide the basis for claims that successive governments have created an 'enterprise culture'. However, this is a much more difficult concept to evaluate. To some extent there has been a debate about whether there has been sufficient changes in society to talk about the creation of an enterprise culture. We will now briefly consider some of the contributions to the debate.

THE ENTERPRISE CULTURE: DOES IT EXIST?

We concentrate on whether successive governments (since 1979) have successfully changed the attitudes to enterprise in the UK. Obviously implicit in this claim is that there have been some change in the attitudes and beliefs of society since then. To claim that there has been this change it is necessary to show that society, in

1979, had different perceptions and attitudes. Before 1979, it is claimed that society did not provide an environment that fostered entrepreneurship and enterprise development; that enterprise skills were insufficiently rewarded; that there was insufficient motivation and reward to start your own business; and that existing businesses were stifled for lack of opportunity and the right climate for development and growth. It is claimed that the development of enterprise skills, whether in large or small organizations, was not fostered by the culture and environment that existed in 1979.

Lord Young and subsequent government ministers have claimed that there were sufficiently significant changes in the attitudes and environment of society by the mid-1980s. There has been a subsequent academic debate about whether this 'enterprise culture' does exist. The claim is that the spirit of enterprise has been freed (53).

The debate has drawn comments from a wide academic background; contributions have ranged from theologians to sociologists (54, 55), to economists (56) and to politicians (57). Advocates of the existence of the enterprise culture have been enthusiastic in their claims. For example, Bannock (58) has gone so far as to call this a 'sea change' in social attitudes in the 1980s.

Claims for the creation and existence of an enterprise culture suffer from a number of problems. Firstly, it is difficult to define precisely what is meant by 'enterprise culture'. It is a term which is full of ambiguities and has led to different attempts at definition (59). MacDonald and Coffield (60) have compared the term 'enterprise' to 'Heffalump'—the mythical creature of supposed vast importance but which no one has ever seen. Secondly, as pointed out in this chapter, evaluation reports on the effectiveness of state initiatives give misleading impressions of their effectiveness and impact. Mills (61), on a comment on the EAS, says:

> The rhetoric of the EAS claims to create an Enterprise Culture and encourage the growth of entrepreneurs in Britain. In practice it seems to have been a means of reducing the unemployment statistics. (p. 93)

Thirdly, it is very difficult to assess the much more tenuous question of whether there has been any noticeable change in the culture of society. For example, Amin and Tomaney (44) in their study of the North East assess the impact of enterprise initiatives and comment that it has been the: 'expressed aim of the Conservative administration to foster an entrepreneurial culture and to use this as a main plank for local economic generation' (p. 479). This study is critical of the government initiatives (such as enterprise zones) and the gradual rundown of state regional grant aid. Even the creation of the Nissan plant in the region comes in for criticism as being a relatively costly investment. Other initiatives are criticized for encouraging investment in property rather than manufacturing, such as the Tyne and Wear Urban Development Corporation.

Fourthly, long-term changes have been taking place in the structure of the UK economy. The decline of traditional industries and structural change involving a shift out of manufacturing was in evidence long before 1979. Similarly economic and social changes were underway before 1979, for example, increased economic activity rates by women.

An attempt to change cultural attitudes to entrepreneurship has been undertaken in Scotland, through a national strategy targeted at changing attitudes in institutions and in the population. A national enquiry in Scotland (62) (as discussed in Chapter 1) revealed that entrepreneurs (and entrepreneurship) were perceived as low status (and as a career) and that this was a factor affecting the low rate of participation. After five years of a major campaign in Scotland to influence attitudes to entrepreneurs and to starting a business, the strategy does seem to have had an effect. For example, a repeat of the Mori opinion poll showed a significant increase in the numbers 'committed to starting a business' (63). This seems to show that a major campaign targeted at improving the profile of entrepreneurs, and the education system, can have effects on society attitudes to enterprise. Secondly, a study by the IPPR (64) has suggested that a range of government measures still need to be taken if the UK is to develop an entrepreneurial society. The authors of this report comment:

> Our proposals range from broad measures to foster a culture of enterprise to some of the detail of business support schemes . . . which are certainly in need of reappraisal and overhaul. (p. v)

It is likely that forces for change in society's attitudes are much more complex and if changes have taken place they have been set in train by forces in society that were changing before 1979. It may be that the enterprise initiatives introduced by the Government have given these changes a boost and brought them forward. However, many of the claims for the impact of these initiatives must be treated with caution.

CONCLUSIONS

In the 1980s the development of a support network of 300 enterprise agencies, 82 TECs and 20 LECs saw a large private and public sector investment in new and small businesses. Whether this investment will ever be adequately evaluated is doubtful. Despite the additional creation of Business Links, the level of support is confusing and suffers from a number of inadequacies. We are still a long way from the German model of effective intervention, collaboration and networking that supports the creation of viable and high quality small businesses.

Business Links were a move in the right direction in terms of refocusing enterprise support. However, the development of the EA movement has left the UK with an unplanned and confusing mixture of public and independent support that owes more to historical accidents of provision and individual promotion than to any policy of consistent and planned support targeted to specific areas and firms. Duplication of support provision remains a problem in the UK. TECs and LECs, although arguably too small, have in some cases been beneficial in acting as a catalyst to force agencies to work together. Limited co-operation still remains a problem which Business Links have not been able to solve.

State enterprise initiatives have met with limited success, but often the true cost of these initiatives is not appreciated (or admitted), e.g., there are many people who would not be in business if more jobs were available. Wider criteria need to be applied to evaluation of state schemes, i.e., the quality of jobs created, longitudinal criteria (how long do the jobs last for?), assessment of the externalities of the schemes, and suggestions for improvement of the schemes.

There is welcome change, however, when considering whether the right type of people are being encouraged into business. In the past, the associated suffering of families of the people who are encouraged to start their own businesses, that later fail, has been ignored. These business failures, which were at record levels in the previous recession, are often accompanied by the loss of personal equity, property and homes. Families which may have enjoyed a good standard of living have, in some cases, been left destitute and with large personal debts. The social costs of this greater concern with the enterprise culture have sometimes been ignored. The 'downside' aspects are often not appreciated by the people who are encouraged to start their own businesses due to an emphasis on success and achievement. The associated social costs include strains on married life and family relationships, long hours of work and the lack of fringe benefits such as non-contributory pension schemes. While it remains true that the UK needs to promote an enterprise culture, this needs to be done in a balanced way that ensures appropriate people are encouraged to enter entrepreneurship.

Learning outcomes

At the end of this chapter students should be able to:

1. Appreciate the range and diversity of government enterprise initiatives designed to encourage and foster the development of the enterprise culture.
2. Discuss the roles of support agencies and the level of UK support provision.
3. Describe the advantages of networking between agencies and other institutions involved in the support of new ventures.
4. Compare UK levels of networking to the German and French experience and the role of German and French chambers of commerce.
5. Discuss criteria that can be used to evaluate state schemes.
6. Appreciate and discuss problems with the term 'enterprise culture'.
7. Recognize the contribution of official studies and independent writers when assessing the development of an enterprise culture.
8. Appreciate both positive and negative aspects of the attempt to create an enterprise culture.

REFERENCES

1. BIRCH, D.L. (1979) 'The job generation process', *MIT study on neighbourhood and regional change*, MIT, Boston.
2. LORD YOUNG (1992) 'Enterprise Regained', in Heelas, P. and Morris, P. (eds) *The Values of The Enterprise Culture: the moral debate*, Routledge, London.
3. *The Guardian*, 25th November 1997.
4. HM GOVERNMENT (1998), White Paper, *Regional Development Agencies*, HMSO, London.
5. SCHLEGELMILCH, B.B., DIAMANTOPOULOS, A. AND MOORE, S.A. (1992) 'The Market for Management Consulting in Britain: An Analysis of Demand and Supply', *Management Decision*, vol. 30, no. 2, pp. 46–54.
6. HRD PARTNERSHIP REPORT (1992) 'UK Management Consultants and the Small/Medium Firm; HRD Study of the BGT Option 3 Programme', Esprit Consulting, London.
7. PAYNE, A. (1986) 'Effective Use of Professional Management Services', *Management Decision*, vol. 24, no. 6, pp. 16–24.
8. SEGAL, QUINCE, WICKSTEED (1994), *Evaluation of the Consultancy Initiatives*, 4th stage, HMSO, London.
9. SCHEIN, E.H. (1987) *Process Consultation, Vol II*, Addison-Wesley, Massachusetts, USA.
10. DEAKINS, D., LEVINSON, D., O'NEILL, E. AND PAUL, S. (1996) *The Use and Impact of Business Consultancy in Scotland*, Paisley Enterprise Research Centre, University of Paisley, Scotland.
11. HM GOVERNMENT (1995), White Paper, *Competitiveness: Forging Ahead*, HMSO, London.
12. SEAR, L. AND AGAR, J. (1996) *A Survey of Business Link PBAs*, Small Business Centre, Durham University Business School, Durham.
13. JONES, M. (1996) 'Business Link: A critical commentary', *Local Economy*, vol. 11, no. 1, pp. 71–8.
14. DEAKINS, D., GRAHAM, L., SULLIVAN, R. AND WHITTAM, G. (1998) 'New Venture Support: an analysis of mentoring support', 1st stage report to Renfrewshire Enterprise, Paisley Enterprise Research Centre, University of Paisley, Scotland.
15. DEAKINS, D., MILEHAM, P. AND O'NEILL, E. (1998) 'The Role and Influence of Non-Executive Directors in Growing Small Companies', research report for the ACCA, Paisley Enterprise Research Centre, University of Paisley, Scotland.
16. DEAKINS, D., GRAHAM, L., SULLIVAN, R. AND WHITTAM, G. (1998) 'New Venture Support', 2nd stage report to Renfrewshire Enterprise, Paisley Enterprise Research Centre, University of Paisley, Scotland.
17. SEGAL, QUINCE, WICKSTEED (1988) *Encouraging small business start-up and growth: creating a supportive local environment*, HMSO, London.
18. CARSWELL, M. (1990) 'Small firm networking and business performance', *Proceedings of the 13th National Small Firms Policy and Research Conference*, Harrogate.
19. SMALLBONE, D. (1990) 'Success and failure in small business start-ups',

International Small Business Journal, vol. 8, no. 2, pp. 34–47.

20. DEAKINS, D. (1993) 'What Role for Support Agencies? A case study of UK Enterprise Agencies', *Local Economy*, vol. 8, no.1, pp. 57–68.

21. BENNETT, R.J., WICKS, P.J. AND McCOSHAN, A. (1994) *Local Empowerment and Business Services: Britain's Experiment with TECs*, UCL Press, London.

22. EMMERICH, M. AND PECK, J. (1992) *Reforming the TECs: Towards a New Training Strategy*, final report of the CLES TEC/LEC Monitoring Project, CLES, Manchester.

23. TOPHAM, N., PADMORE, K. AND TWONEY, J. (1994) *English TECs: Ranking, Requirement and Resources*, Salford University, Salford.

24. CURRAN, J. (1993) 'TECs and Small Firms: Can TECs Reach the Small Firms Other Strategies have Failed to Reach?, paper presented to the House of Commons Social and Science Policy Group, Kingston University, Kingston.

25. CURRAN, J., BLACKBURN, R., KITCHING, J. AND NORTH, J. (1996) 'Small Firms and Workforce Training', paper presented to the 19th National Small Firms Policy and Research Conference, Birmingham.

26. SMALLBONE, D. (1990) 'Enterprise Agencies in London—a public private sector partnership?', *Local Government Studies*, Sept/Oct, pp. 17–32.

27. FULLER, T. AND HANNON, P. (1992) 'Information Technology and Business Networks; navigation systems, theory and practice' in *The Entrepreneur in the driving seat*, proceedings of the 22nd European Small Business Seminar, Amsterdam.

28. CASSON, M. (ed.) (1990) *Entrepreneurship*, Edward Elgar, London.

29. BUSINESS IN THE COMMUNITY (1985) *Small Firms: survival and job creation: the contribution of enterprise agencies*, BITC, London.

30. BUSINESS IN THE COMMUNITY (1988) *The future for enterprise agencies*, BITC, London.

31. MOORE, C. (1988) 'Enterprise Agencies: privatisation or partnership?', *Local Economy*, vol. 3, no. 1, pp. 21–30.

32. CENTRE FOR EMPLOYMENT INITIATIVES (1985) *The impact of Local Enterprise Agencies in Great Britain: operational lessons and policy implications*, CEI.

33. STOREY, D.J. (1994) *Understanding the Small Business Sector*, Routledge, London.

34. PA CAMBRIDGE CONSULTANTS (1995) 'Evaluation of DTI-funded TEC Services in Support of SMEs', HMSO, London.

35. DEAKINS, D. AND PHILPOTT, T. (1993) *Comparative European Practices in the Finance of Small Firms: UK, Germany and Holland*, University of Central England, Birmingham.

36. COOPERS AND LYBRAND DELOITTE AND BUSINESS IN THE COMMUNITY (1991) *Local support for enterprise*, BITC, London.

37. BENNETT, R.J. (1996) 'SMEs and Public Policy: present dilemmas, future priorities and the case of Business Links', paper presented to the 19th ISBA National Small Firms Conference, Birmingham.

38. CUTLER (1994) 'Gearing Up for Business Link', *Local Economy*, vol. 8, no. 4, pp. 365–8.

39. BENNETT, M.J., KREBS, G. AND ZIMMERMAN, H. (1993) *Chambers of Commerce in Britain and Germany and The Single Market*, Anglo-German Foundation, Poole.

40. DALY, M. AND McCANN, A. (1992) 'How Many Small Firms?', *Employment Gazette*, April, pp. 47–51.

41. DALY, M., CAMPBELL, M., ROBSON, G. AND GALLAGHER, C. (1992) 'Job Creation 1987–89: The Contributions of Small and Large Firms', *Employment Gazette*, April, pp. 589–94.

42. VYAKARNAM, S. AND JACOBS, R. (1995) 'TEAMSTART, Overcoming the Blockages to Small Business Growth', in Chittenden, F., Robertson, M. and Marshall, I. (eds) *Small Firms: Partnerships for Growth*, Paul Chapman Publishing, London, pp. 192–205.

43. FREEL, M. (1998) 'Policy, Prediction and Growth: picking start-up winners', *Journal of Small Business and Enterprise Development*, vol. 5, no. 1, pp. 19–32.

44. AMIN, A. AND TOMANEY, J. (1991) 'Creating an Enterprise Culture in the North East? The Impact of Urban and Regional Policies of the 1980s', *Regional Studies*, vol. 25, no. 5, pp. 479–87.

45. GRAY, C. (1990) 'Some Economic and Psychological Considerations on the Effects of the Enterprise Allowance Scheme', *Small Business*, vol. 1, pp. 111–24.

46. SIMKIN, C. AND ALLEN, D. (1988) *Enterprise Allowance Scheme Evaluation: second eighteen month national survey—Final report*, MSC, London.

47. CHARLES BATCHELOR (1993) *Financial Times*, 23 March.

48. BANK OF ENGLAND (1997) *Finance for Small Firms*, Bank of England, London.

49. COWLING, M. AND CLAY, N. (1994) 'An Assessment of the Loan Guarantee Scheme', *Journal of Small Business and Enterprise Development*, vol. 1, no. 3, pp. 7–13.

50. NATIONAL ECONOMIC RESEARCH ASSOCIATION (1990) *An Evaluation of the Loan Guarantee Scheme*, Department of Employment, London.

51. SEGAL, QUINCE, WICKSTEED (1989) *Evaluation of the Consultancy Initiatives*, HMSO, London.

52. MASON, C., HARRISON, J. AND HARRISON, R. (1988) *Closing the Equity Gap? An Assessment of the Business Expansion Scheme*, Small Business Research Trust, Milton Keynes.

53. MORRIS, P. (1991) 'Freeing the Spirit of Enterprise', in Keat, R. and Abercrombie, N. (eds) *Enterprise Culture*, Routledge, London, pp. 21–37.

54. MORRIS, P. (1992) 'Is God Enterprising? Reflections on enterprise culture and religion', in Heelas, P. and Morris, P. (eds) *The Values of the Enterprise Culture: the moral debate*, Routledge, London, pp. 276–90.

55. ABERCROMBIE, N. (1991) 'The privilege of the producer', in Keat, R. and Abercrombie, N. (eds) *Enterprise Culture*, Routledge, London, pp. 171–85.

56. RICKETTS, M. (1987) *The Economics of Business Enterprise*, Wheatsheaf Books, London.

57. LAWSON, N. (1984) *The British Experiment*, Fifth Mais Lecture, HM Treasury.

58. BANNOCK, G. (1991) *Venture Capital and the Equity Gap*, National Westminster Bank, London.

59. RITCHIE, J. (1991) 'Chasing Shadows: Enterprise Culture as an Educational Phenomenon', *Journal of Education Policy*, vol. 6, no. 3, pp. 315–25.

60. MacDONALD, R. AND COFFIELD, F. (1991) *Risky Business: Youth and the Enterprise Culture*, Falmer Press, London.

61. MILLS, V. (1991) 'Review of Some Economic and Psychological Considerations on the Effects of the EAS', *International Small Business Journal*, vol. 9, no. 4, pp. 91–4.
62. SCOTTISH ENTERPRISE (1993) *Scotland's Business Birth Rate: A National Enquiry*, Scottish Enterprise, Glasgow.
63. SCOTTISH ENTERPRISE (1998) 'The Business Birth Rate 5th Anniversary: press release', Scottish Enterprise, Glasgow.
64. GAVRON, R., COWLING, M., HOLTHAM, G. AND WESTALL, A. (1996) *The Entrepreneurial Society*, IPPR, London.

RECOMMENDED READING

For the debate on the enterprise culture two collections of contributions to the debate are recommended:

HEELAS, P. AND MORRIS, P. (1992) *The Values of The Enterprise Culture: The Moral Debate*, Routledge, London.
KEAT, R. AND ABERCROMBIE, N. (eds) (1991) *Enterprise Culture*, Routledge, London.

Other reading on the enterprise culture:

AMIN, A. AND TOMANEY, J. (1991) 'Creating an Enterprise Culture in the North East? The impact of Urban and Regional Policies of the 1980s', *Regional Studies*, vol. 25, no. 5, pp. 479–87.
MacDONALD, R. AND COFFIELD, F. (1991) *Risky Business: Youth and the Enterprise Culture*, Falmer Press.
RITCHIE, J. (1991) 'Chasing Shadows: *Enterprise Culture* as an Educational Phenomenon', *Journal of Education Policy*, vol. 6, no. 3, pp. 315–25.

For a more recent discussion of the attitudes in society:

GAVRON, R., COWLING, M., HOLTHAM, G. AND WESTALL, A. (1996) *The Entrepreneurial Society*, IPPR, London.

For an evaluation of TEC services to SMEs:

PA CAMBRIDGE CONSULTANTS (1995) *Evaluation of DTI-funded TEC Services in Support of SMEs*, HMSO, London.

9. Entrepreneurial and Growth Firms

INTRODUCTION

There is a basic distinction between the person or entrepreneur who wishes to go into self-employment to pursue their own interests (and perhaps enters self-employment because there is no or little alternative) and the person or entrepreneur that enters small business ownership because they have desires to develop their businesses, to achieve growth, expand employment and grow into a medium-sized or large firm. The former type of small business owner has very different managerial objectives from the latter. The objectives of the first will be concerned with survival and maintenance of life-style, whereas those of the second type will be concerned with growth and expansion with the entrepreneur eventually owning several companies.

Many people who were made redundant due to 'downsizing' of traditional manufacturing firms in the 1980s entered self-employment as small business owners. They were normally sole traders, employed few or no people and their major objectives were likely to be concerned with survival and maintaining sufficient income to ensure that the business provided them and their family with sufficient income. These small businesses, which are the overwhelming majority of small firms in the UK, are sometimes called 'life-style' businesses. In other words the owner-manager is only concerned with maintaining a life-style that he or she may have been accustomed to in a previous form of employment. A minority of small firms may be called 'entrepreneurial firms'; their owners will be concerned mainly with the managerial objective of achieving growth, and will often go on to own more than one firm.

There has been much speculation about whether such 'entrepreneurial firms' can be identified *ex ante*, that is, before they achieve growth, rather than *ex post*, after they have demonstrated growth. This presents a problem for researchers and policy makers and for investors such as venture capitalists who will want to identify high growth and high performer firms. It is a classical adverse selection problem created by uncertainty and limited (if not asymmetric) information. Despite the inherent built-in difficulties of identifying such growth firms, this has not stopped policy makers from establishing agencies such as the Business Links to support existing small and medium-sized firms that have the potential for growth. This problem has also not stopped researchers from attempting to identify the characteristics and features of such growth firms and their entrepreneurs.

There is no agreement on exactly what measure to use to distinguish a high performing firm. Should performance be measured on the basis of employment created or by some other criterion, such as profits, turnover or financial assets? Attention has, nonetheless, focused on identifying growth firms rather identifying constraints which may block the growth potential of many entrepreneurs and small firms. The inherent problem for policy makers, however, is that environments that favour the expansion of some firms may not remain stable. There are only certain windows of marketing opportunity that can lead to success of entrepreneurs and to growth firms. The right timing has proved to be crucial in many circumstances, even if other equally crucial factors might be in place. We saw with the Aquamotive case that the right product may not lead to growth and success if the timing is wrong and the environment has not been supportive. Even very successful entrepreneurs such as Bill Gates may not be able to recreate their success. There may be a unique combination of circumstances and perhaps the right combination of people that produce the high growth firm. The rest of this chapter reviews theory, evidence and approaches to growth firms.

Almost forty years ago Edith Penrose (1) classically noted that:

> The differences in the administrative structures of the very small and the very large firms are so great that in many ways it is hard to see that the two species are of the same genus . . . we cannot define a caterpillar and use the same definition for a butterfly. (p. 19)

Yet, as a logical imperative, there exists a process through which small becomes large. This process of growth, and growth firms themselves, have been and remain one of the main foci of research into entrepreneurship and small firms. The focus is further heightened by the contention that only a small number of small firms enjoy the bulk of growth in any given period. That is to say: '. . . job creation amongst small firms is heavily concentrated within very few such firms.' (2, p. 35)

This view, drawing impetus and support from the work of Gallagher and others (3, 4, 5), has, in effect, become accepted wisdom in the small firms literature. As a rule of thumb, 'out of every 100 small firms 4 will be responsible for 50 per cent of the employment created'. Further, this body of research has had considerable influence upon small firms policy. Accordingly, blanket and early-stage support schemes, such as the Enterprise Allowance Scheme, have all but been abandoned in England, left to the discretion of TECs, while in Scotland many of the LECs, though persisting with versions of these schemes, have begun to shift a proportion of their resources towards targeted support. In essence the aim now is to 'pick winners' or, in Scottish Enterprise parlance, 'create winners' (6)[1].

---

[1] It is of interest to note that Scottish Enterprise (6) persist with the conviction that '. . . improving the number of new ventures is a prerequisite to increasing the number of fast-growing businesses' (p. 16)—a notion running counter to the Storey and Johnson (2) contention that '. . . policies which artificially raise the number of business formations lead to higher death rates of businesses and to a radical reduction in the number of successful firms and hence of employment' (p. 39).

Given limited resources and the desire to maximize returns or minimize losses, the attraction of a satisfactory predictive model, or growth theory, to policy makers, financial institutions, support services and potential investors is clear. As a result, a commendable amount of research has attempted to articulate the process of growth or identify those characteristics which distinguish growth firms from their stable or declining counterparts. The purpose of this chapter is to review some of the issues and main factors that affect growth in this area.

Additional material on management issues in the growth process and case study are provided in the tutor's manual.

STAGE MODELS OF GROWTH

During the 1970s and early 1980s much of the theoretical and empirical work attempted to conceptualize the metamorphosis of Penrose's caterpillar in terms of stage, or lifecycle, models of firm growth. These models, normally incorporating five stages, envisage an inevitable and gradual movement along a known growth trajectory (Fig, 9.1). At each stage the organization undergoes changes in management practices and style, organizational structure, degree of internal formality of systems and strategy, in such a way that the Stage 5 firm is truly distinct from the Stage 1 firm from which it derived.

In this section we will briefly discuss, specifically, two of the most commonly cited stage models of growth: Greiner (7) and Churchill and Lewis (8). Taking them chronologically, the Greiner model posits a linear, continuous relationship between time and growth postulating periods of incremental, trouble-

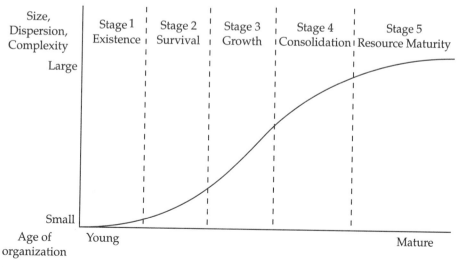

Figure 9.1   Lifecycle growth models

free growth (evolution) punctuated by explicitly defined crises (revolution). Each period of evolution has a clear set of attributes which characterize it and each stage, which ultimately degenerates into crisis, is a solution to the crisis of the previous stage, as shown in Table 9.1.

The crises outlined by Greiner form the bottom row of Table 9.1.

Crisis of leadership   The shift from a Phase 1 firm to a Phase 2 firm is triggered by a crisis of leadership. More sophisticated knowledge and competencies are required to operate larger production runs and manage an increasing workforce. Capital must be secured to underpin further growth and financial controls must be put in place. The company must hire additional executive resource and restructure to meet these challenges.

Crisis of autonomy   The control mechanisms implemented as a result of the first crisis become less appropriate as the physical size of the company increases. Line employees and line managers become frustrated with the bureaucracy attendant upon a centralized hierarchy. Line staff are more familiar with markets and machinery than executives and become 'torn between following procedures and taking initiative' (p. 42). It has become necessary for the company to delegate to allow sufficient discretion in operating decision making.

Crisis of control   Top executives begin to perceive a loss of control as a consequence of excessive discretion resting with middle and lower managers. There exists little co-ordination across divisions, plants or functions—'Freedom breeds a parochial attitude' (p. 43). Top management must seek to regain control, not through recentralization, but through the use of [undefined] 'special co-ordination techniques'.

Crisis of red tape   The 'watchdog' approach adopted by senior management, in Phase 4, and the proliferation of systems and programmes leads to a crisis of confidence and red tape. Line managers object to excessive direction and senior managers view line managers as unco-operative and disruptive. Both groups are unhappy with the cumbersome paper system which evolved to meet the challenges of the previous period. The company has become too large and complex to be managed through an extensive framework of formal procedures and controls. Movement to Phase 5 requires a shift to 'interpersonal collaboration'.

Crisis of ?   The crisis into which Phase 5 degenerates remains undefined in Greiner's model. He can find no 'consistent' empirical evidence which points to the nature of this crisis and the subsequent Phase 6. However, he hypothesizes that this crisis will revolve around the 'psychological saturation' of employees which will occur as a logical result of the information age. Consequently organizations will evolve with dual structures of 'habit' and 'reflection', allowing employees to move periodically between the two for periods of rest—or some alternative format whereby 'spent' staff can refuel their energies.

The revolutionary components of Greiner's paradigm are perhaps atypical of the broader set of stage models (although Scott and Bruce (9) imply a similar set of

Table 9.1 Greiner's stage model of growth

Attribute	Phase 1 Creativity	Phase 2 Direction	Phase 3 Delegation	Phase 4 Co-ordination	Phase 5 Collaboration
Management focus	Make and sell	Efficiency of operations	Expansion of market	Consolidation of organization	Problem solving and innovation
Organization structure	Informal	Centralized and functional	Decentralized and geographical	Line staff and product groups	Matrix of teams
Top management style	Individualistic and entrepreneurial	Directive	Delegative	Watchdog	Participative
Control system	Market results	Standards and cost centres	Reports and profit centres	Plans and investment centres	Mutual goal setting
Management reward emphasis	Ownership	Salary and merit increases	Individual bonus	Profit sharing and stock options	Team bonus
Crises	Crisis of leadership	Crisis of autonomy	Crisis of control	Crisis of red tape	Crisis of ?

crisis triggers). By contrast, Churchill and Lewis, although commenting upon Greiner, present a more general depiction of growth models where transition from stage to stage has no explicit trigger, as shown in Table 9.2. Further, Churchill and Lewis include a sixth stage by dividing the standard 'Success', or 'Growth', stage into growth firms and what may be described as 'comfort firms'—(stage 3–D)— which, having achieved economic viability and chosen not to proactively seek further growth, can be assured of average or above-average profits in the long run, providing managerial incompetence is avoided and the environment does not change to destroy their market niche.

In addition to those represented in Table 9.2, Churchill and Lewis include a further two factors in their paradigm which do not allow for easy tabulation: 'Organization' and 'Business and owner'. Addressing 'Organization' first, the authors posit an internal organizational structure of progressively increasing horizontal and vertical complexity, thus allowing for greater managerial sophistication and delegation. Secondly, the 'Business and owner' factor tracks the importance of the original owner-manager from an initially increasing central role to an eventual peripheral capacity when the organization has reached 'Resource maturity'.

Following both tables, along individual rows, from left to right we see a logical progression in the sophistication of the individual factors. The implication appears to be that firms move from an informal and *ad hoc* birth, through a quasi-functional state, culminating in the highest level of managerial and organizational refinement yet imagined. Whilst there are obvious differences in the nuances of these models, they are sufficiently alike to belong to the same school of thought on the growth process. These models are intended to facilitate owner-managers and senior executives in recognizing the stage at which their organization stands and consequently identifying the skills required for further progression or, in the case of Greiner, the likely impending crises. Yet whilst these models have the advantage of highlighting the notion that managerial skill requirements are not of a 'once and for all time' nature, there are fundamental flaws associated with the rigidity of them. From the literature (10, 11), the standard critique is fourfold:

1. Most firms experience little or no growth and therefore are unlikely ever to reach Stages 3, 4 or 5. Whilst Greiner allows for the conscious decision to remain in a particular stage and Churchill and Lewis provide numerous 'break-off' paths for disengagement or failure, it nonetheless remains implicit that the 'norm' for growth firms is to follow and complete the process.

2. The models do not allow for a backward movement along the continuum or for the 'skipping' of stages. It is surely conceivable that many firms will reach 'take-off', only to find themselves plunged back into a struggle for survival due to unexpected changes in markets, technology or consumer preferences. In addition, the requirement for the firm to complete each stage before moving forward to that stage immediately following seems excessively limiting. In the case of the Churchill and Lewis model, we can envisage some firms moving from 'Existence' to 'Growth' with such speed that either 'survival' is negligible or non-existent. We can also conceive of a start-up, which is sufficiently large, as to fulfil the criteria for Churchill and Lewis' Stage 3–G.

Table 9.2 Churchill and Lewis: Lifecycle growth model

	Stage 1 Existence	Stage 2 Survival	Stage 3–D Success– Disengage	Stage 3–G Success– Growth	Stage 4 Take-off	Stage 5 Maturity
Management style	Direct supervision	Supervised supervision	Functional	Functional	Divisional	Line and staff
Extent of formal systems	Minimal to non-existent	Minimal	Basic	Developing	Maturing	Extensive
Major strategy	Existence	Survival	Maintaining profitable status quo	Get resources for growth	Growth	Return on investment

3. Perhaps most significantly, the models do not permit firms to exhibit characteristics from one or more stage, to become hybrids. As brief illustrations: from Greiner we can conjecture a situation whereby top management style is participative (Phase 5) whilst the organization structure is informal (Phase 1); from Churchill and Lewis, a situation such that formal systems are either maturing (Stage 4) or extensive (Stage 5) and yet the major strategy is survival (a new franchisee may be one such example).

4. The idea that firms are occasionally able to learn and adjust with greater effect in response to crises than in periods of relative stability seems entirely plausible, yet that crises occur in the non-random manner suggested, given the inherent uncertainty within which firms operate, is far less credible. It is conceivable that some firms will lurch from crisis to crisis and that these crises will not be of leadership, autonomy, control and red tape, but of market stagnation, market saturation, technology, finance or skills. It is further conceivable that other firms will enjoy smooth growth over a relatively uninterrupted horizon.

Stage models do place a welcome emphasis on the role of history in defining the future shape and success of an organization. Greiner explicitly notes the importance of 'historical actions . . . [as] . . . determinants of what happens to the company at a much later date' (pp. 45–6). Difficulties arise in the interpretation of this historicity, path dependency and crisis stimulated growth. The frameworks suggested are overly rigid. The inevitability of each stage and each crisis is implausible. To assume that firms move from one stage to another along a narrow path, shaped only by periods of regularly recurring crises, ignores the variability and complexity of firm growth.

PREDICTIVE MODELLING OF GROWTH

In his final criticism of stage models, Storey (10) notes that the '. . . models describe, rather than predict' (p. 122). Accordingly, it is the body of literature concerned with predictive modelling of firm growth that we briefly consider in this section.

Financial Models

The early work undertaken by Storey *et al.* (12) concentrated on the role of standard financial variables in predicting successful small firms. This method, adapted from use with large corporations, adopted an inverted approach to predicting small firm success—predicting failure and identifying success by implication. After initial testing of 'univariate ratio analysis' (consideration of individual financial ratios in progression rather than as a composite) proved inappropriate, Storey and colleagues shifted their focus towards methods of multivariate inquiry (principally 'multiple discriminant analysis'). Whilst univariate analysis suggested, predictably, that low profitability and high gearing ratios were positive correlates of small firms failure, the researchers' 'optimum' multivariate model utilized cashflow and asset structure variables as their primary predictors. On the basis of this final model Storey *et al.* (12) claimed a 75 per cent success rate in distinguishing between failed firms and survivors.

Several criticisms can be levelled at this technique[2]. Firstly, the technique offers no historical insight. There is little consistent evidence to suggest that the variables alter significantly as the companies approach failure, nor is their any indication of the underlying causes of failure. Secondly, as a predictive model for rapid growth firms the technique would appear inadequate. Since its purpose is to identify firms which will fail, the model is unable to distinguish between the small proportion of growth firms and the bulk of survivors. Finally, the model takes little account of the human capital factors which play a considerable role in determining survival and growth (13, 14).

Characteristics Approach

Subsequent efforts to distinguish growth firms from their stable or declining contemporaries have tended to place a greater emphasis on non-financial characteristics of the owner-manager and the firm. In a comprehensive review and synthesis of the research literature[3], Storey (10) postulates that small firm growth is driven by three integral component sets: characteristics of the entrepreneur (identifiable pre-start), characteristics of the firm (identifiable at start) and characteristics of the corporate strategy (identifiable post start). From the empirical studies reviewed, Storey isolates those factors where 'consistent' evidence of influence was available, as shown in Table 9.3.

Table 9.3 The 'characteristics' approach to growth

The entrepreneur	*The firm*	*Strategy*
Motivation	Age	External equity
Education	Legal form	Market positioning
Managerial experience	Location	New product introduction
Teams	Size	Management recruitment
Age	Market/Sector	
	Ownership	

The Entrepreneur

Motivation It is suggested that individuals who are 'pulled' into business ownership, and whose motivation is consequently positive, are more likely to develop growth firms. However, in common with other areas of entrepreneurship, motivation is likely to be a more complex process, often the result of an interplay of factors (15). Simplifying motivation into an artificial dichotomy of 'pull' and 'push' factors can be misleading.

---

[2] For a more detailed critique see Reid and Jacobsen (1988, pp. 78–83).
[3] Summarized effectively in Barkham *et al.* (17, ch. 2).

Education   There are two contrasting hypotheses presented for this factor. Firstly, ignoring any relationship between education and competency, it may be argued that education provides a foundation from which the entrepreneur can undertake the personal and professional development necessary for successful entrepreneurship and that education will endow the entrepreneur with greater confidence in dealing with bankers, customers and suppliers. It may also be argued that on aggregate education can be taken as a [fallible proxy for intelligence. Conversely, it may argued that '. . . business ownership is not an intellectual activity' (p. 129) and that the educated entrepreneur will quickly become wearied with the many tedious tasks which form the remit of most owner-managers. In Storey's review, evidence is found to support the former hypothesis in preference to the latter. From his work on a database of surveyed NatWest Bank clients, Cressy (16) suggests that whilst a first degree in a science or engineering subject may be most appropriate for high technology entrepreneurs, it is more likely that a trade qualification is optimal for mainstream firms. Logic would dictate that education, not to a level but of a type, would influence the entrepreneur's ability in the given environment and, consequently, the firm's chances of growth. Yet as a component of a predictive model, relative consistency is a prerequisite. Of the eighteen studies reviewed by Storey, nine show no impact and eight show '. . . some form of positive relationship' (p. 129). For Storey this provides 'fairly consistent support'. However, since little effort is made to explain the effect education has on firm processes we cannot explain why various types or levels of education *occasionally* influence growth. For instance Barkham *et al.* (17), in their four-region study of the determinants of growth, note that 'Education matters . . . but in an indirect way, and the disadvantage of poorer education can be overcome by those who adopt similar strategies to graduates' (p. 140)—the authors suggest that education *per se* does not influence growth, but rather education influences strategic choice which, in turn, influences growth. Accordingly, there seems very little basis for prediction, other than excessively subjective prediction, using this variable.

Managerial experience   It is conjectured that in all but the very smallest firms the principal activity of the entrepreneur is the co-ordination of the work of other individuals. Hence prior managerial experience and, consequently, experience in the co-ordination role will allow the entrepreneur to attend more effectively to his remit and subsequently meet business objectives. There is also a parallel argument regarding the higher 'minimum wages' those with managerial experience are likely to have. Individuals with high minimum income are unlikely to enter into self-employment without a corresponding high degree of confidence in a successful outcome. To counter this hypothesis, small firms are emphatically not large firms and managing in a small firm is likely to require a very different set of skills than the, often functional, competencies required for large firm management. Thus managing in a large firm, whilst raising minimum income requirements, is unlikely to represent a dependable proving ground for small firm owner-management. So will experience of managing in a small firm act as suitable predictor of success or growth? Again, given the high levels of uncertainty in which small firms operate and accepting the axiom that 'Small firms are not homogeneous. Each is different and has special characteristics' (18, p. 5), it is unlikely that any 'acceptable' consistency will be detected in the influence of this factor. The 'consistency' Storey (10) notes is that, of eleven studies, four have a positive impact, six have no impact and one has a negative impact. As with most of these factors, our contention is not that there is no impact. Rather the consistency and degree of influence of this factor are subject to levels of variation which negate prediction.

Teams   In light of the evidence viewed, it is postulated by Storey (10) that

> Since the management of a business requires a range of skills . . . businesses owned by more than a single individual are more likely to grow than businesses owned by a single person.
> (p. 130)

This view is often taken to be axiomatic. However, from his research with high technology firms (often viewed as the industrial sector representing greatest growth potential) Oakey (19) noted that '. . . rapid firm growth is strongly related to "single founder" businesses' (p. 16). On a different note, but perhaps as significantly, Vyakarnam *et al.* (20) argue that the core competence of successful entrepreneurs is the ability to build and manage effective teams—not the team itself. This hypothesis would appear to offer scope for team dynamics and the evolution of the team *from* start-up. It is further argued by Vyakarnam *et al.* that the team-building process itself is '. . . non-linear, chaotic and unique . . .' thus negating the possibility of artificially manufacturing teams as a policy measure.

Age   In support of the evidence viewed by Storey (10), Cressy (16) argues that the critical characteristics of growth firms are associated with human capital variables—most significantly founder(s) age and team size. With regards to age, it would seem clear that, since 'time is not simply time elapsed but has a chronology and a history' (21), being of a certain age cannot, in itself, act as a predictor of growth. It is the substance of an individual's life not the accumulated number of years which is important. Thus any paradigm which incorporated an age component would be subject to inconsistency.

The Firm

Legal status   In his review, Storey (10) finds overwhelming support for the contention that 'United Kingdom studies consistently point to more rapid growth being experienced by limited companies' (p. 140). Credibility with customers, suppliers and financial institutions is argued to be the principal benefit of incorporation. Although limited liability is often circumvented through the provision of personal guarantees to funding providers, it is difficult in the face of the evidence to dispute this hypothesis. However, from the perspective of predictive modelling it should be noted that legal form is, by no means, stationary. As Storey points out, '. . . we cannot reject the hypothesis that current legal status is a consequence rather than a cause of growth' (p. 141).

Age and size   The issues of firm size and age may be dealt with concurrently since it can be safely assumed that they are often related variables.

Whilst the relationship between size and age is by no means linear, we can plausibly suggest that in aggregate 'the more a firm grows (the bigger it is) the more likely it is to survive another period (the older it is)' (22). With regards to growth, accepted wisdom states that small firms grow faster than large firms and that younger firms grow faster than older firms. From the point of view of policy, logic would seem to endorse the support of small, new firms as a means to achieving employment policy objectives. On a cautionary note it should be understood that most studies deal with changing *rates* of growth and not with absolute growth. To illustrate: a firm employing one individual which recruits an additional member of staff has grown 100 per cent, yet a firm with 100 employees which appoints an additional 10 members of staff has enjoyed only 10 per cent growth. The first firm has enjoyed faster growth, but in terms of net employment gain the latter firm is the greater contributor. An additional caveat would be to note that, since in practice all failures are omitted from empirical samples, there is a tendency to overestimate small firm growth rates in relation to their larger counterparts (23). Further, as recent research has noted, employment growth within the small firm sector is primarily a result of existing business expansion rather than new firm creation (24, 25). Indirectly allied to this is the notion that 'The probability of a firm failing falls as it increases in size and as it increases in age' (13, p. 17).

Location Storey suggests that, since the bulk of small firms operate in localized markets, location will logically be a factor influencing firm performance. Simplistically then, the argument proffered for this variable is that firms in accessible rural areas grow faster than firms located both in urban areas and in remote rural areas. However, more recent work by Westhead (26) found that '. . . the majority of firms suggested more than half their customers were located outside the county region of the businesses main operating premises' (pp. 375–6) and that '. . . urban firms had recorded the largest absolute and standardised employment increases since business start-up' (p. 375). The literature is decidedly equivocal on this point. Even the studies reviewed by Storey fail to reach consensus. Regardless, this factor does little to enhance our understanding of cause and effect. Location itself does not directly influence growth, rather a number of inconsistently related variables, such as physical and support infrastructure, resource munificence and availability of skilled labour, are the 'true' factors for which location acts as a fallible proxy variable.

Market/Industry sector With regards to industrial sector, high technology small firms are often viewed as a corrective for unemployment caused by the decline in traditional industries which has marked the past twenty years. This view is reflected in the plethora of policy initiatives directed at this sector of the economy. However, as Oakey (19) stresses, what little evidence is available to support this contention has been extrapolated from mainly American data. Contextual issues remain over the ability to replicate this phenomenon.

Ownership It is hypothesized that a considerable amount of small firm growth is inorganic, i.e., growth through acquisition and through the development, by individual entrepreneurs, of other distinct business. The latter notion, often called 'portfolio entrepreneurship', has enjoyed a surge in popularity recently (27, 28, 29). Scott and Rosa (30) contend that the predilection of small firm researchers for firm-level analysis fails to recognize the contribution of the individual entrepreneur to wealth and capital accumulation. Whilst this might be true, the survey-based methodologies employed have a tendency to overstate the case. For example, such remote and often *ad hoc* studies are unable to distinguish those who have started another trading business from those who have merely registered another company for legal reasons. In addition, regardless of the merits of identifying portfolio entrepreneurs and shifting the focus of research from firm-level to individual-level analysis, the substance of the research findings to date, perhaps as a consequence of the methodology employed, do not 'explain' the process through which wealth and capital are accumulated.

The Strategy

External equity   Logically, the sources of finance accessed and the corresponding financial structures of small firms will influence their propensity to grow. The relative reliance of firms on short-term, often overdraft, debt finance (31) is clearly sub-optimal with regards to long-term growth. The argument advanced by Storey is that those firms who have either shared external equity or have been willing to allow an external holding in their company are more likely to grow than those who have, or are, not. Thus capital for equity allows firms to circumvent the constraint imposed by short-term debt funding. Yet we note three points which indicate the need for caution. Firstly, as Storey himself points out, it may be the case that the only firms which attract external equity are those which have grown or exhibit obvious potential for growth. Consequently there is no indication of the direction of causation. Secondly, it is unlikely that such a questionable measure as 'willingness to share equity' has been included in research studies. Thirdly, most small firm researchers would be able to provide anecdotal evidence of a firm which stated its willingness to share equity yet when the occasion arose either procrastinated or declined the opportunity. Correspondingly there remains the much cited 'equity gap' (<£250 000) (32) whereby small firms, regardless of desire and strategic stance, are unable to obtain equity funding. It may be that this factor is, in part, not a true measure of strategy but is, instead, a measure of the nature of the external environment.

Market positioning   The temptation has always existed to characterize small firm competition as 'pure' or 'perfect competition' (33). In this way firms become price takers and are bereft of any market power, consequently unable to adopt price competition strategies, erect entry barriers and are overly vulnerable to the vagaries of the ensuing market uncertainty. Since perfect competition requires, *inter alia*, perfect knowledge about present and future states, perfect factor mobility and perfectly rational maximizing actors, this has always been a surprising and implausible assertion. Pure competition, which does not require the first and second of these assumptions to hold true[4], is slightly more credible

---

[4] Nor in practice is the assumption of perfectly rational maximizing actors held to be true.

and is attractive given that, superficially, we can identify in many industries or markets a large number of small firms competing. The argument then, for market positioning, is that growth firms overcome this lack of market power and pricing discretion by inhabiting niches. Competition becomes monopolistic and the firm is able to make above normal profits to finance growth and to increase relative market share, thus reducing uncertainty. Yet, intuitively, price competition is becoming less common. It is likely that most firms undertake some form of differentiation strategy, be it direct product characteristics, customer demographics or product quality. It is also possible for firms inadvertently to occupy market niches. Consider the village shop. As the only shop in a small village it is able to charge slightly higher prices than would otherwise be possible. Whilst most residents will choose to travel outside the village for the bulk of their shopping, it is likely that they will visit the local shop when purchasing occasional items. Geography, rather than conscious market positioning, has allowed the shop owner a degree of discretion when setting prices. Although a niche strategy is undoubtedly advantageous, on aggregate it is likely to be neither a sufficient nor, indeed, a necessary condition for growth. There is a further concern over the appropriateness of niches to sustainable growth. For instance, Barber *et al.* (33) suggest that:

> the challenge facing the growing firm can be stated in terms of a move from relatively narrow market niches in which it exploits a narrow range of distinctive assets into a situation in which it serves a larger number of market segments with a much broader skills and knowledge base. (pp. 15–6)

Another related component of market position involves competitor characteristics. It may be plausibly argued that fast growth firms, occupying market niches, see their primary competitors as other small firms occupying the same or adjacent niches (33). Conversely, poorer performing firms would be in direct competition with large firms where no niche exists. Accordingly, the large firms are able to take advantage of a relatively large market share to the detriment of the small firms. Whilst there is an internal logic to this argument the empirical evidence is, once again, inconclusive. For instance, Westhead and Birley (35) note that:

> [Growth] firms are associated with a strategic stance of competing with large employment sized firms rather than a decision to operate in markets saturated by fellow new and small firms. (p. 28)

New product introduction New product introduction is, as a means of differentiating one firm's products from another's, related to the above discussion of product differentiation and market niches. It is not clear whether the measure addresses products new to the market and industry or simply those new to the firm (i.e., an extension of an individual firms product range). Truly new products (i.e., those new to the market and/or industry) are often taken as a measure of innovative activity and it is suggested that innovative firms perform better than non-innovative firms (36, 37). If we recall, from the discussion of market/industry sector above, Oakey (19) finds little evidence to support the contention that innovative firms enjoy super-growth. This is supported, in part, by Wynarczyk and Thwaites (38) who find that '. . . strong growth in employment is not a strong feature of the average innovative firm' (p. 186). Admittedly Wynarczyk and Thwaites do find that innovative firms grow in terms of assets, turnover and retained profits, yet in general the evidence is inconclusive.

Turning to the second sub-factor, i.e., products new to the firm only, one would logically suggest that the broadening of product or service portfolios would insulate the firm against localized market shocks and consequently improve survival chances and increase likelihood of growth. Yet it is difficult in practice, using remote surveys, to dichotomize between 'truly' new products and those merely new to the firm. As such, little or no work is available to support this final hypothesis.

Management recruitment   Recalling the stage models discussed in the earlier part of this chapter it can be seen that, as the firm grows, the managerial function becomes progressively more complex. The manager can no longer maintain effective control over the minutiae of day-to-day operations and is required to delegate certain tasks to waged employees within the firm. The owner-manager's task becomes the identification or recruitment and motivation of suitable individuals who can 'manage' in his/her stead. This is linked to the Penrose competence theory of firm growth (the link may also extend to the earlier discussion of teams). Penrose (39) argued that the presence of sufficiently experienced executive resource was required for confident planning and subsequent growth. However, in the Penrose model executive resource would ideally be internally experienced, whereas Storey suggests that growth firms are more likely to recruit managers externally. Regardless, as Storey notes, there has been insufficient research in this area. Intuitively, it is likely that management recruitment is both a consequence and a cause of growth and any subsequent growth will be significantly influenced, not by the presence of, but by the efficacy of, new management.

In addition to his triumvirate, Storey notes the importance of the 'wish to grow' in achieving growth (pp. 119–21). This conjecture is supported by Smallbone *et al.* (40) who contend that 'One of the most important factors [in influencing growth] is the commitment of the leader of the company to achieving growth' (p. 59). Whilst it can be plausibly argued that all small firms which grow do not do so willingly, occasionally being 'dragged' by a growing dominant customer, it would nonetheless seem logical to include this factor in any predictive growth model.

On a more general note, but perhaps most significantly, there are criticisms concerning the series of studies selected by Storey to develop his paradigm[5]. Firstly, there exists little consistency of criteria or findings across the research from which to formulate a dependable model. Secondly, and more significantly, the work without exception is quantitative in nature—in common with most research in the area. This may be explained, in part, by the lack of generalizability in more

---

[5] Storey himself (10) highlights much of the inadequacy and fallibility of the data from which the model is derived.

qualitative methodologies. In essence, given that growth is a process, there appears to be an implicit trade-off between generalizability and explanatory power with research favouring the former. As a result, at best we are able to develop a representative growth firm. While this model may provide an aggregate depiction of growth firms, it is not essential for any one firm to match these characteristics precisely. In fact, it is conceivable for growth firms to exhibit all, some or none of the characteristics listed. Thus we have little understanding of causation[6].

It should be noted that it is by no means our intention to suggest that any of the factors discussed above do not influence firm growth—they undoubtedly do. It is merely that treating them as binary variables (e.g., incorporated or not, positive or negative motivation, urban or rural, and so on) ignores the complexity of interaction and is consequently limited. Fundamentally their influence is neither consistent nor, by consequence, predictable. Storey's model, and models of this ilk, neither describe, predict or, more importantly, explain very well. In concord with Smallbone et al. (40) we would suggest that: 'While it may be possible to identify key success factors that affect the growth of SMEs, it is unlikely that a comprehensive model with predictive capability will emerge'.

BARRIERS TO GROWTH

At the same time as the predictive modelling literature has grown, other commentators have argued that the focus of research and policy should be towards relieving barriers to growth for small firms rather than identifying generic characteristics or sets of characteristics (15). Although such an approach does not concern itself directly with growth theories, it has merits which recommend its inclusion in a review chapter of this type. The suggestion that 'artificial' barriers to growth exist and that firms may grow more readily were these barriers to be removed, may be viewed from a different perspective. Implicitly this approach suggests that a particular external state or internal structure is more appropriate for growth than that which prevails in the absence of suggested interventions.

As part of an ACARD (The Advisory Council for Applied Research and Development) and DTI-sponsored study designed to examine the barriers to growth faced by 'high flyers', Barber et al. (34), summarizing the literature, suggest that these constraints consist of three types: management and motivation; resources; and market opportunities and structure[7]. Specifically these would include, *inter alia*: lack of management training, relatively low qualifications,

---

[6] It is an interesting paradox that aggregate level studies are used to formulate firm level interventions.

[7] The work of the ACARD and DTI-funded study was built upon by the later ACOST (Advisory Council on Science and Technology) study (41). The findings of this second study served to support those of the first. In particular it suggested that '. . . the ultimate barriers to growth relate to strategic management and lack of internal resources to make key business transitions' (p. v).

reluctance to delegate, and the need for new management skills and techniques as the organization grows; access to finance, access to skilled labour and access to technology; market growth rates, size and frequency of purchases, degree of segmentation and opportunities for collaboration or merger. Many of the factors in this list are complementary, or related, to variables discussed in the previous sections. For example, lack of management training may equate with prior management experience, low qualifications with education, degree of segmentation with market positioning, and so on. The variable which sits least comfortably, although arguably loosely related to the earlier discussion of external equity, is that of access to finance. This is also the most commonly cited and vigorously debated 'barrier' to growth.

Although the issue of finance was discussed in greater detail in Chapters 5 and 6, the following represents a brief recounting with a view to the current context. The argument generally focuses upon either the 'equity gap', discussed earlier, or access to bank finance—since most firms rely principally upon the latter method of funding.

With regards to banks, it is often argued that some form of market failure or 'finance gap' in the provision of debt to small firms exists. In short, small firm demand for bank loans exceeds supply and the market fails to reach equilibrium at prevailing prices (interest rates set, by the Bank of England, below market equilibrium price). Such an argument, however, assumes homogeneous loan proposals which is unlikely to be the case. Undoubtedly some proposals will be of greater inherent worth than others. It is more likely that any difficulties relate to the relationship between small firms and their banks. Due to the nature of the banking relationship, in the presence of information asymmetries and moral hazard, adverse selection and credit rationing are liable to prevail. The risk averse character of banks favours potentially not selecting 'good' proposals in preference to potentially selecting 'bad' proposals (42). As a 'remedy' it is suggested that there exists scope to improve information flows between small firms and their bankers (43). There are further issues regarding the inconsistency of criteria used in, and the often subjective nature of, bank appraisal procedures (44). Regardless of the plausibility of the above argument, and the laudability of the suggested response, there exists little empirical evidence that access to finance represents a significant barrier to growth (45).

On a more general note there exists a counter argument to the suggested lifting of presumed barriers to growth. It is implied that entrepreneurs, or small business owner-managers, trading in hostile environments are more likely to develop the characteristics of self-reliance and determination required to succeed (46). Consequently, policy should avoid lowering barriers or providing incentives which dull the development of these attributes. This is a generally untested hypothesis built upon principally anecdotal and *ad hoc* observations and it is doubtful whether such an extreme position would be of value in the generality of policy. Whilst we might feel a policy of erecting or maintaining barriers is a step too far, Cressy's (16) suggestion that we should adopt a stricter German model which, by making start-up more difficult, aims at raising the threshold quality of new ventures seems eminently sensible.

CONCLUSION

If this chapter were to provide a comprehensive review of all contributions to our understanding of small firm growth it would require a dedicated text in itself. Instead we have contented ourselves with presenting the three strands which have had greatest influence on public policy and mainstream academic debate. Of these, less attention has been given to the often criticized stage models of growth and the under-developed barriers to growth literature. Whilst implausibly rigid, stage models are truly process oriented and grant due attention to the role of history in determining the actions and structures of firms. However, we concur with Storey; the models describe rather than predict or, more significantly, explain (unless through equally implausible, non-random, defined crises).

On the other hand, the characteristics or predictive modelling approach to small firm growth has, itself, reached an impasse. The factors influencing growth are innumerable and are likely to defy classification in a simple, usable model. Attempting to isolate those where evidence of effect is 'consistent' appears fruitless. To illustrate from recent research, consider Westhead and Birley (35); having identified *eighty-eight* variables hypothesized to influence firm growth, and subsequently conducted a large-scale postal survey, they found two (in the case of manufacturing) or three (in the case of services) factors exerted a statistically significant influence on growth rates. The authors acknowledged, however, that these factors '. . ."explain[ed]" a relatively small proportion of the variance [in sample firm sizes]' (p. 28). Perhaps more importantly, whilst many of the factors incorporated in such models *may* have considerable influence on the growth of small firms, any influence is likely to be contingent upon the given context.

More recently emphasis has begun to shift from static analysis of categorical, often binary, variables towards a more dynamic analysis of the processes of adaptation and learning (47, 21, 48). Simplistically, it may be suggested that, since growth necessitates change, those firms which have enjoyed sustainable growth are those which were most receptive to change and/or have managed change most effectively. Within this context, learning is seen as a process of adaptation to changes in internal and external environments. Such a shift in focus is consistent with the current fashion for 'learning organizations', growth theory and 'education, education, education'—all of which seek to emphasize the pivotal role played by human capital in the development of firms. The aim of such research is to discover and delineate the underlying processes of adaptive learning and growth, irrespective of context. Or indeed, to determine whether such processes exist. Unfortunately no coherent testable model has been developed to date. The development of a suitable process theory of [small] firm growth remains one of the major challenges in entrepreneurship and the wider social sciences.

Suggested assignments

Assignments are provided on case studies in the tutor's manual.

Learning outcomes

At the end of this chapter you should be able to:

1. Discuss the strengths and weaknesses of the main small-firm growth theories.
2. Identify and describe some of the important factors which may affect growth in small firms.
3. Explain the importance of understanding the process of growth to the development of small firms policy.
4. Appreciate the complexity of growth.
5. Recognize the current developments in growth theory and how these hope to supplement existing knowledge.

REFERENCES

1. PENROSE, E. (1959) *The Theory of the Growth of the Firm*, Blackwell, London.
2. STOREY, D. AND JOHNSON, S. (1987) *Are Small Firms the Answer to Unemployment?*, Employment Institute, London.
3. GALLAGHER, C. AND STEWART, H. (1985) 'Business Death and Firms Size in the UK', *International Small Business Journal*, vol. 4, no. 1, pp. 42–57.
4. DOYLE, J. AND GALLAGHER, C. (1987) 'Size Distribution, Growth Potential and Job Generation Contributions of UK Firms', *International Small Business Journal*, vol. 6, no. 1, pp. 31–56.
5. GALLAGHER, C. AND MILLER, P. (1991) 'New Fast Growing Companies Create Jobs', *Long Range Planning*, vol. 24, no. 1, pp. 96–101.
6. SCOTTISH ENTERPRISE (1993) *Improving the Business Birth Rate: A Strategy for Scotland*, Scottish Enterprise, Glasgow.
7. GREINER, L. (1972) 'Evolution and revolution as organisations grow', *Harvard Business Review*, vol. 50, July–August, pp. 37–46.
8. CHURCHILL, N. AND LEWIS, V. (1983) 'The five stages of small business growth', *Harvard Business Review*, vol. 61, May–June, pp. 30–50.
9. SCOTT, M. AND BRUCE, R. (1987) 'Five Stages of Growth in Small Business', *Long Range Planning*, vol. 20, no. 3, pp. 45–52.
10. STOREY, D. (1994) *Understanding the Small Business Sector*, Routledge, London.
11. BURNS, P. AND HARRISON, J. (1996) 'Growth', in Burns, P. and Dewhurst, J. (eds) *Small Business and Entrepreneurship*, Macmillan, London.
12. STOREY, D., KEASEY, K., WATSON, R. AND WYNARCZYK, P. (1987) *The Performance of Small Firms: Profits, Jobs and Failures*, Croom Helm, London.
13. HALL, G. (1995) *Surviving and Prospering in the Small Firm Sector*, Routledge, London.
14. GALLAGHER, C. AND ROBSON, G. (1996) 'The Identification of High Growth SMEs',

paper presented to the 19th National Small Firms Policy and Research Conference, Birmingham.

15. FREEL, M. (1998) 'Policy, Prediction and Growth: picking start-up winners?', *Journal of Small Business and Enterprise Development*, vol. 5, no. 1, pp. 19–32.

16. CRESSY, R. (1996) 'Are Business Start-ups Debt Rationed?', *The Economic Journal*, vol. 106, no. 438, pp. 1253–70.

17. BARKHAM, R., GUDGIN, G., HANVEY, E. AND HART, M. (1996) *The Determinants of Small Firm Growth*, Jessica Kingsley, London.

18. BURNS, P. (1996) 'The Significance of Small Firms', in Burns, P. and Dewhurst, J. (eds) *Small Business and Entrepreneurship*, Macmillan, London.

19. OAKEY, R. (1995) *High-Technology Small Firms: Variable Barriers to Growth*, Paul Chapman, London.

20. VYAKARNAM, S., JACOBS, R. AND HANDELBERG, J. (1996) 'Building and Managing Relationships: The core competence of rapid growth business', paper presented to the 19th National Small Firms Policy and Research Conference, Birmingham (unpublished, amended version).

21. COSTELLO, N. (1996) 'Learning and Routines in High-Tech SMEs: Analysing Rich Case Study Material', *Journal of Economic Issues*, vol. 30, no. 2, pp. 591–7.

22. JENSEN, J.B. AND McGUCKIN, R.H. (1997) 'Firm Performance and Evolution: Empirical Regularities in the US Microdata', *Industrial and Corporate Change*, vol. 6, no. 1, pp. 25–47.

23. JOVANOVIC, B. (1982) 'Selection and the Evolution of Industry', *Econometrica*, vol. 50, no. 3, pp. 649–70.

24. ENSR (1994) *The European Observatory for SMEs: 2nd Annual Report*, ENSR/EIM.

25. SMALLBONE, D. AND NORTH, D. (1995) 'Targeting Established SMEs: Does Their Age Matter?', *International Small Business Journal*, vol. 13, no. 3, pp. 47–64.

26. WESTHEAD, P. (1995) 'New Owner-managed Business in Rural and Urban Areas in Great Britain: A Matched Pairs Comparison' *Regional Studies*, vol. 29, no. 4, pp. 367–80.

27. BIRLEY, S. AND WESTHEAD, P. (1994) 'A Comparison of New Businesses Established by "Novice" and "Habitual" Founders in GB', *International Small Business Journal*, vol. 12, no. 1, pp. 38–60.

28. SCOTT, M. AND ROSA, P. (1996) 'Existing Business as Sources of New Firms: A missing topic in business formation research', paper presented to the Babson *Entrepreneurship Research Conference*, Seattle, USA.

29. WESTHEAD, P. AND WRIGHT, M. (1997) 'Novice, Portfolio and Serial Founders: are they different?', paper presented to the Babson *Entrepreneurship Research Conference*, Boston, USA.

30. SCOTT, M. AND ROSA, P. (1996) 'Has Firm Level Analysis Reached its Limits? Time for a Rethink', *International Small Business Journal*, vol. 14, no. 4, pp. 81–9.

31. DEAKINS, D AND HUSSAIN, G. (1994) 'Financial Information, the Banker and Small Business: A Comment', *British Accounting Review*, vol. 26, pp. 24–31.

32. MURRAY, G. (1994) 'The Second 'Equity Gap': Exit Problems for Seed and Early Stage Venture Capitalists and their Investee Companies', *International Small Business Journal*, vol. 12, no. 4, pp. 58–76.

33. STOREY, D. AND SYKES, N. (1996) 'Uncertainty, Innovation and Management', in

Burns, P. and Dewhurst, J. (eds) *Small Business and Entrepreneurship*, Macmillan, London.

34. BARBER, J., METCALFE, S. AND PORTEOUS, M. (1989) 'Barriers to growth: the ACARD study', in Barber, J., Metcalfe, S. and Porteous, M. (eds) *Barriers to Growth in Small Firms*, Routledge, London.

35. WESTHEAD, P. AND BIRLEY, S. (1995) 'Employment Growth in New Independent Owner-managed Firms in GB', *International Small Business Journal*, vol. 13, no. 3, pp. 11–34.

36. ROTHWELL, R. AND ZEGVELD, W. (1982) *Innovation and the Small and Medium Sized Firm*, Francis Pinter, London.

37. GEROWSKI, P. AND MACHIN, S. (1992) 'Do Innovating Firms Outperform Non-Innovators?', *Business Strategy Review*, Summer, pp. 79–90.

38. WYNARCZYK, P. AND THWAITES, A. (1997) 'The Economic Performance, Survival and Non-Survival of Innovative Small Firms', in Oakey, R. and Muktar, S. (eds) *New Technology-Based Firms in the 1990s: Volume III*, Paul Chapman, London.

39. PENROSE, E. (1971) 'Limits to the Size and Growth of Firms', in *The Growth of Firms, Middle East Oil and Other Essays*, first published in *American Economic Review*, vol. 45, no. 2.

40. SMALLBONE, D., LEIGH, R. AND NORTH, D. (1995) 'The Characteristics and Strategies of High Growth SMEs', *International Journal of Entrepreneurial Behaviour and Research*, vol. 1, no. 3, pp. 44–62.

41. ACOST (1990) *The Enterprise Challenge: Overcoming Barriers to Growth in Small Firms*, HMSO, London.

42. DEAKINS, D. AND HUSSAIN, G. (1991) *Risk Assessment by Bank Managers*, Birmingham Polytechnic Business School.

43. BINKS, M. AND ENNEW, C. (1996) 'Financing Small Firms', in Burns, P. and Dewhurst, J. (eds) *Small Business and Entrepreneurship*, Macmillan, London.

44. DEAKINS, D., HUSSAIN, G. AND RAM, M. (1992) 'Overcoming the Adverse Selection Problem', paper presented to the 15th National Small Firms Policy and Research Conference, Southampton.

45. CRESSY, R. (1996) 'Small Business Failure: Failure to Fund or Failure to Learn', paper presented to the ESRC Network of Industrial Economists meeting on *Entrepreneurship and Small Business*, University of Durham, December.

46. DEWHURST, J. (1996) 'The Entrepreneur', in Burns, P. and Dewhurst, J. (eds) *Small Business and Entrepreneurship*, Macmillan, London.

47. FREEL, M. (1998) 'Evolution, innovation and learning: evidence from case studies', *Entrepreneurship and Regional Development*, vol. 10, no. 2, pp. 137–49.

48. WIKLUND, J. (1998) *Small Firm Growth and Performance: Entrepreneurship and Beyond*, dissertation series No. 3, Jönköping International Business School.

RECOMMENDED READING

ACOST (1990) *The Enterprise Challenge: Overcoming Barriers to Growth in Small Firms*, HMSO, London.

BARKHAM, R., GUDGIN, G., HANVEY, E. AND HART, M. (1996) *The Determinants of Small Firm Growth*, Jessica Kingsley, London.

CHURCHILL, N. AND LEWIS, V. (1983) 'The five stages of small business growth', *Harvard Business Review*, vol. 61, May–June, pp. 30–50.

FREEL, M. (1998) 'Policy, Prediction and Growth: picking start-up winners?', *Journal of Small Business and Enterprise Development*, vol. 5, no. 1, pp. 19–32.

GREINER, L. (1972) 'Evolution and revolution as organisations grow', *Harvard Business Review*, vol. 50, July–August, pp. 37–46.

STOREY, D. (1994) *Understanding the Small Business Sector*, Routledge, London.

10. International Entrepreneurship and the Global Economy

INTRODUCTION

The previous chapter examined some of the factors in the growth process. One factor likely to be involved in an entrepreneurial growth firm is the ability to export or to internationalize through overseas operations. For many fast growth firms, establishing overseas markets is an essential part of the growth process. Trading overseas requires some understanding of different cultures, different economies and different ways of 'doing business'. In this chapter we examine some of the characteristics of different cultures, which affect entrepreneurial behaviour, risk taking and economic production methods in other nations. These are factors that need to be taken into account by entrepreneurs in the UK who are seeking to expand in overseas markets. We begin by noting the importance of the global economy, a trend, it is argued, that cannot be ignored by all small firm entrepreneurs, whether trading internationally or not.

Global markets

As we have stated a number of times before, the majority of small firm entrepreneurs do not wish to grow (and, by definition, do not wish to export or expand overseas). However, it is arguable that all entrepreneurs are affected by the globalization of the economy. A number of forces have led to increased 'globalization' that cannot be ignored. All entrepreneurs today have to trade in an economy that is affected by the trends or forces forming the global economy. Even if a firm's market is restricted to its local geographical area, it may face competitors that are based overseas and trading locally. Equally, the firm may be part of a supply chain whose end markets are global. For example, the West Midlands is well known for the number of small firms that produce car components, supplying to local car manufacturers. All firms in the supply chain will be part of the global market and will be unable to ignore trends in that market. A small firm producing car components in Coventry is probably affected more by events in Japan than by the local economy. Curran and Blackburn (1) among others have claimed that firms operate in global networks.

Nowadays we are all affected by economic events in other markets whether they are taking place in Japan, Russia or closer to home. Ability to respond to these events, to manage in the increasing pace of change, will affect the sustainability and viability of all small firms; part of that increasing pace of change is the globalization of the economy. A number of factors have contributed to the development of the global economy, factors which are increasing in importance. Some of them are listed below. This list is not meant to be exhaustive, but includes:

- The development of the knowledge economy
- Improved forms of communication (and information)
- New technological developments that favour smaller firms (e.g., biotechnology/micro-technologies)
- Reduction of barriers to trade, through agreements formed under the General Agreement on Tariffs and Trade (GATT) and the increased importance of common trading areas such as the EU
- Increased pace of change requiring flexible and speedy responses
- Privatization and reduced barriers in emerging nations, with the development of economies in transition, the emergence of 'tiger economies' and the emergence of China as a major overseas market
- Increased mobility of labour force and other resources
- Growth of global capital markets
- Growth of the sovereign individual and greater consumer choice
- Reduction of cultural barriers.

Implications for entrepreneurs who export

Growing companies have to assess how to tackle globalization and the penetration of overseas markets as a result. Operating abroad usually involves one of three approaches:

1. Production at home and exporting.
2. Entering into a joint venture agreement or strategic partnerships to exploit overseas markets.
3. Owning and controlling overseas operation, through either a *de novo* operation or buying an existing operation.

These options represent different strategic choices for the entrepreneurial growth firm. The strategy chosen will depend on factors such as cost, availability of finance, regulations in different countries, risk involved, availability of strategic partners and exchange rate risks, but not least, the entrepreneurial culture of different areas and nations. We have insufficient space for an adequate discussion of these factors; however, drawing on the example of the Aquamotive case, we saw there that the firm operated in global markets (supplying control feeding systems to fish farms). The strategy adopted to exploit such global markets was to seek strategic partnerships. Aquamotive was at an early stage of the development of the product, was still operating on a small scale and with limited resources. Seeking strategic partners represented the best strategy for the firm, given its stage of development and given the resources it had available or could access. For a different firm in a different technology a different strategy might be preferable. For example, there are fast growth information technology firms who have quickly established overseas operations through expansion abroad, by setting up overseas offices and production facilities and operating subsidiaries as a multinational enterprise. Factors such as the need to be near to their customers (users of new software) and lower cost of operating abroad were important to such firms.

While noting the importance of such factors, for this chapter we focus on different cultures and how such cultures can affect entrepreneurial behaviour, a factor which will affect the strategy adopted by entrepreneurial firms to exploit the globalization of local economies.

DIFFERENT ENTREPRENEURIAL CULTURES

In Chapter 1 we discussed how the entrepreneur is increasingly seen as a key actor in the economy and as an *agent* of economic change. To perform this function the entrepreneur becomes a *problem solver*; reconciling limited resources with the environment. The entrepreneur may be seen as having the same function in each economy yet the environment and resources will vary. In different economies, different cultures will affect the degree to which the entrepreneur is able to be the key actor and hence influence economic change. Some economies are perceived to contain environments which are more conducive to entrepreneurship than others. For example, the USA and Japan have economies that are regarded as 'entrepreneurial', that is, favouring the entrepreneur as the key agent of economic change. In this section we examine some of the factors that determine the nature of the environment and culture in different economies.

ADVANCED ECONOMIES

Casson (2) has attempted to analyse and classify the 'entrepreneurial' cultures of advanced, or developed, economies. He makes a distinction between 'high level' entrepreneurial behaviour, which he claims is associated with the Schumpeterian concept of entrepreneurship, and 'low level' entrepreneurial behaviour, which he claims is associated with the Kirznerian concept of entrepreneurship (see Chapter 1 for an explanation of these contrasting concepts). Casson compares seven advanced industrial economies (USA, Japan, UK, France, Canada, Sweden and Italy) and uses a scoring system for certain characteristics of cultural attitudes and environment, which are discussed below. Using this (weighted) scoring system he finds (2) that Japan and the USA have the highest and most conducive entrepreneurial cultures, whereas (of the seven nations), the UK and Italy have the lowest ratings.

Casson claims that there are two groups of characteristics of national cultures that determine these ratings. Firstly, technical aspects of a culture, which include attitudes to the importance of scientific measurement, to taking a systems view and hence to the degree of sophistication in decision making. Secondly, moral characteristics of a culture, which include the extent of voluntarism, types of commitment and attitudes to achievement. These groups of characteristics determine the extent to which a culture is conducive to 'high level' (Schumpeterian) entrepreneurship as opposed to 'low level' (Kirznerian) entrepreneurship. For example, Japan scores well on a national characteristic of a scientific approach to problems and a systems view of planning, which means a willingness to accept logistical planning and awareness of interdependency. Japan scores lower with voluntarism, the extent of willingness to allow freedom for transactions, an area where the USA scores highly. This is explained by Casson (2) as:

> The philosophy of voluntarism ... supports a political framework within which people are free to transact with whomever they like. Voluntarism opposes the concentration of coercive powers on institutions such as the state. (p. 92)

Casson's hierachy of national entrepreneurial cultures is an attempt to provide objective measurement of subjective assessments of intangible values of different national cultures. As such, they could be subject to widely different interpretations. For example, Germany is a rather surprising omission from Casson's countries chosen for comparison, and might score quite low on some of Casson's criteria, yet it would be accepted by many observers as a nation having a high level of entrepreneurial activity and behaviour. Casson's approach, nevertheless, is an interesting attempt to analyse different levels of entrepreneurial cultures in different economies. In identifying factors which affect attitudes to scientific endeavour, to moral codes, to commitments, the approach provides a useful framework for discussion of features of different national cultures and different levels of entrepreneurial activity.

It would be a mistake, however, to view certain economies as 'model' or prototypical entrepreneurial economies. Quite different cultures with different systems, attitudes and infrastructures can result in high-level, advanced entrepreneurship. For example, the Scottish Enterprise Birth Rate Enquiry (3) investigated two advanced regional economies to examine factors that accounted for their relatively high levels of entrepreneurial behaviour. The two contrasting regions, Massachusetts in the USA, and Baden-Württemberg in Germany, had quite different attitudes, characteristics and environments, Massachusetts was characterized by little state intervention and a dependence on private sector venture capital to provide the risk capital to finance new ventures. Baden-Württemberg, however, was characterized by (regional) state-funded assistance and a reliance on bank loan finance to provide new venture capital. These two powerful regions demonstrate that different characteristics in society and different infrastructures can produce advanced high-level entrepreneurship.

The importance of developed networks

The common feature of advanced entrepreneurial economies is the extent of networking. As discussed before (see Chapter 8), Baden-Württemberg contained advanced networks focused through local chambers of commerce. Massachusetts also had important networks, through venture capitalists and through integration with Massachusetts Institute of Technology (MIT), which provided an important spinout route for technology-based high value start-ups. The level of networking and co-operative behaviour is not one of Casson's criteria; however, it is a recognized factor behind the success of areas such as the north east of Italy, the *Third Italy* .

Scottish Enterprise (4) following its enquiry, identified networking arrangements amongst new firms as a way to achieve growth and hence job creation:

> Networks are important: many of the solutions will be found in the actions of individual entrepreneurs, backed by their networks of family and friends. An important focus of action for the strategy is to improve the effectiveness of these networks and to make potential entrepreneurs more of what they can do themselves to achieve success. Part of this involves improving the support given by the formal support networks in the private and public sectors. (p. 4.)

Similarly, in its recently published clustering strategy (5), Scottish Enterprise claims:

> To compete, companies will need to build strong partnerships through which information and ideas can flow quickly and to best mutual advantage. Spanning customers, suppliers, competitors and other supporting institutions such as the universities, colleges, research bodies and the utilities, these specialist networks or 'clusters' create more of the sparks that fuel innovation and generate synergies that power them to greater competitiveness. (p. 1)

The benefits which can accrue to new firms operating in partnerships/networks/clusters are the potential advantages of economies of scale. Services and inputs, such as advertising, training, access to loan finance at advantageous rates, consultancy advice, financial services—items which a single firm cannot easily afford or secure when operating independently—can be secured when operating as part of a larger group. Whilst the organizational structure of firms operating in some kind of cohesive way may be given the title 'networking', firms producing in any economy take on some of the attributes of a networking structure. For example, by engaging in production and trade a firm deals with suppliers and customers which necessitates a degree of co-operation and trust. These factors are regarded as essential attributes to the successful functioning of a network. There is also an element of risk and uncertainty within any business relationship. Trust arises in response to the threat of risk and uncertainty. When trust exists it minimizes the potential risk and opportunism. Thompson (6) underlines the importance of trust:

> Co-operation is more secure and robust when agents have a trust because of the reputation of themselves and other agents in the network for honesty and consistency. (p. 58)

Risk and opportunism can also be reduced via contracting but, as Macaulay (7) notes, whilst detailed clauses are often written into contracts, they are seldom used:

> . . . contract and contract law are often thought unnecessary because there are many non-legal sanctions. Two norms are widely accepted.
> (1) Commitments are to be honoured in almost all situations; . . .
> (2) One ought to produce a good product and stand behind it. (p. 63)

In other words an environment can develop where implicit contracting ensures a degree of trust and co-operation. Other more established relationships can develop beyond that of a purely contractual kind. Sakou (8) identifies two other kinds of trust: competence trust, being the belief that a trading partner will fulfil a particular task, and goodwill trust, which occurs in situations where initiatives are undertaken beyond the specific remit of a contract: 'the role of goodwill trust extends beyond existing relations and includes the transfer of new ideas and new technology' (9, p. 218).

Whilst we have identified trust and co-operation as two attributes of an advanced economy, they can be strengthened to ensure the efficient operation of the network. This can be the key to the development of advanced entrepreneurial economies such as the *Third Italy*. For this to happen, contractual trust must be developed into goodwill trust. Economists using a game theoretical framework have demonstrated that where firms attach sufficient weight to future interactions, then punishment strategies can be employed to secure co-operation. When joining a formal organization such as a network defectors and unco-operative players can be excluded. The problem with over-reliance on punishment strategies is that it could lead to distrust which would threaten co-operation. 'If you trust me, why are you monitoring my behaviour?' Axelrod (10) suggests that co-operation can evolve over a period of time as firms gradually learn rules and norms of behaviour leading to co-operation. In other words, through continual interaction and the belief of further interaction, the temptation to cheat diminishes. The firms build up reputations for co-operation and these reputations have to be protected.

We have indicated that where established networks exist, this can take the form of policing in an attempt to prevent opportunistic behaviour on behalf of the member firms. Where no existing meaningful networking arrangements exist, policy bodies could attempt to facilitate such developments. In local economies where this has proven to be more successful, such as the industrial districts of the *Third Italy*, this has occurred in conjunction with the key agents in the region, such as the small firm entrepreneurs themselves, the equivalent of the local chambers of commerce, the relevant financial institutions and the local authorities. In other words, the key players in the local economy have been involved in the design and implementation of the strategy, which is a major factor in that they take on ownership of the organization.

Thus it has been argued that the level of co-operation, trust and networking is a key factor determining the level of entrepreneurship in different cultures. This networking may be characterized by different forms, but it seems to be a necessary condition for advanced levels of entrepreneurship.

ECONOMIES IN TRANSITION

With the collapse of communism in Eastern Europe and the old USSR, attention has focused on whether such nations can successfully transform into entrepreneurial economies (whether high level or low level). Such nations are regarded as emerging economies, as potential new areas for entrepreneurs seeking new markets. Therefore, if they can achieve the features of advanced economies that have been discussed in the previous section, new opportunities for firms seeking growth become available. Such economies have been grouped together with the rather optimistic term of 'economies in transition'. As in Western Europe, this term hides a great diversity of development; different nations are at different stages in the transition process. This partly reflects the situation before the break-up of the old Soviet bloc, where some states had semi-market economies (such as Poland) and others were completely government controlled, such as the Baltic States. It also partly reflects the different features and characteristics of the nations.

These emerging economies have certain features which include:

- High levels of uncertainty and lack of information implying opportunities for the Kirznerian entrepreneur
- A lack of formal financial infrastructure and sources of finance
- Limited markets and spending power within internal economies
- No formal regulation, e.g., for regulating new firms/companies.

While there are considerable opportunities for entrepreneurship to flourish in such nations, innovative or *high level* entrepreneurship is difficult because of the lack of infrastructure that can provide the level of finance or risk capital required, the lack of networks and co-operative behaviour (identified above as important features of advanced entrepreneurial regions) and the lack of infrastructure to support the small firm entrepreneur. In some nations a tradition of co-operative ownership has also led to problems with the establishment of individual entrepreneurship (11).

Given the newness of 'economies in transition', there is still a limited literature on the characteristics of their culture and the way this affects entrepreneurial behaviour in such nations. However, a paper by Roberts and Tholen (12) gives some insights into differences within these nations. For example, their research showed considerable differences in Russia compared to other former Soviet bloc nations, with business development in Russia being more *ad hoc* and unplanned, compared to other Eastern European countries. Common characteristics across Eastern European nations included:

- Unstable political régimes and hence the need for businesses to grow quickly
- A lack of tradition of business ownership and comparatively few family firms
- The absence of support services.

Differences were likely to be:

- Source of new entrepreneurs (in Russia new entrepreneurs were

former workers, whereas in other Eastern European nations they
were more likely to come from management levels)

- Higher growth ambitions in Eastern Europe compared to Russia
- Fewer female entrepreneurs in Russia (in other nations female
  entrepreneurs accounted for around 30 per cent of new business
  ownership)
- Attitudes could vary to 'doing business' (entrepreneurs in Russia
  were likely to seek the 'big deal', whereas in nations such as
  Poland a more realistic incremental development was adopted by
  entrepreneurs).

The transition economies of Eastern Europe and Russia can be seen as containing
a wide spectrum of different stages of progression to higher levels of
entrepreneurship. Undoubtedly, much of it is low level, characterized by Casson
as Kirznerian, with some areas struggling to shake off attitudes that restrict
creativity and innovative behaviour. In a statement that is probably representative
of many transition economies of Eastern Europe, one native writer (13) on
Slovenia comments perceptively that:

> Traditionally, Slovenians have not been classified as exhibiting
> entrepreneurial traits. The collectivist culture, dependency upon
> the state, historical subordination by external powers and strong
> egalitarian values relative to the even distribution of social and
> material gains have combined with a conservative formal education
> system that rewarded obedience and diligence, and suppressed
> innovation and creativity. (p. 108)

Western European nations have been involved in assisting the development of
infrastructures in transition economies in Eastern Europe. However, as one writer
comments (14):

> It may well be that in the longer term, borrowing ideas which lead to a
> change in values and attitudes towards enterprise and small business
> and which change norms of behaviour, is a critical task in ensuring
> that a culture sympathetic to small business is created. (p. 26)

Transition economies, for the time being, remain at very different individual
stages of development, characterized by different levels of entrepreneurship. They
face unique problems in transforming their society and cultures from former state
dependency to ones where individual risk taking is accepted and supported. The
diversity of development, however, is such that to treat such economies
collectively is a mistake. Each nation, and indeed each region, will evolve their
own entrepreneurial characteristics and activity. It would also be a mistake to
prescribe solutions from the West. Lessons from emerging nations suggest that
unique developments and infrastructures are required to overcome some of the
barriers to entrepreneurial development. Some of these lessons are examined in
the next section.

How important small firm entrepreneurs are in such transition economies has been the subject of some disagreement. For example, one writer (15) at least has claimed that small firms are still unimportant in such economies. Others (16) have claimed, in the case of Poland, that small firms entrepreneurs have become the engine of the Polish economy. Such diametrically opposed opinions will take some time to reconcile as the transition economies continue to evolve.

EMERGING ECONOMIES

In contrast to transition economies, the emerging economies contain examples of nations in which the small firm has always played a role in their economic development. In India the small firm sector has been a prominent part of the economy for the past fifty years (17). Other emerging nations, of course, provide examples where entrepreneurial behaviour has been far longer in developing. For example, Kenya is still considered to have low levels of entrepreneurial activities (18).

There are obviously vast differences which exist in cultures and concomitant entrepreneurial levels of activity in different emergent nations. We do not attempt to discuss such diversity here. However, it is worth noting examples of successful entrepreneurial behaviour, how certain groups have overcome barriers to entrepreneurial development and factors in such success. Such examples may have wider applications and lessons for advanced and transition economies.

In India a high need for co-operation to overcome substantial limitations on resources has been observed and seems to be characteristic of entrepreneurial behaviour (19). High levels of trust and co-operative behaviour have provided the basis for micro-credit unions (20), examples of micro-business finance that have provided the basis for models of investment trusts in cities in advanced nations (21). Such attributes of entrepreneurial behaviour were discussed in our earlier section. India provides examples of flourishing networks and clusters (22).

Other emergent nations often have complex factors that may have arisen from their history and inheritance as former colonial states, and which affect cultural attitudes to entrepreneurship. For example, South Africa, according to one writer (23):

> . . . with its many cultures and dynamic and transforming socio-political environment, represents a particularly problematic case study with respect to the application of arguments. (p. 27)

The legacy of apartheid in South Africa has caused some black entrepreneurs to respond entrepreneurially to adversity, while enterprise in other members of the black population has been stifled (23).

The diversity of emergent economies is such that it is difficult to draw coherent patterns of factors that affect the level of entrepreneurship. Factors which may be important and conducive to entrepreneurial behaviour in one culture, such as co-operative behaviour and networks in India, may be restrictive in others.

For example, a study of small firm entrepreneurs in Turkey (24) found that networks were dependent on traditional values, sectarian affiliations and the family environment. The researcher claimed that such networks enforced their own inertia preventing innovation in small firms in Turkey.

This complexity of factors reveals the infinite variety of entrepreneurial behaviour in emergent nations, variety to which we can give only the briefest of indications. In many cases we are just beginning to learn about and appreciate this diversity. What is apparent is that we cannot apply 'Western' solutions to such diversity.

CONCLUSIONS

In this chapter we have argued that individual entrepreneurs cannot isolate themselves from the globalization of the economy. Every business trades in a global economy, which effectively means adopting strategies that enable the entrepreneur to optimize opportunities. These strategies will depend on resources available, key staff, type of product and the nature of technology. It may mean adopting joint venture strategies; it may mean adopting quality benchmarking techniques as part of a network of firms in a supply chain. It may mean forming networks to share resources, information and gain externalities. Entrepreneurs must think globally, even if they operate only in local markets.

Entrepreneurs who do 'internationalize', by operating in more than one country, must be aware of different entrepreneurial cultures in different nations. We have examined how, in advanced economies, different regions can have very different cultures yet still be successful. We have suggested that advanced networks may hold one key to successful entrepreneurial development in advanced economies. In transition economies the legacy of communism and state control has affected entrepreneurial development in different nations. Some have been more successful at overcoming this legacy; in others lack of a recent history of business ownership has been more of a hindrance. Similarly, in emergent nations entrepreneurs have reacted in different ways to historical legacies, whether this is apartheid in South Africa or colonialism in the Indian subcontinent.

Casson has suggested that it is possible to identify characteristics in the cultures of different nations that will determine whether they have high or low levels of entrepreneurship. However, we have also seen that the infinite variety of international entrepreneurship defies classification and it can be claimed that inconsistent factors affect the level and success of entrepreneurial activity (such as networks). All entrepreneurs need to be aware of the global economy, but all who wish to operate internationally must also be aware of the infinite variety of cultures that still exist in that economy.

Learning outcomes

At the end of this chapter students should be able to:

1. Describe how different cultures can affect entrepreneurial activity.
2. Apply criteria to determine different levels of entrepreneurship in different nations, such as high level and low level.
3. Understand some of the factors that affect the level of entrepreneurship in different nations.
4. Understand how all entrepreneurs are affected by the global economy.
5. Discuss opportunities and threats posed by the global economy.
6. Describe examples of entrepreneurial activities in advanced, transition and emergent economies.

Suggested assignments

Students are required to work in a small group with an identified small firm entrepreneur in their locality. They are required to assess how the firm could be affected by the global economy and produce a group report which covers the following:

- Introduction with case material on the firm
- Analysis of strengths and weaknesses
- Analysis of opportunities and threats within a global economy
- Research with potential markets (DTI provides publications on overseas markets)
- Conclusions.

REFERENCES

1. CURRAN, J. AND BLACKBURN, R. (1993) *Local Economic Networks: The Death of the Local Economy*, Routledge, London.
2. CASSON, M. (1990) *Enterprise and Competitiveness*, Clarendon Press, Oxford.
3. SCOTTISH ENTERPRISE (1993) *The Business Birth Rate Enquiry*, Scottish Enterprise, Glasgow.
4. SCOTTISH ENTERPRISE (1993) *The Business Birth Rate Strategy*, Scottish Enterprise, Glasgow.
5. SCOTTISH ENTERPRISE (1998) *The Clusters Approach*, Scottish Enterprise, Glasgow.

6. THOMPSON, G. (1993) 'Network Coordination' in Maidment, R. and Thompson, G. (eds) *Managing the United Kingdom*, Sage, London.

7. MACAULAY S. (1963) 'Non-contractual relations in business: a preliminary study', *American Sociological Review*, vol. 45, pp. 55–69.

8. SAKO, M. (1992) *Prices Quality and Trust: Inter-Firm Relations in Britain and Japan*, CUP, Cambridge.

9. BURCHELL B. AND WILKINSON F. (1997) 'Trust, business relationships and the contract environment', *Cambridge Journal of Economics*, vol. 21, no. 2, pp. 217–37.

10. AXELROD, R. (1981) 'The emergence of cooperation among egoists', *American Review of Political Science*, vol. 75, pp. 306–18.

11. CARLISLE, B. AND GOTLIEB, A. (1995) 'Problems, Training and Consultancy Needs in SMEs in Russia—An Exploratory Study', paper presented to the 18th ISBA Small Firms National Conference, Paisley, November.

12. ROBERTS, K. AND THOLEN, J. (1997) 'Young Entrepreneurs in the New Market Economies', paper presented to a conference on Enterprise in the Transition Economies, Wolverhampton, September.

13. GLAS, M. (1998) 'Entrepreneurship in Slovenia' in Morrison, A. (ed.) *Entrepreneurship: An International Perspective*, Butterworth-Heinemann, Woburn, MA, pp. 108–24.

14. BATSTONE, S. (1998) 'SME Policy in Slovakia: The Role of Bi-Lateral and Multi-Lateral Aid', paper presented to a Conference on Enterprise in the Transition Economies, Wolverhampton, September.

15. SCASE, R. (1998) 'The Role of Small Businesses in the Economic Transformation in Eastern Europe, *International Small Business Journal*, vol. 16, no. 1, pp. 13–21.

16. ERUTKU, C. AND VALLÉE, L. (1997) 'Business Start-ups in Today's Poland: Who and How?', *Entrepreneurship and Regional Development*, vol. 9, no. 2, pp. 113–26.

17. DAS, K. (1998) 'Collective Dynamism and Firm Strategy: a study of an Indian industrial cluster', *Entrepreneurship and Regional Development*, vol. 10, no. 1, pp. 33–50.

18. DONDO, A. AND NGUMO, M. (1998) 'Entrepreneurship in Kenya', in Morrison, A. (ed.) *Entrepreneurship: An International Perspective*, Butterworth-Heinemann, Woburn, MA, pp. 27–41.

19. SCHMITZ, H. (1990) 'Small Firms and Flexible Specialisation in Developing Countries', *Labour and Society*, vol. 15, pp. 257–85.

20. KASHYAP, S.P. (1988) 'Growth of small-scale enterprises in India: its nature and content', *World Development*, vol. 16, pp. 667–81.

21. NICHOLSON, B. (1998) 'Aston Reinvestment Trust', paper presented to the ESRC Seminar Series, The Finance of Small Firms, University of Middlesex, October.

22. DAS, K. (1996) 'Flexibility together: surviving and growing in a garment cluster, Ahmedabad, India', *Journal of Entrepreneurship*, vol. 5, pp. 153–77.

23. ALLIE, F. AND HUMAN, L. (1998) 'Entrepreneurship in South Africa', in Morrison, A. (ed.) *Entrepreneurship: An International Perspective*, Butterworth-Heinemann, Woburn, MA, pp. 27–41.

24. ÖZCAN, G.B. (1995) 'Small Business Networks and Local Ties in Turkey', *Entrepreneurship and Regional Development*, vol. 7, no. 3, pp. 265–82.

RECOMMENDED READING

CASSON, M. (1990) *Enterprise and Competitiveness*, Clarendon Press, Oxford.

MORRISON, A. (ed.) *Entrepreneurship: An International Perspective*, Butterworth-Heinemann, Woburn, MA.

SCASE, R. (1998) 'The Role of Small Businesses in the Economic Transformation in Eastern Europe, *International Small Business Journal*, vol. 16, no. 1, pp. 13–21.

11. Sources of Information and Research Methodology

INTRODUCTION

This chapter should be read as an introduction to Chapter 12 on business plans. It examines some of the research methods which may be necessary as background preparation to provide information for either a feasibility study or the strategic business plan. We also mention briefly some of the secondary sources of information which are now commonly available. One of the problems that entrepreneurs face is that often they do not have the time to research market opportunities properly. Obviously they will not have either the resources or the time to spend on collecting data. In recent years some institutions have utilized the potential of student assignments with local entrepreneurs which may have helped with this problem. Assignments are given at the end of the chapter with suggested guidelines and outlines of requirements. For entrepreneurs who wish to carry out research to write their own business plans, there are still a lot of sources that can be accessed quickly and even if some primary market research can be undertaken, this will improve the assumptions and market forecasts which are used for the business plans and be more likely to influence potential funders in a positive way.

This chapter aims to provide some guidelines only for carrying out basic research for a business plan. It does not attempt to provide a comprehensive survey of research methods. There are adequate books which can be examined on research methodology and we cannot do justice in the confines of this chapter to a full discussion. However, it is probably true to say that the majority of business plans are put together with either no or very little research and, in consequence, this will affect the information in the business plan, the way that it is presented and the way that it is received by potential funders.

For students, if you can provide a methodology section for the business plan (or feasibility study), then its quality will be improved. It is important to give some attention to the methodology adopted to carry out your research. It is insufficient to explain methodology in terms of either secondary or primary sources of data. Research methodology is concerned with whether you have used quantitative methods, how you analysed them, and whether you used qualitative methods. If you can use a mixture of both quantitative and qualitative survey methods, as well as secondary sources of data where relevant, this will improve the quality of information that is presented in the business plan. It may not be appropriate, however, to use both quantitative and qualitative methods, although a section on methodology should explain why you decided to adopt one or both methods.

Research methodology is dealt with in more detail later. We begin with a brief survey of some secondary data sources that you may wish to consult.

THE IMPORTANCE OF INFORMATION

All organizations operate in conditions of uncertainty. There will always be only a limited amount of information about competitors, the price of their products or services, strategic decisions of competitors, preferences of customers and costs of operation. However, uncertainty can be reduced by obtaining information which will reduce the possibility of making mistakes regarding crucial business and strategic decisions. The entrepreneur and small firm can be at a disadvantage because they do not have the same resources as large firms to enable them to carry out information gathering, particularly where this might involve obtaining primary data. Nevertheless much information can now be obtained through secondary sources and the availability and content of these sources continues to grow. In addition, the development of the Internet with search techniques has put the on-line user in touch with a vast number of sources of secondary information.

The appetite for information, especially by large firms, continues to grow. For example, the development of loyalty cards by chain store retail outlets has been one method of obtaining details on consumer spending. Information on consumer spend is becoming more sophisticated and allows large firms to target goods at niche markets and to tailor advertising campaigns accordingly. Despite the growth of different methods of improving market intelligence, firms still rely on secondary data and trends displayed by such data. For example, in the construction industry, builders are only recently adjusting to the increased demand for single-occupancy dwellings, reflecting demographic changes in society which become apparent only on examination of secondary data.

A business is often at its most vulnerable when launching, because it will not have the same knowledge or information as its competitors. It will need to establish a range of contacts with suppliers and buyers; its credit rating will inevitably be low, it may not be aware of what credit it can take advantage of, and what are the best sources of advice. There may also be shortages of skilled labour and it will still have its reputation to establish. These problems can at least be reduced if a new business takes advantage of the wide range of sources of information that are now available. The purpose of this chapter is to examine some of these sources briefly. There is such a wide and expanding range of secondary sources that we will only provide brief notes on these.

Information and technology note   The acquisition of information becomes particularly important for firms that employ high technology or are engaged in fields in which technology is rapidly changing. Thus the importance of successful R&D becomes crucial to the success of firms in high technology fields. Recent studies have pointed out that R&D itself may be carried out by firms merely to gain information and knowledge. See in particular, Cohen and Levinthal (1).

SECONDARY DATA SOURCES

Sources of information are conveniently classified as either primary or secondary. All secondary information sources include officially published data, provided by the Government or their agencies or by other institutions such as banks, CBI, trades unions, local authorities and chambers of commerce. Most institutions also have on-line Web pages, which may provide access to sources of information. For example, the DTI provide information via the Internet through their 'Enterprise Zone', containing information on Business Links and their services.

It is likely that, in the future, printed sources of statistical data will become redundant as on-line access methods are developed. However, at present we still review the main sources of published data. Some indicative and brief notes follow on the main official publications of the Office for National Statistics (ONS). These are conveniently classified as either general or (more) specific sources.

General Sources

National Income and Expenditure Year Book

The so-called 'Blue Book'. It contains the main components of national income and expenditure in the form of summary tables. It is useful if you wanted to know national or regional data on say output, incomes, wages or prices.

Annual Abstract of Statistics

Again this is a comprehensive source of secondary data, containing summary tables on population, national income and the labour force. It is more comprehensive than the blue book, containing more details on regional characteristics and financial data.

Census

The national census is the ultimate secondary data source and the most comprehensive demographic information source. For businesses it represents a valuable potential data source for their marketing campaigns and data on potential markets. It will contain a lot of socio-economic data on standard of living, material possessions and life styles. The census data is analysed and published in a more useful form through separate publications on particular demographic features of the population. For example, Ballard and Kalra have published a breakdown of ethnic minority demographic data (2).

As we have mentioned, these sources are only indicative. In practice it is more likely that you will need and use more specific sources which provide detailed information on such topics as, say, the proportion of women who are under 25, married, with children, in socio-economic category B. Also we would want more recent information because there is an inevitable time lag with the publication of general sources of information. The following sources could be included in this category.

Specific Sources

Monthly Digest of Statistics

An up-to-date survey of the main components of national income, including wages and prices. This is less comprehensive than the general sources above, but has the advantage of being relatively recent.

Economic Trends

Summaries of the main economic indicators with articles on changes and forecasts where appropriate. Again this is a monthly publication and as an indicator of future trends in the economy is thus one of the more useful of the official sources for businesses.

Regional Trends

Similar to *Economic Trends* but with the emphasis on regional variations with indicators of differences in standards of living between the regions. Obviously this could be a valuable source of information for a small business seeking to obtain regional data on employment, income and market trends.

Population Trends

Up-to-date demographic data with articles on birth rates, death rates etc., and their implications for the future characteristics of the UK population. We indicated above that such data can be important, for example, to the construction industry. It will give indications of lifestyle changes (e.g., increased numbers of single people living alone) which will be important for consumer spending patterns.

Financial Statistics

Contains the main financial indicators, including money supply and dealings in the security markets; bank and building society advances, data on non-bank financial intermediaries, interest rates and data on the wholesale money markets.

Bank of England Quarterly Bulletin

Money supply data but including the balance sheets of the banks and the Bank of England.

New Earnings Survey

An annual publication that gives detailed information on earnings, hours worked, overtime, holidays and general labour market information including unemployment and job vacancies. The detail in the survey can be quite valuable for businesses. For example, it gives wage rates by occupation for men and women and the hours that they work.

Business Monitors

The business monitors are a valuable source of reference for entrepreneurs wishing to start a new business or expand an existing business. They provide valuable information on particular business sectors and can be obtained from many of the larger reference or university libraries. They contain output data on industries and sales. It will give information on output in the industry and thus some information on competitors. Business monitors are a very good reference source for general trends within an industry. For example, on the car industry a business monitor will provide recent information on production, sales of different models, output levels, exports and imports and market share of the main producers.

Census of Production

Output figures and tables, including concentration measures. This publication also contains the Standard Industrial Classification (SIC) which is periodically updated in the Department of Employment's *Labour Market Trends* and is a useful reference for researchers.

Labour Market Trends

A monthly publication that often contains articles of interest to small businesses. For example, it gives periodic articles on the number of new firms (and deaths). It contains details on labour force statistics, including earnings, unemployment and hours worked.

On-line Databases

The development of on-line databases gives advantage in terms of direct access and downloading data. Many of the official sources above are now available as databases accessed by computers. For example, a university may have access to a ONS database at Manchester University which holds data from most of the ONS publications. One of the advantages of these 'on-line' databases is that the full, time series data can be downloaded onto a micro or for analysis straight into a statistical package, if students are working on researching feasibility studies and business plans at the university. Thus statistical analysis can be carried out easily and immediately.

EXSTAT provides micro-level data on individual companies including profit levels, turnover, asset size, shareholdings and general financial/accounting data. These EXSTAT databases are a development of the EXTEL cards which used to be available in a published form in some libraries. They are, effectively, brief summaries of an individual company's financial and trading record. For entrepreneurs and small businesses they are a potentially valuable source of information on the profitability and performance of existing competitors. However, they only provide information on limited companies, so do not include information on small 'micro-businesses' which are partnerships or sole traders.

A number of commercial databases are now available where information at the micro-level can be obtained for a fee to the commercial company that compiles and markets the database. These include DATASTREAM which contains detailed financial and share price information, and KOMPASS, a powerful pan-European database containing detailed information on companies throughout Europe.

CD/ROM Databases

Most libraries now have databases that store basic statistics on a CD disk. These may be databases of literature, journal articles or statistical and financial information. The development of these databases has made 'literature searches' far easier and nowadays there is an increasing amount of information and basic data which is available on CD/ROM.

One financial database which is available on CD in some libraries is FAME. After a little practice it can be used as a valuable source for financial data on the SME sector and the performance of firms.

There are obviously many other secondary sources of information. Local authorities often publish useful local economic reports. These may also be available from other agencies such as the Training and Enterprise Councils (TECs) in England and Wales and the Local Enterprise Companies (LECs) in Scotland. They will often be a valuable source of local 'intelligence'. In some cases this local information may also be available on CD/ROM.

It is impossible to list or discuss all that is available in the confines of this short section. The quality and value of the information will also vary from one area to another. However, the advantage is that it is often freely available, whereas to obtain some information, e.g., on CD/ROM, may either involve a fee or the purchase of the database itself. We would encourage the researcher to seek out what is available locally. Breakdown of local economic information is often made available on enquiry, even though it may not be published.

One source of secondary data that may be either overlooked or under-rated is the trade and industry journal which is appropriate to the business proposition. Again the value of these publications is variable, but they can be an important source of market intelligence.

Trade and Industry Publications

Apart from commercially available on-line databases, there are a number of private sector publications which can be useful to entrepreneurs and small firms which need to research new market opportunities and assess existing or potential competition. Trade periodicals will provide *qualitative* information on prospects and performance of companies in their industry. This is often quite useful and provides an alternative to the *quantitative* information that is available through the secondary sources given above. For example, an interview with a managing director in a trade publication can often give an insight into the strategic decisions and planning of the company. These publications may also be useful for names of contacts, who to approach when dealing with a company. More detailed quantitative information may occasionally be published through their own survey of subscribers, perhaps by a questionnaire survey.

Mintel Reports

If either access to a good library is available or one can afford the fee, then there are the valuable Mintel reports which provide market intelligence reports on particular products or sectors. They use market research methods to provide information on competitors' products and sales figures. They are obviously very valuable for potential or existing entrepreneurs and they can provide information that would otherwise be difficult to collect. However the Mintel reports are expensive (it's large firms and libraries that can afford to pay for them) and for the vast majority of small firm entrepreneurs it is more likely that they will have to rely on primary sources of data and research in order to obtain market research information.

The Internet

An alternative approach to gathering information on competitors may increasingly be through the Internet. Most, if not all, large firms have their own Web page, and with the search engines that now exist, information can be obtained and downloaded on potential competitors. The Internet will become more important in the future as more organizations develop their own Web pages and an increasing range of sources of information become available. At present, however, printed versions of secondary sources are still in demand, because of the time taken to search the Internet and the variation in quality on Web pages. For example, until a Web address is accessed, at present the researcher is unlikely to know the extent and quality of information that is made available. Until there is more published information about the quality of different sites, this will always remain a problem. The Internet is a valuable source, but only if the researcher has time to search it.

Other Secondary Sources

A number of agencies operate an intelligence service and databases specifically designed to provide information for small firm entrepreneurs, for example, sources of finance or sources of assistance. The quality and availability varies from region to region and may be affected by institutional arrangements in any one area. For example, local government reorganization can affect the range and quality of sources of information available from the local authority.

Institutional arrangements will vary from region to region, but there are also Euro-information centres in selected localities which provide a range of information on European funding and assistance.

This area is rapidly changing and with the development of on-line databases more information is becoming available, although there may often be a fee to use some of the services. Some centres now provide a patent database which allows potential users and entrepreneurs to search for existing patents in a particular product/field, but there is a fee for using it.

PRIMARY SOURCES

Although there is a vast range of secondary sources of information, it will be appreciated that they often do not provide the right combination of data or perhaps the data is incomplete. There are many situations where this is going to happen when entrepreneurs are searching for specific information regarding products and potential demand. If you are considering launching a new product, the only way to find out information concerning potential demand is to carry out your own market research using survey techniques and questionnaires.

There are a number of ways that primary information can be obtained, the most obvious being through the use of questionnaires using a variety of methods including postal, telephone and face-to-face interviews. Data may also be obtained by observation, e.g., traffic surveys; by interview over a long period of time (longitudinal research) to establish, say, whether there are changes in social attitudes; by records of respondents, e.g., purchases of families recorded by the Family Expenditure Survey. A brief survey of some of the methods of obtaining primary data is given below.

Survey Methods

In the feasibility study and/or subsequent business plan, you may wish to organize a survey of potential customers for yourself or your client. There is a danger that these surveys will be done superficially, by using questionnaires that only reveal the most basic information. You will need to aim for high quality information and that can only be achieved if your questionnaire and survey is well designed. Since the information obtained from any survey is going to form the basis of conclusions and recommendations in your final business plan, the quality of this plan is going to depend crucially upon your research techniques and the design, of your questionnaire. Past experience has found that entrepreneurs/ students who carry out their own research pay insufficient attention to the design of questions and the survey method used. Some careful consideration to both of these aspects will improve the quality of analysis that can be carried out subsequently in either a feasibility study or business plan.

Survey methods include questionnaire-based surveys, normally postal or telephone, and interview-based surveys which may be more open-ended.

Postal Surveys

Although postal questionnaires can be carried out more cheaply than interviews and can be used where a large survey might be required relatively quickly, they suffer from a number of disadvantages which means that they are better avoided unless there is no alternative. However, in conjunction with a smaller interview-based survey they can provide useful basic data.

The disadvantages of postal surveys are that:

- Response rates are usually very low (even with incentives provided for respondents)
- Replies may be unreliable, consequently samples are biased
- Responses will be self-selecting—those that do respond will probably have particular motives to reply
- The extent of questions that can be asked is limited and the questionnaire must be constructed very carefully to avoid misinterpretation by respondents
- Some responses may be incomplete making analysis quite difficult.

These disadvantages, however, need not necessarily rule out postal surveys in appropriate circumstances. For example, if you obtain a mailing list of the members of a particular association you may wish to test how many of the members might buy a new product or service. If the mailing list consists of several thousand names, a postal questionnaire may be the only option which will allow you to survey the full membership.

Note It is stressed that great care should be taken on the use and design of postal questionnaires. Get advice from someone who has had experience of using this research method. Use reply-paid envelopes and pilot the questionnaire beforehand. Use incentives to encourage replies if at all possible and do not rely solely on this survey method. Combine it with interviews of a small sample of the population which will provide more reliable data and provide a check on the value of the postal survey. Use 'closed' rather than open-ended questions as described below.

Telephone Surveys

Telephone surveys can be used where time is of the essence and you wish to ensure that the response rate is reasonable. However, telephone surveys still contain many disadvantages:

- The range and type of questions are severely limited since replies are given over the telephone, although the questions can be posted in advance so that the respondent has them available when you phone
- Some people object to answering questionnaires over the phone
- The respondent has little time in which to consider replies and this limits the type of question that can be asked
- If data is required the respondent may not have this easily available, which can lead to incomplete responses.

Telephone surveys probably suffer from more disadvantages than any other method, but they are useful occasionally, and should not be ruled out, e.g., in situations where you need to obtain some basic and limited data quite quickly. They can also be used in conjunction with a more comprehensive postal survey.

Interviews

Face-to-face interviews have the advantage that issues can be explored in more depth. They can provide qualitative data on values and opinions of respondents as well as the more basic quantitative data. However, interviews can be difficult to carry out and the researcher needs to have some method of recording responses. For full in-depth interviews a small tape recorder is normally the way to record all the information provided by the respondent. Face-to-face interviews are therefore desirable but they still have a number of disadvantages:

- Interviews are subject to the personal bias of the interviewer. Questions need to be carefully designed and even then the interviewer can affect the outcome by placing his/her own interpretation and explanation of the questions.
- The survey will by its nature be limited in the coverage of respondents and unless they are chosen carefully this can provide a further source of bias. Without access to unlimited resources the number of interviews that can be carried out is going to be relatively small.
- If the interview is open-ended and assuming that some acceptable method of recording is found, there is still the problem of adequate analysis and categorizing of responses.

Focus Groups

A focus group involves the selection of a small number of respondents that meet together with the interviewer and opinions are provided in an unstructured way to promptings from the interviewer/facilitator. They have the advantage that they can avoid bias on the part of the interviewer, but their disadvantages include:

- They can be difficult to arrange and organize with a group that is representative.
- It is difficult to get a balanced group that will not be dominated by one or two individuals. If focus groups work they have to have synergy, that is, the group (or sum) contribution should be greater than the parts.
- It is difficult to record the outcomes of the group in a coherent way. As a result, analysis of outcomes can be difficult.

Focus groups can be a useful method of obtaining additional qualitative data and are often used in market research to discover customer opinions and preferences about particular products.

Any survey method will depend, for accurate and coherent subsequent analysis, on the research design which will include the questionnaire design. It may be acceptable to combine these different survey methods, for example, short interviews of a reasonable sample may be combined with more in-depth material with a small number of respondents. In-depth interviews are designed to obtain qualitative information whereas larger surveys are designed to obtain quantitative information.

Research Design

The research design and survey method used will depend on the aims and objectives of the research. For example, a full feasibility study undertaken in advance of a business plan will aim to provide both quantitative data and analysis and more in-depth qualitative information so that a combination of methods will be appropriate. A brief survey required by an entrepreneur to prepare a business plan will need a quick response survey and may involve a mere telephone survey of potential clients. Whatever the objectives of the research, however, some attention should be paid to research design, sampling method and questionnaire design.

Research design involves the selection of the appropriate survey method(s), the sample and the design of appropriate questions. The design involves matching the survey method or combination of methods to the aims of the study and research. Good research design and some thought to the survey method used will pay dividends later in analysis and the production of the final business plan. This is shown in diagrammatic form in Fig. 11.1.

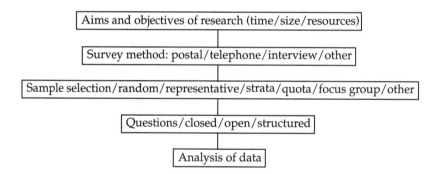

Figure 11.1 Research design

Sampling method

Some attention should be paid to how you are going to choose your sample. The sampling frame may be provided, such as a membership list of an association; you may then decide to survey the whole membership, the population, or choose a sample. How this sample is chosen will affect the interpretation that can be placed on the final results.

The sample will be drawn from some sampling frame such as *Yellow Pages*, a membership list, or perhaps the electoral roll in a local area. Samples may be of the following types:

- *Purely random* To select a true random sample each member of the population must have the same chance of being selected. One way to choose a random sample is to generate random numbers using a computer program. You use the numbers to select respondents from your sampling frame.

- *Representative sample* A representative sample contains a microcosm of the features of the population in their appropriate proportions. Thus if you are surveying firms, you may wish to have representations of different firm sizes in true proportions to their numbers in the population of all firms. That is, 95 per cent of your sample should employ less than 20 employees. The extent to which your sample can be representative will depend on having information about the population. Samples can only be representative if features of the full population are known, such as the proportion that earn less than 'X' per week, or the proportion that are male/female, married/not married and so on.

- *Stratified sample* A stratified sample attempts to break down the population in a coherent manner using one or two criteria. One example might be size of organizations which are respondents. The sample is not representative in having true proportions but you use the criteria of, say, size of firm as a way of ensuring some representation is included from each group or 'strata' of the population. Samples may be chosen randomly from each strata if the sampling frame permits this.

- *Quota sampling* Quota sampling is a commonly used technique in market research where a a characteristic of the population (often age/sex) is used to provide quota numbers for interviewers to ensure a minimum number of respondents is identified in each category. In contrast to stratified sampling this method is often used where no sampling frame is available.

Given limited resources and time the entrepreneur may have little scientific basis for the selection of the sample. A small amount of research will pay dividends, however, and prevent the business plan appearing as though it has been 'thrown together'. A short methodology section in the business plan (or feasibility study) will indicate that some thought has gone into the research behind the plan and that assumptions are well founded, have a good basis and the strategic plans and projections are not haphazard or just 'dreamt up' by the entrepreneur. This can make a tremendous difference and also affects the confidence in which you can present a business plan to any potential funders. Good research will not leave any 'holes' that can be picked upon by potential backers of the proposition.

Question Design

As before, some care devoted to question design will pay dividends when analysing results of any research. There are some simple rules which can be found in any statistical textbook, for example, questions should be:

- Unambiguous
- Relatively short

- Not biased or leading in some way
- Achieve the objectives of the research
- May be structured/semi-structured or open-ended, but open-ended are generally avoided with postal questionnaires.

It is desirable to have some method of *coding* questions. This enables analysis to be carried out with, preferably, a statistical package on computer or using a calculator.

Coding questions   An example best illustrates the value of coding questions. Suppose you were carrying out some research into customer preferences when buying a product/service. You could ask a question in the following way:

Please indicate which of the following factors is important to you when buying 'X' (tick box as appropriate):

(a) Price   ☐
(b) Quality   ☐
(c) After-sales service ☐
(d) Speed of delivery   ☐

The problem with this question is that it does not allow the respondent to distinguish between the factors that might be important when buying 'X'. A better question would ask the respondent to rate the importance of each factor on some scale. For example the question could also be worded in the following way:

Please indicate the importance of the following factors to you when buying 'X' according to the scale provided. Enter your rating in the box provided:

Scale: *Most important*   *Least important*
                      10   1

(a) Price   ☐
(b) Quality   ☐
(c) After-sales service ☐
(d) Speed of delivery   ☐

The advantages of the coded response are that they can be entered numerically and it is easy to calculate the average score for each response and percentages in each category.

There are a wide variety of acceptable questions that can be used, including the standard YES/NO which are sometimes called *filter* questions. The less categories that are used, however, the more we are forcing the respondent into a pigeon-hole of our own choosing. Although such closed questions are desirable, their limitations mean that we would want to combine any analysis from these questions with more open-ended questions that can be used in an interview situation or with interview-based research.

Open-ended questions should still aim to be neutral and avoid bias. It is often difficult to do so and therefore it is strongly recommended that some time should be spent on *testing and piloting* the questionnaire. Questions can then be either omitted or redesigned in the light of the pilot test. Of course, piloting does take time and resources. If you do not have the time to do piloting, it is worth mentioning, again in the methodology section, that this was at least considered.

Analysis

Having taken care with the research design that underpins the eventual business plan (or feasibility study) it is important to pay some attention to the analysis of research and, more important, to the presentation of that analysis. The analysis stage will directly affect the quality and presentation of your final feasibility study and the business plan. If the research design is strong, this will be reflected in good analysis and presentation. If too many yes/no questions are used or insufficient probing is carried out on respondents in the survey, this too will be reflected in the quality of material that is presented in the final business plan.

We are not looking for sophisticated statistical analysis; there is a danger that blinding people with science may put off potential investors. Good presentation of basic analysis such as percentages and averages will go a long way to persuading readers that the research behind the business plan is serious. It must not be presented in a way that leaves the reader baffled.

Thus in the analysis stage the student or the entrepreneur should aim to ensure, in a relatively simple way, that the reader can understand basic data, percentages and assumptions behind the income forecasts that are used for the cashflow forecasts. Where a computer package is used for analysis, it will be relatively easy to produce bar charts and pie charts that illustrate the basic data that lie behind the projections in the cashflow. As discussed before, depending on the design of the research, you may have quantitative and/or qualitative analysis.

Quantitative analysis

Statistical measures which are presented include the arithmetic means, medians or mode. These measures often appear to mean very little on their own and it is useful to present them in conjunction with the standard deviations where these are easily available, say, from a standard computer package. Standard deviations can tell us much more about the characteristics of the sample of respondents than the arithmetic means. They indicate the degree of variance behind a statistical measure. Using the example above of the coded question on factors affecting purchase, if the standard deviations are known as well as the arithmetic means this will enable some knowledge of the degree of variance of respondents' replies. If price has a high mean score (of importance) but a high standard deviation this would mean that there are some respondents that do not think that it is important and it would be worth investigating in more detail with them why that is the case.

For students, this information should also be written up as part of your methodology section in the feasibility study and business plan. The methodology section will include the sources of information that you used, for example, secondary, as well as the survey methods.

Qualitative Analysis

Small sample sizes of less than 30 respondents may be used for qualitative analysis. Yet this form of analysis is often powerful and of more use to the entrepreneur or potential funder. Qualitative analysis aims to look at process and causes of actions. For example:

- Why do respondents buy or not buy a particular product or service?
- What do respondents think of the service or product provided by the client?
- Do they have any complaints?
- How do they think that the service or product could be improved?
- If they buy a different service or product, why?
- You may want to ask questions about the range of provision, for example, can they obtain the product? are opening times suitable?
- What do they think about the quality of the product?

By the nature of the investigation, qualitative analysis usually (but not always) involves open-ended questions. The interview will last for a lot longer; 30–60 minutes is typical, and you must have some method of recording the interview.

RECORDING INTERVIEWS

Recording the interview provides the basis for the analysis and again affects the quality of your feasibility study and the final business plan. A useful methodology is to carry out a quick quantitative survey for the feasibility study and then a more in-depth qualitative survey for the business plan. You may wish to hold interviews with existing customers as well as potential customers. There are two methods of recording interviews:

1. If you are working as a team and carrying out the interviews together you can afford to have one member making notes and another member of the team asking the questions. A third member can be used to record other information such as the reaction of the respondent to certain questions, the nature of the surroundings and how these might affect the interview. All this information is valid for qualitative analysis.
2. A better method is to record the interview with a small tape-recorder. This allows one member of the team to carry out the interview and enables all the information to be recorded. Nowadays tape-recorders can be relatively unobtrusive. However, the permission of the respondent should always be obtained first. Respondents are not always agreeable to having their interview recorded.

Analysis of Interviews

Qualitative analysis should not be unstructured. There needs to be some purpose to the questions and if they are structured this will allow for meaningful analysis afterwards. One or two short quotes are sometimes a powerful way of backing up the quantitative analysis. However, do not overdo this since more than minimal use of quotes from the interviews will tend to obscure the principal factors that you wish to emerge in the overall analysis of the research.

CONCLUSIONS

The final business plan is only as good as the research that underpins the projections. The purpose of this chapter has been to ensure that research is not done on a haphazard basis. Research should have a sound methodology. While any investor will not be looking for a full research study with a full explanation of research methodology and sophisticated analysis, he/she will expect that assumptions used for forecasts have a sound basis. If this basis is rooted in appropriate methodology and survey methods and you can demonstrate that some original (primary) research has been carried out, then the confidence of both you as the entrepreneur and the investor will be that much better. This can be particularly important if the business plan is going to a venture capitalist or perhaps a business angel for funding where they will be much more concerned (than, say, a banker) with the extent of primary research and the way in which that research has been carried out.

The value of the research to the entrepreneur is that, apart from making projections in the business plan more accurate, it can provide the following advantages:

- It gives increased confidence in the presentation of the business plan to potential funders/investors
- It can provide revised calculations of the potential success of the business or the market opportunity
- It provides basic calculations which will serve as a planning document to measure performance of the business over a number of years into the future—without sound methodology and research this will not be possible or will be extremely unlikely
- It can provide a database of potential customers which can be returned to later to carry out further market research on extensions to the business or research into the viability of new products.

We have tended to favour small qualitative surveys as being a valuable method of research. However, we do not wish to be prescriptive. The survey or research method used will depend upon the objectives set by the entrepreneur and by the nature of the business proposition. A self-employed tradesman that wishes to start his own small business and borrow £1000 will not require a sophisticated research study. However, even for a small business proposition some time spent on a little research will pay dividends by improving forecasts and make the business plan an accurate and workable document.

Learning outcomes

At the end of this session entrepreneurs/students should be able to:

1. Appreciate the range of secondary sources available to entrepreneurs and small business owners and the SME sector.
2. Carry out a research study involving the use of structured questionnaires.
3. Discuss the potential of on-line databases for information gathering.
4. Evaluate the role of information in reducing uncertainty.
5. Evaluate the potential of primary and secondary sources of information for entrepreneurs.
6. Realize the importance of different sources of information for carrying out a feasibility study.
7. Appreciate the importance of carrying out both quantitative and qualitative research for both a feasibility study and a business plan.
8. Realize the importance of qualitative research for the business plan.
9. Understand the important statistical measures in quantitative analysis.
10. Appreciate the range of secondary sources of information.
11. Understand the concept of on-line databases.
12. Be willing to record and undertake interviews as part of the research for a feasibility study or business plan.
13. Be willing to revise cashflow forecasts in the light of research undertaken.

Suggested assignment: feasibility study

Students are separated into groups to research and produce a feasibility study for an existing firm/entrepreneur. The feasibility study may involve a new market opportunity or a change of strategy perhaps involving diversification from existing markets. The firm will be local and identified as a potential client by the university/college. Students work as consultants to the client entrepreneur and are required to:

1. Negotiate and agree terms of reference with the entrepreneur.
2. Use appropriate research methods including market research with a questionnaire.
3. Identify and analyse existing and potential competition.
4. Identify the additional costs/resources that will be required to exploit the opportunity.

5. Examine the local labour market as appropriate if additional staff are required.
6. Produce a feasibility study as a written report with sections that include: introduction/terms of reference, research methods, findings, conclusions and recommendations.
7. Make an interim presentation of the findings to the entrepreneur and obtain feedback.

Note: This assignment should be coupled with a follow-up business plan as suggested at the end of the final chapter.

REFERENCES

1. COHEN, W.M. AND LEVINTHAL, D.A. (1989) 'Innovation and Learning: the two faces of R & D', *Economic Journal*, vol. 99, pp. 569–96.
2. Ballard, R. and Kalra, V.S. (1994) *Ethnic Dimensions of the 1991 Census*, University of Manchester.

RECOMMENDED READING

MASON, R., LIND, D. AND MARCHAL, W. (1998) *Statistical Techniques in Business and Economics*, 10th edn, McGraw-Hill.
PREECE, M. (1990) *Qualitative Research Methods*, Sage, London.

12. Business Plans: Design and Implementation

INTRODUCTION

Designing and writing the business plan should be seen as the outcome of a careful research process and subsequent planning procedure—it should be regarded as part of that procedure but not as the end of that process. The business plan is part of the ongoing process of strategic planning for the entrepreneur and small business, whether produced for a start-up business or for an existing business. It can have several purposes: it may be to raise funding from banks or venture capitalists, or to obtain grant funding from an agency such as a TEC or a LEC; or the business plan may serve as a strategic planning document for the entrepreneur, to guide the business and serve as a basis for taking strategic decisions and also as a subsequent monitoring device.

Nowadays there are many guides produced by banks, enterprise agencies, accountants and published books on this ongoing planning process (1). This chapter does not attempt to replicate these guides which are often excellent summaries of the essential first steps in starting in business for new entrepreneurs. These guides are often a framework for organizing ideas and formulating a skeleton business plan. Many agencies and bankers would say that most new business start-ups now are required to produce an elementary business plan. This is a major advance on what might have existed only ten years ago, when a person with a business idea could talk it over with a bank manager and produce some rough 'back of the envelope' calculations and walk out of the bank with a start-up overdraft. The majority of start-ups and even expansions of existing businesses are still planned on the basis of some cashflow forecasts with a few introductory pages of explanation. Although there have been major improvements, partly as a result of the expansion of the agency movement, discussed in Chapter 8, there remains tremendous variety in the standard of business plans that are produced with many that are severely limited in scope. There is, as yet, no research into the quality and effectiveness of many business plans. There is an oft quoted statement that a business plan is 'out of date as soon as it is produced'; yet if a business plan is to be effective this should not be the case. This chapter aims to explain how a business plan can be used effectively as an ongoing monitoring and strategic planning document which, although it may need revision, should be effective for several years as a tool for the entrepreneur. After all, if considerable effort has been expended on research, as recommended in the previous chapter, then this should have some pay-off in the future planning and monitoring of the business.

One problem, when designing and writing a business plan, is that different funding bodies can have different requirements. We have seen in Chapter 5 that even among different bank managers there were considerably different expectations in terms of what was expected and required from entrepreneurs when producing a business plan for a start-up business (2). In addition, venture capitalists will require a much more detailed business plan and perhaps more market analysis than a bank manager, for the obvious reason that the venture capitalist will not be able to take security to safeguard his/her investment. An enterprise agency or a TEC/LEC will also vary in its requirements if a business plan is required to secure grant-aided funding. Thus the advice to potential and existing entrepreneurs before writing the business plan is to seek to determine what format is preferred by the potential funder in terms not of content, but of presentation. This will avoid unnecessary re-writes of the business plan or changes to the presentation. It is best to have a full business plan that you are satisfied with and will serve you as the entrepreneur when taking strategic decisions for the business. Remember that the business plan should be produced for yourself, not for the potential funder; it can be modified, shortened, summarized or extended for different potential funders (or users) and you should be prepared to make these changes. Some additional hints on the presentation of business plans are given at the end of this chapter.

NEW DEVELOPMENTS

As well as extensive guides that can be purchased or are easily available, it is strongly advised that you have access to, or purchase, a modern PC (preferably with laser printer). This will make a tremendous difference to the quality of the final printed version of the business plan, making it easy to produce forecasts on a spreadsheet, or to produce illustrations of market research through bar charts (as recommended in the previous chapter). In addition software is available that will provide a full business planning package. This will contain the essential sections and help you to produce financial forecasts. One package that is recommended is the *Business Architect* software package which can be operated on any PC, is relatively inexpensive and provides a detailed dialogue to enable users to navigate their way through the various sections of a comprehensive business plan. Of course, any amount of software cannot replace the basic planning process that requires adequate research. A business plan, however well produced and presented, will only be as good as the quality of data and information entered into the software that is being used. Obtaining impressive software should not blind the entrepreneur or user (if a student or consultant) to the need to provide good quality research and reliable data that will be processed by the software into a business plan that will serve as a valuable tool for a number of years.

DESIGNING THE BUSINESS PLAN

There are a number of standard sections that would normally be included in any business plan. These should include sections on aims and objectives, competitive analysis, marketing strategy and SWOT analysis. However, the sections required for the business plan will vary depending on the nature and sector of the business. A manufacturing business requires a different business plan from a service sector-based business. An exporting firm requires a different business plan from a components supplier who relies on large UK customers. A small start-up concern requires a different business plan from a medium-sized firm that is planning an expansion into different products. This is one of the problems faced by software manufacturers who aim to provide a standard package that can be used by any business. A business plan has to be flexible and it is impossible to be prescriptive since every business plan will be different and will be produced for different requirements. Having said that it is impossible to be prescriptive, there are certain sections and guidelines that can be discussed and we attempt to do this below. We discuss what might be expected from any business plan. You may not wish to include all of the sections—not everyone will have the time or resources to produce a full and detailed business plan. However, the following suggestions will help to plan for possible different scenarios, competition and future changes that will be faced by the entrepreneur. Some thought at the research and design stage will improve the process of decision making which is one of the main purposes of any business plan.

The following sections are recommended when designing the content of the business plan. As stressed above, these sections are not prescriptive and can be modified to suit the purposes of individual entrepreneurs and business plans.

1. Executive Summary

If your plan is carefully researched, constructed and written, then an executive summary will be very useful to the users of the business plan, who may be potential funders or partner entrepreneurs in the business. Although the executive summary should be the first section, it is likely to be the last section to be written and it can be the most difficult because you have to summarize the main contents of the plan. You will find it useful to build the executive summary around the competitive strategy.

2. Introduction

A short introduction should give some background to the business, the key people and an introduction to the nature of the business and the industrial sector. This section can be used to give the main aims and objectives of the business. You will need to explain the purpose of the business plan. Is it to map out an expansion plan for the business? Or is it to provide a strategy for the launch of a new business? The aims and objectives could be placed in a separate section. You can also use this section to explain the rationale for the business and the business plan. Deciding how to differentiate between what are aims and what are objectives of your business can be difficult. A general guide is that aims can be considered to be quite broad and less specific than objectives. Objectives should be written in terms of specific outcomes. For example, an aim of, say, a five year-business plan would be to:

- provide a strategic planning process to become a major competitor in the industry.

Whereas an objective of the same business plan might be to:

- achieve a fourfold growth in sales within five years.

In the introduction you can provide additional information such as the nature of incorporation if a start-up, whether the company is registered, whether you have registered for VAT, in which case a VAT number should be quoted, starting employment levels, resources and whether there is a need for recruitment of staff and personnel.

3. Market Analysis and Research

In this section you can report the findings of market research that might have been undertaken, if primary research has been completed along the lines suggested. Avoid the temptation to give too much information, although as suggested before, illustrations of the main findings can be quite useful for presentation purposes and for potential readers of the plan. However, those readers will not want to wade through a large amount of information and data. If the questionnaire that has been used as the basis for the research has been well designed, it should be possible to present the information and analysis in the form of summary tables with brief comments on the significance and importance of market analysis and summaries of the potential total market and market share.

Some of the software packages mentioned above will give a market opportunity analysis. For example, *Business Architect* will provide a useful market opportunity matrix which gives a score and an interpretation of the value of that score for the importance of the market opportunity. Additional analysis provided by such software can be a useful way of impressing any potential funder.

This section should be used to explain the assumptions behind income generation in the cashflow statements. Are the income levels based upon the market research findings? Or perhaps based on other factors such as seasonality? State of economic levels of activity? Capacity levels if a manufacturing concern? Other factors should also be included, such as the basis of payment—income may be generated on the basis of commission, fees or sales. If sales of product and services are involved, then some form of normal credit period will be assumed. Standard practice is, of course, 30-day credit periods between the sale taking place and income shown in the cashflow. If your business is subject to strong seasonal factors, such as high sales in the Christmas period, then this should be shown in the income statement of the cash flow with allowance made for any credit period.

You may wish to consider outlining a brief marketing and distribution plan. This can be contained within the business plan, or if distribution is a major part of the firm's operations, then it is recommended that a separate document is produced. The marketing plan effectively sets out how sales are to be achieved. It may include all aspects of the 'marketing mix':

- Pricing policy
- Promotion (advertising and other forms of promotion)
- Production. The outlets and marketing strategy should reflect the production capabilities of the business. It is important to get these aspects of the business integrated, so that distribution channels and outlets do not overburden the production process and capabilities and that the outlets are appropriate to cope with production capacities.

An example is illustrative. A small firm had produced a form of hanging basket bracket that was produced to a new design and to a high quality. Yet the marketing strategy adopted bore no relation to production capabilities. The hanging bracket was marketed through a major chain gardening store and as soon as one order was placed the firm could not cope with the production quantities required by a major multiple retailer. This problem of matching production to outlets and distribution channels cannot always be resolved, but planning for different outcomes in the business plan can help to resolve it if it does arise and a separate marketing plan can be a valuable planning tool for any business.

- Place. How are the goods going to be distributed and how are they to be sold? What outlets are being used? Are direct selling methods to be used or are agents being used, perhaps working on commission?

Access to retail outlets can be a problem for some businesses. You should demonstrate that you have given some thought to this and that you have secured retail outlets if the product is new.

4. Production Strategy

If your business is concerned with manufacturing and production, a separate section should be devoted to the planning of production. If the business is concerned merely with expanding using existing production facilities, through perhaps obtaining new market outlets, then a separate production plan will not be necessary. However, you may need to plan for additional production facilities, new machinery and increased capacity. You will need to identify the additional resources and capabilities that will be required for new production levels. Additional skilled staff may be required and recruitment policies should be explained.

For a new start-up business that requires production facilities the business plan will need to describe how these are to be obtained and how staff are to be recruited.

The assumptions described in this section will form the basis behind the projections in the expenses of the cashflow statements. Some research may be necessary in order to predict these forecasts accurately. You should not rely on your own estimates but obtain quotations for ordering supplies and equipment that is required.

Timing

An important element of any manufacturing business is timing production to co-ordinate with sales orders and to match supply of materials with production capabilities and sales orders. This means integrating market predictions and sales back through the production process and ensuring that the supply of materials and components is of the quality required to ensure that your customers are satisfied with the product. It must be stressed that orders can be lost if insufficient attention is paid to quality in the production process and from suppliers. This can be a particular problem for a new (producing) firm which can be vulnerable if certain specifications have been laid down to suppliers with no guarantee that these are going to be met. Although this may use up some resources, try to get some prototypes made to check the quality. This will be a particular problem where new technology or new production techniques are being employed, which is one of the reasons why financing new technology firms contains different and special issues from other types of start-ups.

Timing is important because resources and finance will be required before products are made, before sales are made and certainly well before income is received. This should be reflected in the cashflow statements. Any manufacturing and producing firm is certain to have a negative balance in the first part of the cashflow. It is better to plan properly for this, so that financial resources can either be set aside if internal resources are available, or funding requirements can be made clear in the business plan.

Action plans

To aid the planning process it is worth providing an action plan. The purpose is to map actions against time and the production process. This will allow you to plan different requirements into the production and marketing stages as they are required over time.

An action plan can be produced for any type of business and modified to produce a Gantt Chart, which maps out the sequential timing of decisions against production/sales levels and can serve as an action plan for the business.

5. Swot Analysis

A section on SWOT analysis involves the identification of strengths, weaknesses, opportunities and threats for the business. There can be some dispute over how the analysis can be presented and explained. To some extent, a SWOT analysis should consist of a series of short bullet points so that the reader can see quickly the main strengths and weaknesses of the business and the opportunity. However, the bullet points should not be so short that they become perfunctory statements and the reader is left wanting and wishing for further explanation or elaboration. Again a balance has to be struck between keeping the statements short (and preferably punchy) and providing an adequate explanation that the reader or user of the business plan can understand and comprehend.

A long list of strengths and weaknesses is not necessary; the list should be relatively short, perhaps half-a-dozen bullet points under each heading. It is also better to be honest. A long list of strengths followed by a short list of weaknesses is more likely to raise suspicions from potential funders rather than impress them.

The SWOT analysis should 'fit' the business plan. If many strengths are shown but other aspects of the business plan are perhaps weak (such as limited analysis of market projections), then the SWOT analysis will look out of place in the context of the rest of the business plan.

There are few guidelines that can be given for the SWOT analysis. You as the entrepreneur are the best person to write the SWOT analysis but, bearing in mind the points raised above, you should not be afraid to put down your strengths. These may include extensive experience in the industry, a reputation for quality, a high knowledge of working practices and employment conditions in the industry, existing contacts with potential customers and knowledge of new techniques/technologies that can be applied to existing production processes.

A SWOT analysis will always remain subject to personal preferences and views. The reader of the business plan should be aware of this and will make some allowances for it. A different individual could interpret strengths and weaknesses in different ways. Unless a business plan is put together by an independent consultant, a SWOT analysis will remain a personal statement by the entrepreneur(s) of their view of the strengths and weaknesses of the business and the opportunities provided by the business creation or development.

6. Competition

The competition and a section dealing with competitive analysis will follow the identification of threats in the SWOT analysis. The extent of knowledge on competitors will probably vary, but it should be possible to identify the major competitors and what their relative strengths. It is also useful to identify what strategies they have used to establish their market position. For example, have they used market nicheing strategies? Or perhaps more aggressive market penetration strategies? Or have they established their position merely by reputation and word of mouth?

In this text we have considered some of the reasons for the success of small firms in the 1980s and 1990s. Often the reason for the start-up of a new firm by an entrepreneur is that they have recognized a market niche in an industry that is not being catered for by existing (large) firms. A small firm/entrepreneur will have the flexibility to respond to new market opportunities and market niches, while it is likely that the competition may consist of well established firms that may not have the flexibility to respond quickly to new opportunities and challenges.

The analysis of competition should match the market analysis that is presented in the business plan as discussed above. If you are predicting a relatively large market share, this will not fit with an analysis which suggests that the major competitors are strong, well established and that the market can be difficult to penetrate. This analysis should also fit the marketing strategy. A market nicheing strategy will probably aim for high quality services or products and likely outlets that are willing to take your products, or potential customers if a service is being marketed, should have been identified.

You should also give some thought to potential competition. As opportunities develop, you may face competition either from additional entrepreneurs who are starting up or from retaliation in the existing competition. If the business plan is to be a valuable document over a three- or five- year planning period, then some thought must be given to future competition and the likely sources of that competition.

It is possible to provide contingency plans but, given that the number of different scenarios is infinite, you will not be able to provide one which will cope with all possible eventualities, reactions and strategies of the competition. All that can be done is to recognize that the outcomes that are predicted in the business plan can change and that the plan should be used to monitor operations and then adjust predictions and/or strategy according to circumstances. As we will see later it is desirable to conduct a limited amount of sensitivity analysis which will demonstrate to potential funders that you have thought about different outcomes and the reaction of existing and potential competitors.

7. Competitive Strategy

In some ways this is the most important section of the business plan, since it should map out the strategy for the survival, development and growth of your business. A strategy should be identified that will enable the business to meet the aims and objectives which will have been set out in the early part or sections of the business plan. The development of competitive strategy will be the natural outcome of the process of researching the market opportunity, the nature of the product or service, the SWOT analysis and the competitive analysis. Porter (3) has provided a well known taxonomy of generic market strategies which are indicated below. It is likely that your strategy will fall into one of these three categories. Porter shows that competitive strategies are a response to the environment in which the business operates, in other words they are generic to the environment and the nature of competition faced by the business. Porter's three generic strategies are described below.

Cost leadership

Under this strategy the emphasis is on maintaining a competitive edge through a cost advantage over competitors. It may, but does not necessarily, involve undercutting competitors and maintaining a competitive edge on price. Undercutting through price does have disadvantages. It may lead to some form of price war and even if competitors are at a cost disadvantage they may be better placed to sustain losses that might be incurred through any price cutting war to gain customers. The advantage of cost leadership for entrepreneurs will lie in the generation of additional income that may result from cost reduction and which may be reinvested to provide new production techniques or new products.

Differentiation

This strategy may follow from a need to diversify production or services. It should not be confused with the third (focus) strategy. It is more likely to apply to existing and well established producers where, perhaps, products have entered a maturity stage of their life cycle and there is a need to diversify production to maintain growth in the firm.

Focus

This third strategy is the one most likely to be adopted by new firm entrepreneurs. It recognizes that many market opportunities result from specialization. Small firms have the advantage that they can be flexible as well as specialized. The development of a focus strategy involves the identification of a market niche that has not been exploited by existing producers. The firm should be able to gain a reputation quickly for satisfying this market niche. It is important to identify the correct time to launch and exploit the market opportunity. Thus there are market 'windows of opportunity' that appear at different times. Launching too early or too late can miss this opportunity.

Although Porter's categories have been very influential, they may be seen as a bit limiting. Kay (4) has produced a useful alternative analysis of competitive strategy that focuses on the importance of value-added that a firm can bring to the industry. The extent to which a firm will produce value-added to its costs of production will determine its success. For example, in an analysis of the retail food industry Kay shows that the strategies adopted by Sainsbury and Tesco have been very successful at adding value to their operations through successful marketing. At the time of Kay's analysis, Kwik-Save was also successful with a very different marketing strategy which aimed to capture the low cost end of the market but still provide value-added to its operations. The poor market performer was Asda, who was considered to have a low-value added performance. However, since this analysis, Asda has responded with more aggressive marketing to increase its market share.

These analyses stress the importance of fitting the strategy to the type of market that you are in. There is no right or wrong strategy, but it must be appropriate for the business, the operation, the market and the business development plan.

8. Critical Success Factors

The identification of critical success factors is a useful section that should be included in the final business plan. It can serve as a useful summary and check of factors that have been identified in other sections of the business plan and is best placed towards the end of the business plan. Like the SWOT analysis it will tend to be a personal reflection on the most important factors that are going to be critical to the success of the business. Thus, again, it is impossible to be at all prescriptive about this section but you may like to think about the following factors:

1. What factors does the success of the business hinge upon? Are they concerned with gaining orders or with securing quality from suppliers?
2. How important are the key personnel to the success of the business? If a key member of staff leaves, how will this affect the performance of the business? Can they be replaced?
3. How important is the recruitment strategy of the business? Does the success of the business depend on obtaining appropriate skilled staff?
4. Does the success of the strategy adopted depend on how competitors react?

It is worth considering each section of the business plan and identifying just one or two key factors from each that will be critical to the performance of your firm and to its success. As an entrepreneur this will help you to identify key and critical success factors and at later stages to monitor performance. Having identified such factors you can adopt strategies that can ensure success or lead to alternative arrangements. For example, if a supplier is identified as a critical factor, you may wish to investigate alternative arrangements of ensuring supply.

9. Cashflow Statement

The cashflow statement contains the projected income from sales and other sources and all the expenses concerned with the launch and operation of the business. It is best prepared on a computer spreadsheet package, although business planning software, mentioned before, will have its own spreadsheet and financial analysis built in.

The importance of the cashflow statement is that it shows the timing of income and expenses and should show all these figures for twelve-monthly periods of up to three or perhaps five years, depending on the potential users of the business plan. It shows the liquidity of the business at any one time and reflects the need or otherwise to raise funds and credit. If the business plan is being prepared for a bank manager, then it is unlikely that cashflow forecasts will be required beyond three years. If, on the other hand, it is being prepared for a venture capitalist, it is more likely that five years' cashflow forecasts will be required.

A *pro forma* cashflow statement is shown as an example in Fig. 12.1, but the detail of the cashflow will obviously depend on the individual business. The notes given in the *pro forma* are referred to below:

1. *Income* will consist of sales, fees and commission. It may include income from grants, or loans. The timing of the receipt of this income should be as accurate as possible. A small adjustment to the timing of the income can affect the extent of any negative or positive net cashflow.

HYPOTHETICAL COMPANY YEAR 1

	JAN	FEB	MARCH	APRIL	MAY	JUNE	JULY	AUGUST	SEPT	OCT	NOV	DEC	TOTALS (11)
INCOME (1)													
SALES		3500	4000	5000	5500	5000	6000	3000	6500	6500	7000	10000	62000
FEES	2025	2025	2700	2025	2700	2700		1350	3375	2700	3375	2025	27000
GRANT													0
ENTERPRISE AGENCY	7000												7000
TOTAL INCOME (2)	9025	5525	6700	7025	8200	7700	6000	4350	9875	9200	10375	12025	96000
EXPENSES (3)													
MATERIALS	3500	3000	3000	3500	3000	3000	3500	3000	5000	4000	4000	3000	41500
EQUIPMENT													
MACHINERY	5000	5000	5000	5000									20000
COMPUTERS		3600											3600
PRINTER		1000											1000
VIDEO			750										750
TABLES			600										600
CHAIRS		600											600
BOOKCASES			300										300
WAGES (4)													0
PRODUCTION	2893.75	2315	2893.75	2315	2315	2315	2893.75	2315	2893.75	2315	2315	2315	30095
OFFICE	607.5	607.5	810	607.5	810	810		405	1012.5	810	1012.5	607.5	8100
HEAT AND LIGHT			1000			1000			800			1200	4000
RATES				1000						1000			2000
INSURANCE (5)				1500						1500			3000
TELEPHONE			200			200			150			250	800
CONSUMABLES													0
PRODUCTION	200	200	200	200	200	200		200	200	200	200	200	2200
OFFICE STATIONERY	300	100	100	100	100	100		100	100	100	100	100	1300
VAT (REBATE) (6)						-1575			-1500			-1500	-4575
TOTAL EXPENSES (7)	12501.3	16422.5	14853.8	14222.5	6425	6050	6393.75	6020	8656.25	9925	7627.5	6172.5	115270
NET CASHFLOW (8)	-3476.3	-10898	-8153.8	-7197.5	1775	1650	-393.75	-1670	1218.75	-725	2747.5	5852.5	-19270
OPENING BALANCE (9)	0	-3476.3	-14374	-22528	-29725	-27950	-26300	-26694	-28364	-27145	-27870	-25123	0
CLOSING BALANCE (10)	-3476.3	-14374	-22528	-29725	-27950	-26300	-26694	-28364	-27145	-27870	-25123	-19270	(12)

Figure 12.1 Cashflow forecast for a hypothetical company and *pro forma*

2. *Total income* calculates the total for each month. On a spreadsheet this is easily done by inserting the appropriate formula to sum cells and then copying across different cells.

3. *Expenses* can either be summarized under different headings or shown individually, but they should identify all expenses from the operations of the business. They will include equipment, materials, computing equipment, wages, car leasing, insurance and promotional expenses. Again timing is important and should be as accurate as possible since a small adjustment will affect the extent of the positive or negative cashflow.

4. *Wages* should include national insurance contributions, although NI payments can be shown separately.

5. It is important to consider and include items such as *insurance*. If you are a producer you will need products' liability, public liability and employers' liability insurance. If insurance is a relatively small part of sales, perhaps only 2 per cent, it can be paid in one annual premium.

6. If the business is registered for *VAT*, then it will be entitled to a rebate on VAT payments. These can be claimed every three months. Registering for VAT becomes mandatory over a threshold turnover of £48 000 in 1997, but registration is advisable at levels below this to claim VAT rebates.

7. *Total expenses* merely add up the expenses in each column and this is easily done on a spreadsheet.

8. Subtracting the total expenses from the total income shows the *net cashflow* for each month. A general point to consider is that you will want to take advantage of any credit. This will be reflected in the liquidity of the business as shown in the net cashflow.

9. The *opening balance* for the first month is normally shown as zero, although it is possible to have reserves (from previous operations) shown in the opening balance.

10. The *closing balance* adds the opening balance to the net cashflow. The closing balance is automatically carried forward to become the opening balance in the next month (period).

11. The *totals* are added horizontally. They need not be shown, but they are a useful check on calculations and can show the total income and expenses for the year.

12. The *last closing balance* for the year will become the opening balance for the next year and should be carried forward as in previous months.

13. If drawings are made by the owner/entrepreneur, perhaps as a sole trader, then these are best shown as part of the expenses concerned with the operation of the business. These are likely to be regular withdrawals and they should be shown monthly rather than a total figure at the end of the year.

Note: The cashflow statement is not the same as profit and loss.

As stated before, the net cashflow reflects the liquidity of the business. The cashflow can show additional income, e.g., borrowings which are not part of the profit and loss account.

10. Forecasted Profit and Loss Account

It is advisable but not essential to forecast an end-of-year profit and loss account. This involves adding up all the trading income then subtracting cost of goods sold to find the trading profit and loss. General expenses for the year can be totalled, including depreciation subtracted from the trading profit to find the net profit.

11. Forecasted Balance Sheet

A forecasted balance sheet is sometimes required, particularly by bank managers, and this can be relatively easily calculated from the projections for the end of year.

The balance sheet is a statement of assets and liabilities at any particular time period. As a planning tool it is not very useful, since it only provides a snapshot at any one time, but it may be required by bank managers (5).

A number of financial ratios can be calculated and included in terms of profitability and liquidity. It is not necessary to go into detail on the calculation and usefulness of these but standard business planning software will calculate them automatically.

12. Sensitivity Analysis

The purpose of the sensitivity analysis is to provide a test of the susceptibility of the business to changes, or a test of the robustness of the business proposition to cope with unforeseen changes. We can assume that most of the expense forecasts will be accurate. Despite careful research, income forecasts will still contain some uncertainty and the purpose of sensitivity analysis is to examine the consequences of changing some of the income forecasts on the net cashflow.

There is little point in developing any sensitivity analysis beyond the first year of operation, but it it is worth formulating for the first year what can be called an optimistic and a pessimistic scenario.

The optimistic scenario might increase sales and other income by 10 per cent. Expenses will need to be adjusted to allow for this, for example through increased cost of materials, and perhaps through increased salary costs. The pessimistic scenario might decrease sales and other income by 10 per cent with appropriate adjustments of expenses.

WRITING THE BUSINESS PLAN

As indicated before, the business plan is best prepared on a computer package using a standard word-processing package such as WORD PERFECT or WORD (for WINDOWS) combined with spreadsheet package such as EXCEL or LOTUS (which if using a WINDOWS format can be imported into the final document) for preparing the cashflow. Alternatively, business planning software that is now available will integrate a spreadsheet with a word-processing package that contains the main sections of the business plan. PCs these days are relatively inexpensive; a small outlay will improve the quality and presentation of the final business plan and any intermediate feasibility study.

Some hints and guidelines are given below in terms of the actual writing and presentation of the final business plan.

1. The construction of the cashflow statement should be undertaken at a relatively early stage, perhaps after the analysis of the market research described in the previous chapter. This has the advantage of deciding what information and forecasts need to be justified and explained in the written parts of the business plan. It also allows you to consider whether you have done sufficient research and whether there any additional expenses that need to be calculated.

2. To aid presentation use relatively wide margins—we would recommend at least 1 inch on either side and generous top and bottom margins. This avoids presenting too much information on one page and allows the potential user or funder to make notes.

3. Start each section on a fresh page. Again this improves presentation and enables the user to find sections quickly.

4. Avoid appendices where possible. If appendices are used to provide market research data, it can be difficult for the reader/user to refer to data while reading the appropriate section in the business plan. Appendices may be used sparingly, e.g., to give CVs. These may be left out of some versions of the same business plan.

5. Use illustrations, although do not overdo this. Comments have been made on the illustration of research data in the previous chapter. Illustrations are useful and can help the user assimilate data quickly. Ability to do this, however, may depend on the sophistication of the software being used.

6. Include a contents page at the beginning. This will enable the reader to locate different sections and navigate around the business plan quickly.

7. Most word-processing packages allow the inclusion of headers and footers. By leaving generous top and bottom margins, you can include either a header or footer on each page of the business plan. This could be the name of the business.

8. Include some notes to the accounts, whether you are providing cashflow statement only, or a more detailed set of accounts that may contain profit and loss and a forecasted balance sheet. Even though assumptions will have been given in different sections in the business plan, it will still be necessary to provide some notes on certain figures in the cashflow to explain what additional assumptions have been made on the basis of calculation.

9. Insert contact names on the front or inside page of the business plan.

10. The business plan should not be too long, perhaps 30 pages including appendices is a rough maximum (or 10 000 words). There is no ideal length, although there is little point in producing a very detailed plan if the only aim is to raise a small overdraft at the bank.

11. Bind the business plan securely (not stapled) and provide a cover that will stand up to some wear and tear. You may wish to go to the expense of having

the business plan properly bound by a printer. However, we do not recommend this since you may wish to change certain sections or add pages. A loosely ring-bound document will allow you to modify and produce different versions of the same business plan for different users and funders.

12. Finally, an over-used phrase is that the business plan should 'stack up'. We defy anyone to explain exactly what this phrase means but it is best expressed by saying, in principle, that different sections should integrate and support the findings. Assumptions should underpin the forecasts. If different sections are out of line this will be transmitted as an unbalanced plan. A strategy section that emphasizes small scale and quality should match other sections such as the market research and marketing strategy and the cashflow forecasts.

IMPLEMENTATION

As stressed above, the business plan should not become out of date as soon as the business starts up. Before operation and trading the business plan is a document that can be read and used by a number of different people—perhaps other partners in the business, perhaps for analysis by potential funders. It should also enable planning of the launch and operation of the first stage of the business.

After start-up or launch of the new product/diversification the business plan can be used to monitor performance against the projections. It can be used to signal better (or worse) performance, dangers, and critical success factors. Timings can be crucial and, if properly planned for, production and marketing plans can be matched against business plan forecasts to give some guide to the performance of the business. Income and expense forecasts can be matched against real outcomes to give an indicator of performance. During the first year any change in performance can be matched against the sensitivity analysis and this will give some indication of the extent to which the business is outperforming or under-performing forecasts in the business plan.

It must be remembered that the business plan is a strategy document as much as anything else. It is not there merely to provide a financial forecast, but to provide the strategy for the survival, development and growth of the business. If forecasts do prove to be substantially different from real outcomes, then the strategy will need to be reviewed and possibly changed and adapted to different circumstances.

Assuming that the business plan has been produced for at least three years, it will need to be reviewed at the end of the first year. If there have been substantially different outcomes, it will be worth changing the business plan, perhaps by revising cashflow outcomes. Assuming that a spreadsheet has been used, this should be relatively easy. The strategy and details provided in the business plan should still be appropriate and should be used (perhaps with some modifications) for the remainder of the planning period. Forecasts should now be more accurate and more reliable. As the business plan is reviewed in subsequent years the advantages of forward planning become apparent. The business plan should serve as a guide throughout the life of the business.

FURTHER HINTS

1. Be confident in presentation of the business plan. Careful research should increase confidence. Potential funders will need to be impressed by your own confidence and knowledge behind the forecasts that are in the business plan. No matter how well the business plan is prepared, potential backers are still influenced by presentation.
2. Prepare for questions on the business plan. Is there anything missed out? If profit and loss is not presented, some rough calculations will give a potential backer an indication.
3. Take the business plan to different agencies and backers and get their opinion on how it 'stacks up'.
4. Don't give up if you cannot raise funding at the first attempt. For example, our own research has shown that bank mangers can have quite different interpretations of the same business plan, despite the advent of expert systems and credit scoring (2).
5. If you can afford it, ask a qualified accountant to verify the contents of the business plan. Again research has shown that bank managers are more (positively) influenced by business plans that have been authorized by accountants.
6. Be prepared to accept a long process of vetting if you are seeking funding from a venture capitalist. The due diligence procedure of a venture capitalist can take six months or more before a decision is made on whether to back a proposition.
7. A venture capitalist will also be looking for exit routes. If you are seeking this form of funding you will need to be prepared for the eventual Initial Public Offering (IPO) (share issue) of the business which is the normal exit route for a venture capitalist.
8. Try to find out what potential funders are looking for. Many agencies that might provide funding have very specific criteria, e.g., that you attend enterprise training sessions (if a new entrepreneur). Whether you need these or not, you will have to attend to qualify for the funding. There can be an assumption on the part of existing managers (in large firms) that they do not need enterprise training. Yet the management of start-up as a small firm needs different management skills from that of a large firm.

CONCLUSIONS

The research, design and implementation of the business plan is part of the ongoing planning process within any firm. If as a start-up entrepreneur you adopt planning policies that are based on sound research and careful consideration of strategy, this will have benefits throughout the life of the business. We have seen in a previous chapter that, during the 1980s, there were high birth rates of new small firms and entrepreneurs, but at the same time these were accompanied by high death rates. One of the reasons for these high death rates has been insufficient thought and time given to planning the strategy of the new firm.

We started this chapter by commenting that business plans are much more common nowadays and much more detailed than they used to be. Only ten years ago properly researched business plans were quite rare. One of the reasons for the growth in their use has been the spread of the agency movement and the request of banks (sometimes working in co-operation with agencies) for business plans if any funding is required. Another reason is that it has become accepted that a carefully constructed business plan is important to the survival and successful performance of any business, whether large or small.

Business plans are very flexible. They can be used for both large and small firms; for start-ups or for expansion; for private or public sector organizations; they can be a few pages or a substantial document running to 10 000 words or more supported by appendices. Yet there is still no overall standard format by which any one individual business plan can be measured. It is because they are so varied and they are relatively new (in evolution and use) that it is unlikely that there will be any standard produced in the near future. So how do we measure the quality of a business plan? We are left with that over-used phrase mentioned before that a good business plan should 'hang together'—that the different sections should be interconnected, that it should be underpinned by careful research, by knowledge of the market opportunity and that the assumptions and research should underpin the financial forecasts.

Learning outcomes

At the end of this chapter you should be able to:

1. Construct the main sections of a business plan.
2. Describe the importance of strategic planning for the successful development of a business.
3. Appreciate the importance of careful research for the accuracy of forecasts in the business plan.
4. Construct a cashflow forecast from some income and expense assumptions.
5. Understand the advantages and limitations of (short) business plans for the adequate monitoring of business performance.
6. Appreciate the wide variety and flexibility of business plans and the need for a coherent national standard.

Suggested assignment: business plan

1. Students are required to complete a business plan through the development of research work carried out for the feasibility study. The business plan should follow the guidelines given in this chapter and include sections on:

   Executive summary
   Introduction
   Market analysis and assumptions for cashflow
   SWOT analysis
   Competition analysis
   Competitive strategy
   Required resources with budget
   Cashflow forecast
   Profit and loss forecast if required by client
   Notes to the accounts
   Conclusions
   Appendices if required

   The business plan will be produced by the students working in small groups and working as consultants for a client entrepreneur/firm. The completed written business plan will need to be of high quality, word processed and produced with a hard cover.
2. Students complete a final presentation to the entrepreneur/client.

Note: This assignment should be coupled with the feasibility study assignment at the end of the previous chapter which should be completed as a precursor to the business plan.

REFERENCES

1. For example: BARROW, C. (1989) *The Small Business Guide*, BBC, London, or any of the commercial banks' own guides.
2. DEAKINS, D. AND HUSSAIN, G. (1991) *Risk Assessment by Bank Managers*, Birmingham Polytechnic Business School, Birmingham.
3. PORTER, M. (1980) *Competitive Strategy: Techniques for Analysing Industries and Competitors*, Collier Macmillan.
4. KAY, J. (1993) *Foundations of Corporate Success: how business strategies add value*, OUP, Oxford.
5. FLETCHER, M. (1994) *Bank Managers' Lending Decisions to Small Firms*, Department of Entrepreneurship, University of Stirling, Stirling.

RECOMMENDED READING

BARROW, C. (1989) *The Small Business Guide*, BBC, London.

BARROW, C., BARROW, P. AND BROWN, R. (1992) *The Business Plan Workbook*, 2nd edn, Kogan Page.

Index